Cotton Wool Kids

Cotton Wool Kids

What's making Irish parents paranoid?

Stella O'Malley

MERCIER PRESS
IRISH PUBLISHER – IRISH STORY

Author's note:

Certain details have been changed in the case studies in this book to protect the identities of those involved.

MERCIER PRESS

Cork

www.mercierpress.ie

© Stella O'Malley, 2015

ISBN: 978 1 78117 320 6

10 9 8 7 6 5 4 3 2 1

A CIP record for this title is available from the British Library

Printed and bound in the EU.

Contents

'Children learn to smile from their parents.'

Dr Suzuki

Introduction

Let's get one thing straight – this isn't another parenting book telling you how to raise your children or what you should be doing better. Instead this book seeks to explore childhood in twenty-first-century Ireland and to examine how the modern approach to parenting is impacting family life. I have been urged to write this book by countless clients who, after a course of counselling and psychotherapy, finally realised that to ensure their family is happy they often simply needed to focus on a pleasant lifestyle that suited their values and beliefs.

The weird and excessive cult of over-parenting that is promoted today as the gold standard of parenting isn't working. An extensive range of extra-curricular activities, constant supervision, intensive schoolwork and expensive games are not only unnecessary, but often do more harm than good. In recent years, increasing numbers of stressed and exhausted clients are arriving at my clinic, primarily because the media, commercial interests and other outside forces have created an environment where both parents and children feel burdened by the weight of expectations and demands. Few among us would deny that parents are trying hard – too hard, perhaps – yet their efforts aren't being rewarded, as a growing number of children feel increasingly consumed by fear and anxiety, and the number of teenagers and young adults also seeking counselling is growing. These 'kidults' don't know who they are or what they want – they're more in touch with what their parents want for them than with their own hopes and dreams. Parents feel embattled and worn out by external pressures, and their children are feeling stressed and anxious; something's got to change … and soon.

It was in 2007, when I became pregnant with my first child, that I began to understand more profoundly the complex issues that face modern parents. After I had told everybody the good news, I quickly became unsettled by the overwhelming avalanche of well-meaning but frankly terrifying advice that came from every corner. This was the year that the Madeleine McCann kidnapping tragedy happened and the world was increasingly perceived as a dangerous place, filled with crazed, homicidal axe murderers. I diligently attempted to read all the baby books, trying to crack the nut that is parenting, but became confused when I realised that they all contradicted each other. I was also left feeling slightly bewildered when I realised that many of the baby books could be renamed simply as their special version of 'what you're doing wrong'.

During my ante-natal classes I was advised not to take my own mother's advice too seriously as childhood is very different now, and was also warned not to listen to my friends, as they would probably tell fibs in a fever of competitive parenting. In addition, parenting books were cautioned against as 'each child is different and you can't do parenting by the book'. I nervously turned to my husband and asked him, 'So where the hell *can* we go for advice?'

I had my second baby in 2009 and the paranoia and warnings continued relentlessly. In the hospital ward I started chatting with my neighbour in the bed beside me. She told me all about the elaborate monitoring system her husband had bought so that they could be sure their child would be safe at all times. This high-powered baby-tracking device was connected with an app to her iPhone and a quick glance at her phone would give her information about her baby's breathing, temperature, movements, blood pressure and heart rate at any time she wanted. She planned to attach a tracking device to the child as soon as he was walking. 'Is the child sick?' I wondered anxiously. 'Is there something wrong with him?' She looked at me as if I was a blithering idiot. 'No, of course not. There's nothing wrong. You just can't be too safe – it's a sick world out there!'

But can you be too safe, I wondered. Is it really necessary for parents to monitor their babies every second of every day? And lying in my hospital bed, I couldn't help but wonder whether childhood really has become so dangerous, or is all this a bit excessive? Has society really deteriorated so much – or are we worrying ourselves needlessly?

A leaflet in the hospital advised me to 'keep an eye on your baby at all times'. 'At all times,' I wondered, feeling pretty fed up at this stage, 'do they really mean "at all times"?' As I was puzzling over this leaflet my husband, Henry, had taken our two-day-old son for a wander down the corridor. Henry was cuddling our little 'un in his arms and generally revelling in that oh-so-special tenderness that we have for our newborns when suddenly a siren started blaring loudly. I was in a public ward and all the mothers looked at each other in horror – wow, this really was a brave new world. Nurses and doctors flew to action stations to see who was trying to abduct a baby. Eventually, after a bit of a kerfuffle, it turned out that it was my husband who was the unknown male on the loose. Our son was tagged and Henry had walked too far along the corridor (not off the ward, not through any doors, merely further down the corridor), so the siren had gone off. When I (and everyone else in the ward) heard my husband's stuttered explanation I thought, 'Mother of Divine, they really do mean "at all times".'

There and then I promised myself that when I emerged from the deep water of the early baby years I would one day do my own research and find out for myself whether parenting really needed to be so intensive, and if childhood really had changed so much since I was a child in the 1970s and 1980s.

Some time later, while writing a thesis on parenting in the twenty-first century, I was startled to discover that, despite the sensationalist stories in the media and hysterical tales of child abduction, the rates of child abduction and child murder by strangers are tiny and not increasing, and the rates of infant mortality in general have plummeted. In addition, the statistical rates of child sexual abuse in the developed world have declined an extraordinary 62 per cent since the early 1990s (even though children today are much more likely to report abuse).[1] The rates for children becoming seriously ill have also tumbled – far fewer children die from accidental death and significantly fewer children experience trauma – so if we look at the actual evidence, it turns out that if it really is a sick world we live in today, it was a great deal sicker when today's parents were children.

These could be the glory days of the parent-child relationship, and parents today have the opportunity to enjoy parenting in a way that our own parents and grandparents could never have dreamed of. But this isn't what's happening – instead parents seem to have missed the party. Psychologists are concerned about research showing that parents today don't enjoy rearing their children as much as former generations did.[2] Robin Simon, a professor of sociology and author of 'The Joys of Parenthood, Reconsidered' surveyed over 11,000 parents and reported that 'Parents of young children report far more depression, emotional distress, and other negative emotions than non-parents'.[3] Clearly something is rotten in the state of parenting.

But it doesn't have to be like this – we parents could learn how to handle our hysterical and consumerist culture and simply enjoy raising our children. Hurrying to get to the latest supervised play arrangement could be swapped for children spending lazy days outside, unsupervised, playing with friends, exploring, building dens and riding their bikes. I can hear the shouts of dismay and derision already: 'No, we just can't do that! Life has changed! Children simply have to be raised in captivity; we have no other option! … You are being naïve, life has moved on!' Yet after reading this book you will realise that life has indeed moved on: with levels of obesity, emotional problems, cyber-bullying, screen addiction, teen suicide, learning and behavioural difficulties increasing at a startling rate, the computer in your living room is much more likely to be a danger to your children than the tree in your local park.

Our perceptions of risk have been completely distorted by commercial interests whose sole reason for existing is to stalk parents and frighten them into buying more stuff. Big business has created a culture of fear and paranoia which has scared parents into thinking that they need to put lorryloads of effort into what comes naturally anyway. Not only that, but parents are now habitually regarded as incompetent fools who need extensive training to make up for their glaring inadequacies. We have gone from 'Mother knows best' to 'the child is king' in two short decades, and consequently parenting today has become incredibly demanding and stressful.

In a world obsessed with safety, progress and development, the culture of over-parenting is being sold by marketing maestros as the road to success, and yet over-parenting doesn't improve the life of either the child or the parent – it merely adds to everybody's stress levels. As Tom Hodgkinson, the author of *The Idle Parent*, has pointed out, 'An unhealthy dose of the work ethic is threatening to wreck childhood.'[4] This would perhaps be forgivable if children were happier but, sadly, they're not. Both parents and children today are more anxious and discontented than ever before, despite children being safer, healthier and cleverer today than ever before.[5] When 250 children aged eight to thirteen years old were asked in an extensive UNICEF study what they needed to make them happy, the results were an eye-opener: children want friendships, their own time and the outdoors.[6] How often do we hear parents stating matter-of-factly, 'It's different now; we can't give our children the freedom we so enjoyed as kids; times have changed'? And yes, in many ways times are different – but it's not more dangerous.

We parents need to fight back against the culture of fear, and instead begin to address the true risks that are impacting our children. We needn't fill our lives acting as social secretaries for our children, we needn't ferry our children from dance class to drama to football, and we needn't wrap them in cotton wool – rather we can simply send them out to play.

When I ask clients in my counselling practice to think back to the happiest moments of their childhood, with most it is the freedom that springs to mind; days spent with their pals on their bikes exploring, or roaming the fields, or building ever more complicated forts. Playing in houses with a responsible adult keeping an eye on the situation so that everyone shares nicely will not be remembered by our children with nostalgia, nor will primary-coloured plastic palaces throbbing with overstimulated children be a feature of our kids' happy memories.

After reading this book, I hope that parents will learn to hold their heads up high and fight back against the creepy cult of over-parenting that has gained epic status for parents in the twenty-first century. This book is a call to arms, because a revolution in child-rearing needs to happen – parents and children need to be free to have fun again!

1

The Culture of Fear – It's All About the Money!

Fear cuts deeper than swords.

George R. R. Martin, *Game of Thrones*[1]

It was 2007 and my husband and I were going shopping for our first baby's cot mattress. We had been given a second-hand cot and even though we already had a perfectly good, barely used mattress at home, it was apparently deemed to be unconscionably dangerous to place my baby's body on the second-hand mattress for even an afternoon nap (according to my experienced mother-friends, there were massive links between second-hand mattresses and cot death).

We were a bit mad at the time, you see, because we had just entered the peculiar la-la-land of the new parent. 'Do you want the standard mattress or the specially designed one that is recommended by the Sudden Infant Death Association?' demanded the sales assistant in a slightly aggressive manner. 'Oh,' I replied airily, 'I'll take the one that gives her cot death.' Lack of sleep had rendered myself and my husband slightly hysterical, and we started laughing at my limp joke like hyenas on crack cocaine. 'Two, in fact,' shrieked my bleary-eyed sleep-deprived husband. The sales assistant wasn't amused; she evidently thought we were cheapskate misers for even speaking about the cheaper, not-recommended-by-anyone mattress. 'The standard mattress is €69 but the one that's recommended by the Sudden Infant Death Association is €130. It's up to you of course,' she intoned.

I blinked. Wow, that was a seriously big difference in price! Was it not enough that I was buying a new mattress in the first place? Dare I defy death and choose the cheaper version (even though at €69, cheap it certainly wasn't)? No, reader, I didn't dare. Despite my gay laughter, I chose the expensive, gold-star, 'recommended by the Sudden Infant Death Association' mattress, all the while knowing that I had just been swizzed out of an extra €61 that we really couldn't afford.

This is an example of exactly how parenting has been hijacked by marketing. Nowadays parents and children are big business – everywhere you look there are books, articles, programmes, websites, forums, blogs, educational toys and endless equipment and accessories that are described as essential for parents. It's no longer enough to muddle through, relying on instinct and family wisdom – nowadays the 'good enough' parent is being replaced by the 'super parent', and clipping at the heels of the 'super parent' is the 'ultra parent'.

And yet a scientific study called 'Track Your Happiness', which seeks to discover what makes life worth living, shows us that all this effort isn't making for happy families. In this study an app is used to track people's emotions as they go about their daily lives (see www.trackyourhappiness.org) and the data shows that on a list of people whose company they enjoy, parents rank their own children as low – very low.[2] As Matthew Killingsworth, the lead researcher of the study, stated, 'Interacting with your friends is better than interacting with your spouse, which is better than interacting with other relatives, which is better than interacting with acquaintances, which is better than interacting with children … Who are on a par with strangers.'[3] Oh dear!

And perhaps this is why the (male) comedian, Louis C. K., developed a cult following among parents when he said in a Father's Day skit, 'You wanna know why your father spends so long on the toilet? *Because he's not sure he wants to be a father.*'[4]

Not only that, but a seminal study led by the Nobel-Prize-winning behavioural economist Daniel Kahneman measured which activities gave working women most pleasure, and it turns out that minding children ranked a lowly sixteenth out of a choice of nineteen – behind exercising, having a nap, watching TV, even *housework*![5] If parents aren't enjoying raising their children very much and children are increasingly falling prey to mental health issues, then we need to take some time to examine why the fun has gone from family life.

WHY PARENTING HAS BECOME SO DIFFICULT

There are many reasons why parenting has become so difficult, but one of the more significant reasons is that children are no longer expected to be particularly useful. Since the end of the Second World War, childhood has been redefined and children have gone from being their parents' unpaid employees to being their non-paying bosses. According to the sociologist, Viviana Zelizer, the modern child is 'economically worthless but emotionally price-less'.[6] There is no longer a system of reciprocity, with parents keeping their children fed and watered until they are old enough to kick something back. Instead, rather like a protected species, parents are nowadays encouraged to treat their children like a hyper-sensitive bonsai tree, which, to be raised successfully, must be kept in a certain climate with exactly the right amount of attention, stimulation and nutrition at precisely the right time.

Another reason parenting has become so difficult is because of the heightened expectations of what the arrival of children will do to their parents' happiness levels. In previous years parenting was a given; you were a child, you grew up, you got married, you had children, you grew old and then you died. But today, because of contraception, parenting has become a choice, and so now when we choose to have children we expect that it will improve our lives in some way. We've seen the Hollywood movies, we've seen the gorgeous pictures in Laura Ashley of blooming expectant mothers in magical nurseries and so we have been taught to picture parenting as this soul-fulfilling and aesthetically pleasing calm journey to nirvana. But if it doesn't turn out like that, we have so much invested in the experience, we tend to fall emotionally from a cliff with disappointment.

In addition, many parents are working too much and this has resulted in, among many other pressures, a lot of fights among husbands and wives about who is doing the childcare, the shopping, the household chores ... and to what standard. The traditional masculine and feminine roles have disintegrated, with nothing to replace them; there is no rule book in this new world, with most couples being forced to slug it out until some sort of balance is found. As Jennifer Senior, author of *All Joy and No Fun: The Paradox of Modern Parenting*, points out, women are working almost as much as men these days, and sometimes more: 'women bring home the bacon, fry it up, serve it for breakfast, and use its greasy remains to make candles for their children's science projects'.[7] When the feminists were chaining themselves to the railings and burning their bras they perhaps didn't give enough consideration to how the modern-day family would work out in practice – if the men and the women are both working, then who is minding the babies?

Sadly (for me, anyway) John Maynard Keynes' prediction about a fifteen-hour working week has not happened. Instead, with the arrival of technology, has come the twenty-four-hour, seven-day week where many of us are pretty much always semi-working. This means that we parents are so time-pressed that we find we have very little time to spend with our children, and so we try to make the available time special. And so everything becomes even more heightened and burdened by expectation. Consequently, we tend to indulge our children during our precious free time to ensure that it is enjoyable for all the family, and perhaps this is why many of our children are spoilt.

Many sociologists argue that raising children has become so challenging because we live in a toxic culture where material goods and status are often given more value than time and pleasure. Cynical advertisers show us pictures of laughing, happy kids playing with the latest plastic crap that will apparently keep them entertained and laughing for hours. It doesn't add up, because we know from bitter experience that the children won't be laughing for hours, but the images are alluring and the children fall for it. And so they are pitted against their parents and begin their campaign of pester power; and maybe this is the biggest challenge for parents today: how to stop spending bucketloads of unnecessary cash when raising our children without feeling as though we're ruining our children's fun.

PARENTS DRIVEN BY FEAR

'Toxic parenthood' is perhaps an accurate description of the pressure cooker that is parenting in the twenty-first century. In one generation, contemporary culture has changed at lightning speed, so that our own childhood bears little resemblance to our children's experiences. Parents are expected to navigate between media soundbites that proclaim hysterically the devastating impact of junk food, sugar highs, couch-potato kids, battery children, electronic babysitters, techno-brats and pester power, and many, many more potential hazards that are even today being dreamed up by sharp-suited, young, single and childless men in high-rise offices in cities like London or New York.

We have no way to compare our children's experiences with our own childhood as we didn't have the same issues to contend with:

child obesity, learning and behavioural difficulties, food issues and child safety simply weren't on the agenda then in the manner they are now. Brendan O'Connor declared in the *Sunday Independent* (14 April 2013):

> *In a balanced life, children wouldn't feel like a chore, and the fact that they do sometimes says more about how modern life is out of kilter than it does about us or them. And that's why we worry, about not creating the memories, about brushing them off, about not giving them enough attention, about being better parents, about not wasting the precious time … But modern life doesn't allow that. Because in modern life we have to have it all. And when you have it all, you have nothing properly.*

Parenting these days is perceived as a huge, momentous mountain to climb and so we parents worry that we will fail. This burden of expectation is crushing parents – but perhaps it is not parenting that has changed so considerably? Maybe it is society and the media's expectations of parenting that have changed.

THE CULTURE OF FEAR

In 1929 Charles F. Kettering, Director of General Motors, wrote an article called 'Keep the Consumer Dissatisfied', which (horribly) became almost a code of conduct for salesmen the world over. According to Kettering, the key to economic prosperity is the organised creation of dissatisfaction: 'If everyone were satisfied no one would buy the new thing.'[8] And this is why salesmen freak parents out with hideously scary stories – perhaps the most significant change that has occurred to parenting since our own childhood is not that childhood has become unsafe or more difficult, rather it is that commercial interests have cottoned on to the idea that they can make serious money from parent's fears and anxieties.

Marketing, as we know, sells the sizzle not the sausage, and parents are being sold the fiendish promise that if they read all the books, the blogs and the forums, watch *Supernanny*, buy the apps, invest in the endless array of educational toys and DVDs, buy all the safety equipment and accessories, the organic brain food and the brain-enhancing multi-vitamins, then their children will be happier, safer, cleverer and more successful. This message is very powerful, but it's not true … and it engenders vast levels of worry and guilt among parents.

WHERE HAS ALL THE FREE FUN GONE?

In many ways, the easy-going nature of the spontaneous fun of children's lives is morphing into a structured, supervised and costly exercise that parents have to work hard to provide. During the hot summer of 2013, the journalist Toby Young wrote nostalgically in the *Daily Mail* about his own childhood while decrying the need these days to make vast amounts of money if we want to entertain our children:

> *I now have four children of my own – three of them boys – and in many ways they have the same opportunity that I did. If they are lucky, and this spell of incredible weather lasts, they'll have six glorious weeks ahead of them. They can ride their bikes, go pond-dipping and build a secret camp. It could be a summer they'll remember for the rest of their lives just like 1976 was for me. But I don't suppose they'll do any of that.*
>
> *For my children, the holidays mean more time to spend in front of screens, the kind you watch and the kind you play on. Instead of joining their friends outside for a game of football, it'll be FIFA 13 and Score. They are products of the digital age; my memories of summers in the great outdoors seem to belong to the analogue era.*
>
> *We have moved just one generation forward, but that summer of endless blue skies belongs to a different world. We queued in the*

street for water. My children expect to drink it encased in plastic. We had water fights with buckets. Mine expect a ride in a log-flume at a theme park.

So is it any wonder my four children can't amuse themselves in the sunshine when they've been surrounded by electronic devices all their lives? Having been brought up on a diet of video games and Hollywood blockbusters, they're unlikely to disappear into the woods to play cowboys and Indians.

At least they have the choice. Others will be penned in by parents worried about the traffic, or by an impossible schedule of improving activities, all organised by adults, most involving a car journey. If they do roam 'free' then they are sure to be linked to the mothership by mobile phone. The only way to persuade my kids to leave the house will be to organise a trip to Legoland or Alton Towers. Unfortunately, I'm not sure my bank manager will allow it. You think I'm exaggerating? When I went to Legoland last month to celebrate my five-year-old son's birthday, the price of admission for two adults and five children was £304.50.[9]

IF IT COSTS, IS IT WORTH IT?

It's a cliché we've all heard – babies and toddlers get more entertainment from the box than the toy inside. Yet we continually fall for the sinister advertisers' canny marketing: Oh yes, *this* toy is educational and creative, blah, blah, blah. My children's favourite toys are several bizarre, flat, foam cushions (acquired by accident after they were used as props for an amateur dramatics performance) from which they can make houses, pretend to be in bed and create fences to jump over. Yes this is their best toy; not the child's pink laptop, not the computerised train set, not even the jigsaws or the artist's easel.

When we look at the rise and rise of the Hollywood-style Christmas experience, the elaborately *egg*sessive Easter egg hunts and the 'supersize me' childrens' birthday parties, we soon realise just how much big business is leading the way in the creation of an unnecessarily expensive standard of operation that is causing crippling financial pressure on loving parents. Children's birthday parties have become such heightened affairs that they are often a significant financial burden on parents. But just how crazy is that? All the children want is some cake and the chance to gather all their pals around for some fun.

And yet, if you are building a friendship with someone new, don't you find that you are delighted to receive an invitation to their house? For me, an invitation to the house of an acquaintance is often a sign that our relationship is deepening. This is exactly how the children feel – they want to go to their friends' houses because they want to know their friends on a deeper level. Just as we shouldn't need to book an entertainer if we throw a dinner party (unless you're on *Come Dine With Me*), we shouldn't feel the need to book a clown or a bouncy castle, or professional cleaners, if we throw a children's birthday party.

PRODUCTS, PRODUCTS AND MORE PRODUCTS

Going into a baby store today, customers are accosted by an enormous array of health and safety products that are 'specially recommended' by some organisation or other. I recently wandered through our local baby store and gazed in bewilderment at the latest gadget that will apparently prevent my child from opening the toilet lid and tumbling down the passageway to certain death.

We lucky parents can now buy stuff that supposedly protects our babies from table corners, electric sockets, steps, windows, taps, toilets, doors swinging shut, cupboards swinging open, containers, drawers and any number of relatively benign commonplace fixtures in our homes. There are also sun tents, sun shades, sun protectors, rain protectors, wind protectors, glass safety-film and elaborate stair gates that no man or beast can open. My husband and I (after much consideration, thought and discussion) didn't buy a stair gate for our babies. We decided that we would prefer to teach our children to come down the stairs on their bum until they were able to walk down safely. Hardly revolutionary, but the look of shock and horror that appeared on other parents' faces when they realised that *There Was No Stair Gate On The Stairs In This House* would have been funny if it wasn't so unsettling. In the end we were given not one, not two, but three, stair gates by concerned friends and relatives. We didn't use any of them.

FACT: The 1969–74 'Sesame Street: Old School' DVD is nowadays recommended 'For Adult Viewing Only'. 'Why?' you may ask. The answer is because it is apparently wildly dangerous. You see, happy children playing Follow the Leader, climbing through a giant pipe, balancing on a piece of wood, and weaving through sheets that are drying on a line is now considered so dangerous that the DVD is banned for children in the twenty-first century. Even though at the time it was considered ideal and even educational.[10]

Thudguard®, a helmet for toddlers to wear when they are learning to walk, costs nervous parents between £21.99 and £29.99, and, by the way, it isn't suitable for 'pedal cyclists, skateboarders and rollerskaters'. This helmet is specifically for toddlers to wear as they are learning to walk. And presumably when the child is deemed fit to walk without a helmet, the responsible parent should then bring the child around the house pointing out dangerous spots where the child might fall and hurt himself – because, of course, the child won't have figured that out for himself.

As well as providing statistics about child head injuries, the Thudguard® helmet is endorsed by testimonials from respected professionals – from neurophysiologists to psychiatrists – which further convince parents that this helmet is an essential part of the kit that every safety conscious parent must buy before any lasting damage is done to their toddlers' heads.[11] The message is very convincing – apparently there are 318,575 baby and toddler head injuries recorded every year. However, what is not stated is how many of these head injuries are minor bruises and scrapes – indeed, I would venture the opinion that in 2009 my daughter (a livewire) might have accounted for approximately 118,000 of those bruises!

IT'S ALL ABOUT THE MONEY

Perhaps the most annoying gadget for the new parent is the new extreme baby-tracking monitor. Yes, it's not enough to hear the baby crying from down the hallway; instead we need to have a fully amplified version right next to our bed so that we jump up in terror six times nightly every time the baby stirs. Not only that, but we now need to be able to view the baby with a video that films it as it sleeps; we also apparently need an app on our phone so that we know how often the baby's body position changes, its heart rate, skin temperature, blood oxygen level and sleep quality at any given moment.

The grand promise with these monitors is they are a means of assuaging parents' worries, giving us peace of mind and freeing us to concentrate on other activities, but of course, as we all know deep down, it's a false promise. In truth, many of these gadgets merely serve to up the ante – they give us more to worry about, create more expectation, and more is then asked of us, which of course, causes more pressure and stress.

The biggest fear of parents of new babies is sudden infant death syndrome (SIDS), and with good reason, as SIDS is a leading cause of early infant death. But unfortunately, the cause of SIDS is still uncertain (though current research points to underlying issues) and hi-tech monitors don't actually cure SIDS. What are we to do? Commercial interests design and advertise products in the hope of triggering parents' fears, some of us fall for it and then talk it up, and the heightened conversation creates a buzz of worry among parents. If we snigger at these extreme-worst-case-scenario products we soon feel foolhardy in the face of other parents' disapproval and so all too often we inwardly roll our eyes and join 'em.

More experienced parents may smirk as they read this, smugly satisfied that they no longer fall for cynical marketing ploys directed at nervous first-timers. However, it is mainly new parents who are the target market, and they're not smirking; the sharp rise in the production of extreme safety gadgets for babies is currently being exploited by canny businessmen. If you were to buy the Owlet Baby Monitor, a 'proactive health monitor', it would set you back a hefty €185. Considering that the estimated spend of parents on babycare products in the UK before the birth is £1,619; which equates to a staggering £492 million every year, this is very big business[12] – a business that makes parents feel anxious, fearful, flawed … and broke.

RISK COMPENSATION

The annoying part of all this emphasis on safe-proofing is that it has been proved that humans tend to compensate for risk when they use safety equipment – they drive faster when they wear a safety belt and take more risks when they feel more protected by the equipment.[13] For example, David Ball, a professor of risk management at Middlesex University, analysed injury statistics and found that 'The advent of all these special surfaces for playgrounds has contributed very little, if anything at all, to the safety of children.'[14] The children don't worry so much about falling on the rubber, so they're not as careful. Don't get me wrong, those rubber floors on the playgrounds are brilliant – they must prevent millions of cut knees every day – but, because of our innate tendency to compensate for risk, human beings tend to behave in a more reckless manner when they have a safety net. And this is why the rubber surfaces don't prevent more serious accidents. Every so often random, freak and tragic accidents occur, and apart from perhaps hoping that we are mentally robust enough to be able to cope should the tragedy land on our shoulders, beyond that there is nothing we can do about it.

Case Study

Fiona attended counselling to treat anxiety related to her only son. Jamie was a bright little nine-year-old boy who was becoming increasingly resentful of his mother's tendency to over-protect him. At our first meeting, Fiona described how she was living on a knife-edge, consumed with dread and fear that 'something terrible' would happen to her child. This irrational anxiety had spilled into every aspect of her life.

She finally decided to attend counselling as a consequence of a school tour that had gone disastrously wrong. 'I had tried to volunteer as a helper for the school tour, just like I had in other years, but they didn't need me this year. I was incredibly fearful of Jamie on the bus on his own and on the school tour – so I decided to follow the bus on the school tour. I know it was a bit mad but I felt so anxious. When we got to the aquarium I noticed the adults present looked a bit harassed so I thought I'd stay nearby in case the children needed some extra supervision. I honestly thought I was being unobtrusive. But the other kids in the class noticed me and they started to mock Jamie that his mother was stalking him. He was absolutely furious with me and he's barely speaking to me now.'

As the counselling process proceeded, Fiona further explored her fears and anxieties about Jamie and it emerged that it was predominantly based on the scary stories she had looked up on Internet news sites. Fiona was unhappy and bored in her job and tended to use the Internet as a means of escape. She would then become gripped by the latest horror story on the net, and fearful for her son. Fiona also worked very long hours and was consumed by guilt that Jamie was more often than not being minded by childcare professionals, and so she tried to make up for her 'neglect' by over-protecting her son when she had the chance. It had become a warped demonstration of her love for him.

Fiona finally learned to loosen the reins on Jamie as we worked together to test the validity of her beliefs. The more she educated herself about the subject, the less she found to fear. Within the counselling context, Fiona also engaged in a regular programme of creative visualisation to help her to envisage a happy future for herself and her child. In addition, we collaborated to challenge her habit of seeking out horror stories to further frighten herself. Eventually Fiona's anxiety reduced to more manageable levels and she now repeats some personal mantras to herself to ensure she keeps her tendency to magnify her fears in check. She also chose to change her job and spend more time with her son, thereby reducing her need to over-compensate.

IF IT BLEEDS, IT LEADS

The media is (mis-)leading the way for parents to believe that children must be cosseted, comforted and kept wrapped up in cotton wool at all times. Papers sell if they have a scary message to deliver – sales don't increase if the headline reads, 'Life is fairly good for many people these days'. And so, even though crime is down, the reporting of crime in the media is up. A recent study of newspaper coverage from the University of Toronto found that there was a new homicide reported every single day in the Toronto newspaper over the course of a year.[15] This was strange, because that year there were 68 homicides in Toronto, not 365. So how could a new one appear every day? The answer was that if there wasn't a local murder to report, the media went outside the city to find one. Simply put, the media needs to sell papers, violent and terrible crime sells papers, hence we read about horrible crimes constantly. For the media, chilling crimes are a money-spinner.

Our parents' generation did not have to negotiate the same levels of anxiety as today's parents. In years gone by, tragedies involving children being murdered, raped and abused were reported as serious news, not as gruesome shockers, magnified and sensationalised so as to sell more papers. Michele Elliot, psychologist and founder and director of the child protection charity Kidscape, points out that 'It is no good asking our own mothers for advice … when they were bringing us up, they didn't seem to be hit by shocking news of yet another child murder.'[16] (And this is why these days grandparents are often even more neurotic than parents, even though when they were raising their own kids they were decidedly laissez-faire – the grandparents too have been infected by hysterical media sensations). But, as we shall see later, neuroscience shows that the more frequently a person views horrific pictures, the more feelings of anxiety they induce, and so the explosion of sensationalist journalism has heightened our sense of anxiety simply to make more money.

In truth, the rates of child abduction remain static: once in a blue moon a child will be abducted; however this is an incredibly rare phenomenon (which will be examined in Chapter 2). Even though the rate of child abduction, just like child murder, remains tiny and constant, our perception of this has changed utterly: it is readily accepted among sociologists and crime experts that it is much safer to be a child in 2015 than it was in 1985, but it is the rare parent who would accept this.

How we've changed

Ireland's dark history of children being abused at the hands of the local clergy, and orphans in institutions being subjected to horrific physical and sexual abuse has left a deep mark on the people and we are now trying to make good the damage caused by the secrets of the past. As a country, Ireland has moved on from being riddled with hypocrisy, lies and dirty secrets to become a nation that is working valiantly to provide a safe and open society. Thankfully, in this new era of enlightened attitudes to sex, children are recovering more quickly from incidences of sexual abuse and appear to be less affected by their experiences as a consequence of counselling and understanding from society. Not only that, but thanks to widespread education practices and safety programmes, children these days are much more likely to tell their parents if they are subjected to unsavoury behaviour, and, unlike in years past, children now are usually believed. And so, unlikely as it may appear, we children of the 1970s, 1980s and 1990s were much more likely to be abused than are our children, and we were much more likely to be deeply affected by the experience.

This is one of the many reasons why it is significantly safer to be a child in Ireland today than it was in the 1980s. In fact, today's kids are the safest kids that have *ever* lived. There was an explosion of interest in the media in 2013 when two Roma children in Ireland were taken from their families by the state because they had a different hair colour and complexion than their siblings.

Then there was a shocked outcry when it emerged that in fact any suspicions about them having been taken from their true family were untrue, and were based on very flimsy evidence that seemed to be a direct consequence of racial profiling. The outcry from the media was enormous; however, there was a strident backlash that argued that strong-arm tactics such as these were necessary. One commentator on national radio argued that we as a society must put up with incidents such as this – 'I don't care if 10,000 children are taken from their homes if it saves just one child's life'.[17]

But what does this mean? Children removed without argument from their homes because of random suspicions on Facebook? A society oppressed by suspicion and paranoia, and communities living in fear and dread of the child-snatcher? Or would it be more beneficial if the media was subject to consistent guidelines set down so as to inform rather than promote suspicion, fear and paranoia in our society? Thinking that anything is allowable 'if it saves even one child' is a crazy thought process. If 10,000 children could be taken from their homes by the police, without their parents' consent, to save just one life, we would be living in a fascist state. It would be a country filled with misery, anger and a deep mistrust of the authorities. If this well-regarded broadcaster really thinks any amount of hassle and distress would be worth it to save just one child's life, then he should really be encouraging us all to stop driving – that would save a child's life within the week.

EXPLORING ROAD SAFETY

Road traffic accidents pose a far greater threat to children's lives than child abduction does. But contemplating risk is a funny thing. We don't like to be reminded that we are all simply part of a statistical mass that will inevitably one day get sick and die. We prefer to forget that more kids die in the back of a car than playing on the streets, and that every time we load the kids into the car we are putting both the children and ourselves at risk. Instead, in a strange way, we prefer to dwell on the unlikely event of child abduction, or the implications of a pylon being erected in the area, or some other rare and random danger.

Living in an area with pylons will probably cause the death of one child through leukaemia every ten to twenty years, and many people become very upset about this. But when we hear that there are an average of fourteen deaths every month on the roads – approximately 168 deaths per year – we don't really do very much about it.[18] We know we could stop driving, but we don't. We shudder inwardly when we hear that 30 per cent of these deaths are of young people aged twenty-five and under, and we shiver when we are reminded that the most dangerous time of the day or night on the roads is between 4 p.m. and 6 p.m. – when parents are most often in the car taking kids to activities – and that most accidents happen within five miles of home.[19] We all know it's all a terrible tragedy. We all know we should slow down. But often we don't. And we won't stop using the car. Absolutely no way. The car is essential. Because we need our cars, we like our cars, and so we are prepared to live with that particular risk. And so the debate rages on.

But road accidents don't sell papers, so the media doesn't explode every time there is a tragedy on the road – a small factual paragraph is usually deemed sufficient. So our culture teaches us to accept road accidents as a necessary but tragic part of life, but to lose our heads over child abduction. Parents react to this culture accordingly; we become obsessed with supervision and the random possibility of child abduction and other unlikely dangers, while dismissing the very real danger of road accidents, saying, 'Sure, you can't live like that, you'd go mad!'

Perceptions of risk

If an adult (in 1885, 1985 or in 2015) wishes to abduct a child there is very little that can be done to prevent this; the adult merely needs to regularly visit areas where children are playing and eventually the chance to abduct a child will present itself. The first child might resist and so might the second, but eventually a child will unquestioningly do as the predator says. But the sad fact is that most predators go to the poorest areas of the world to prey upon children: it is there where we really should worry about children's welfare.

Child sex tourism plays an increasingly large part in the world's tourist market; for example, a UNICEF study has reported that over 30 per cent of children aged between twelve and eighteen in Kenya are involved in the sex tourism business.[20] And an estimated third of all prostitutes in Cambodia are underage.[21] Child sex tourism is estimated to be a multi-billion euro illegal industry which is steadily growing, and a US department has reported on fake fishing expeditions to the Amazon which in reality are child sex tours for European and American paedophiles and sexual predators.[22]

If you were to read a book entirely about the risk of child abduction, then 99 per cent of the book would be about children from places such as Thailand or Brazil being prostituted to wealthy older men from richer countries. Barely even one sentence in the book would be given over to middle-class concerns about the highly unlikely possibility of Irish children from intact homes being abducted – except perhaps to say that parents worry excessively about it. We don't tend to fret over the unlikely event of our children contracting some rare and dreadful disease and dying; and nor should we. In much the same way, we shouldn't spend much time worrying ourselves about child abduction when there are more real concerns regarding children's health, such as depression, anxiety and other mental health issues that are, certainly in comparison to child abduction, quite common.

Rare and random tragedies, such as being struck by lightning or being abducted, are largely unpreventable. But there is much we can do to change the phenomenal suicide rate and the growth in mental health issues amongst young people. Problems with mental health are the largest source of ill health in our young people in Ireland today,[23] and when we realise that ten to fourteen people die by suicide every week in Ireland it soon becomes apparent that our eye seems to be on entirely the wrong ball (see boxed text and Figure 1.1).[24] Joylessness, depression, anxiety and mental ill health are causing more misery in Ireland today than stranger child abduction.

In Ireland every year, approximately:

- 450–700 people die by suicide.
- 12,000 people are admitted to hospital for reasons of self-harm (using methods such as attempted hanging, poisoning and cutting).
- 93,000 adolescents (20%) experience psychological problems.
- 72,000 adolescents (15.6%) are diagnosed with an emotional or behavioural disorder.
- 20,000 adolescents (4.5%) experience a major clinical depression.

Sources: National Office for Suicide Prevention, Ireland; St Patrick's Hospital, Dublin.[25]

Figure 1.1: Child suicides in Europe.
(Note: European age standardised rate per 100,000 aged 0–19 years by sex for EU member states plus Norway.)[26]

Every year in Ireland an estimated 450–700 people die by suicide, while 162 people died by road traffic accidents in 2012.[27] Curiously, we seem to ignore the fact that while road traffic accidents are a huge threat to our lives, nevertheless a good many more people die by suicide than on the roads in Ireland. Similarly, many people do terrible things to children every day, but your child is infinitely more likely to be harmed by someone among your family and friends than by a stranger. That is not to say stranger child abduction doesn't happen – it does – but it is very rare.

However, suicide is not so rare; the suicide rate for teenagers in Ireland is the second-highest in Europe.[28] And when we consider that suicide is the third-highest cause of death among teenagers worldwide, we can see that there are some serious issues to contend with here in Ireland.[29] We need to be more aware of happiness and mental well-being, and less obsessed with child safety, because we ignore mental well-being at our peril.

PARENTS' PERCEPTIONS OF STRANGER DANGER

Most parents will have felt the cold, white fear of a lost child at some point, and so we can identify in some tiny way with the indescribable pain of parents' suffering after a child is abducted. The family and friends are left without closure or understanding, searching for answers, and with a process of grieving that is bewildering. There is hardly a more terrible experience imaginable for parents. But as the parenting expert, Dr John McSharry, pointed out in *The Irish Times*, 'Though incidents of child abduction or harm from strangers receive a lot of media attention, they are remarkably rare events, particularly when compared with other dangers.'[30]

Unfortunately for parents, the media have realised that an abduction of a child by a stranger will send sales soaring and they milk this situation with a shocking cynicism and intensity. As a direct result of media hype, parents' fears of stranger danger in Britain and Ireland have reached feverish levels since the tragic disappearance of Madeleine McCann in Portugal in 2007.

The sad case of April Jones, who went missing from the small town of Machynlleth in Wales in September 2012, is a typical example of the media frenzy that erupts when a child is abducted. The response to this tragedy was phenomenal; the international media descended on the town and hourly bulletins were broadcast worldwide. Sky News became positively obsessive about its coverage, running continuous repeated bulletins about the non-appearance of April. Perhaps as a consequence of the lack of something new to report, Sky News took the step of offering an app that people could download to see the geography of the town and the areas the police and volunteers were searching. Eventually, Mark Bridger, who lived on the same estate and was known to April, was sentenced to life imprisonment for her abduction and assumed murder, as her body has never been found. This wasn't a case of 'stranger danger' – Mark Bridger had lured April to her death with what was believed to be a false promise of a sleepover with his daughter.

The first few weeks of April's disappearance cast a pall over many parents' lives all over Britain and Ireland as we shuddered to think what could happen to our lives should such a random tragedy strike. Eight weeks later there remained a ghostly collection of pink ribbons in a local estate near my children's school in East Galway, a weather-beaten, sad and daily reminder to remember April. And yet, how many other children had died in Britain and Ireland in those eight weeks? It is a sad but indisputable fact that tragedies happen every day; some are perhaps more avoidable than others, but we can't raise healthy, happy children by keeping them imprisoned in our sitting rooms.

However, the level of media obsession with horrible stories

involving children begs the question: can we, as a society, continue to live with constant reminders of harrowing tragedies? Should more time be given to considering how we should handle tragedy in society so that we can respect the departed but don't become obsessed with the sadder elements of life? These are difficult questions but it is important that we face them.

THE IMPACT OF THE MADELEINE McCANN TRAGEDY

Many of us still experience a shudder of horror when we read the name Madeleine McCann in the newspapers, closely followed by a terrible wince of sympathy for her family. Nonetheless, the heart-rendingly sad story of the abduction of this child needs to be explored as it highlights the media's cynically opportunistic attitude towards children today: sad stories about children sell newspapers.

When Madeleine disappeared in May 2007, the media almost detonated with excitement. It could be argued that their fanatical obsession was understandable, because the sales of the English tabloids went through the roof that summer as the public followed the media obsession (guilty, your honour!). Kate McCann had this to say about the media coverage of the case:

> *Although I don't doubt that many of them did genuinely want to help, it was a while before I realised the hard lesson that the media are not about spreading news but selling products. Their overriding concern was not us or, sadly, Madeleine, it was someone shouting down the phone that the editor needed 800 words by 10 o'clock.*[31]

From 3 August 2007 to 10 November 2007, the *Daily Express* dedicated at least a section of every front page to Madeleine's disappearance.[32] This action kept this harrowing story before the eyes of the public when in truth it was dead in the water. If we examine the dates, we can see that Madeleine had disappeared in May, and by August when this hundred-day print run began, there was nothing new to report. The story was over, the media had nothing new to discuss, but the papers continued to use the tragedy to sell papers. Of these one hundred front-page stories, eighty-two were under the main headline, with 'MADELEINE' in red block capitals, and all too often with that very sad photo of Madeleine looking up at the camera with the little mark on the iris of her right eye to further provoke and retain readers' interest and anguish. At this stage the media was accusing anyone and everyone, from Kate, Gerry and the 'Tapas Seven' to the cat next door. With hindsight it becomes likely that the media was cynically accusing these innocent people to give new life to a story with which the public had become obsessed and on which the newspapers had nothing new to offer.

In 2009, appearing before the Media Select Committee in the UK Parliament, the then editor of the *Daily Express*, Peter Hill, was accused of being 'obsessed' with this story, and as we can see from the following excerpt from the House of Commons, it does seem to have been a cynical interest in the case:

Chairman: So you reported a story about Madeleine McCann on your front page over many, many days. Can you tell us in terms roughly of newspaper sales the difference between the sales of the Daily Express on the day when you had a Madeleine McCann story and the days when you did not?

Mr Hill: It certainly increased the circulation of the Daily Express *by many thousands on those days without a doubt. As would any item which was of such great interest. It also massively increased the audiences on the BBC as their Head of News has acknowledged. It did this for all newspapers. The way that newspaper people work is that their job is to report on the events which are of interest to their readers and of course this was of consuming interest to readers of all the newspapers not just the* Daily Express. *Yes, it was a consequence. This is what newspapers do. Their job is to sell newspapers; that is what they do.*

Chairman: *Their job is to sell newspapers as long as they are also telling the truth?*

Mr Hill: *At the time we had no reason to believe we were not telling the truth.*

Chairman: *You also took the decision to run a McCann story day after day. To what extent was that because you had seen the consequence it would have on your circulation?*

Mr Hill: *You have to understand that this was the only show around at that time. We were getting 10,000 messages – I am not just talking about hits – on our website; we were getting at least 10,000 messages a day, comments from people. Nothing like this had ever been seen. It was quite clear to me that this was what the readers wanted to read about. So naturally I would do this because that is what newspapers do.*[33]

According to Hill, 'There was an insatiable clamour for information about what was going on.'[34] Clarence Mitchell (the McCanns' media spokesman) speculated that running a Madeleine McCann story increased newspaper sales by 40,000 or 50,000 copies a day.[35] This media circus ended very badly for the McCanns as the parents had been handed a poisoned chalice by media interest; they had to use the media to get the information relating to the disappearance of their daughter out to the world, but when the media needed further information (as the story became tired) they turned on the parents in a manner that could only be described as vicious. Gerry McCann said later: 'Madeleine, I believe, was made a commodity and profits were to be made.'[36] The McCanns afterwards accepted £550,000 from Express Newspapers over more than 100 defamatory articles in the *Daily Express, Daily Star* and their Sunday titles.[37]

During the summer of 2007, when the hunt for Madeleine McCann's abductor was reaching a global crescendo, with sightings of Madeleine being reported from Agadir to Amsterdam, a well-known radio show in Ireland (*Liveline*, RTÉ 1) was, along with many millions of others, discussing the story. One caller rang in and proudly informed the listeners that her children (aged ten and eleven years old) were supervised every minute of the day, seven days a week:

'I never take my eyes off my kids.'

'Surely not every minute of the day?'

'Oh yes, Joe, every minute they're not in school.'

'But what about when they're doing their homework?'

'They do it in the kitchen with me.'

'And walking home from school?'

'I collect them.'

'And what about when they are outside playing?'

'I go outside and sit on the wall and watch them.'

'Fair play to you!'

But is this good for the children? Does it make them safer or does it increase their anxiety levels? As you will see throughout this book, relentless supervision isn't actually very good for children for a multitude of reasons. Children need lots of different things, and freedom to be on their own is extremely important for their mental well-being.

CULTURALLY APPROVED PARANOIA

Just like jealousy, paranoia and suspicion are powerful emotions, and anyone who has felt the madness of jealousy take hold will understand how irrational it all is. You might logically know it's ridiculous to accuse your partner of having an affair but that doesn't mean you can calm down and act normally; likewise, rationally we know it's ridiculous to worry excessively about child abduction – however, when our emotional brain takes over, all logic, reason and judgement go out the window.

If we analyse media reports we can see how parents have been infected by a culture of paranoia and suspicion. We begin with exhibit A: in June 2012 a mother in Tennessee allowed her children, aged eight and five, to go to the playground a block and a half away.[38] When the children didn't come home at the expected time an hour later she rang the police (!) ... but by the time the police arrived both children had come home (they'd stopped by their friend's house). The enthusiastic law-enforcers then proceeded to arrest the mother for felony child abuse and neglect. They then held her *overnight* in jail on a $5,000 bond – leaving the children to be cared for by others with presumably the guilt trip from hell: 'Oh dear, Mommy is rotting in a prison cell because we didn't go home on time.'

Another random example of peculiar police diligence is from April 2012, when a father in Pittsburgh was charged with child endangerment. A passer-by spotted the man's two children, aged six and nine, playing alone in a park, and this concerned stranger thought this was so odd that she had better call the police.[39] When the father arrived to collect the children, the police were waiting for him – even though the kids were well and happy, if a bit puzzled by the kerfuffle. Thankfully, while he was in trouble as there was widespread coverage in the media, this parent wasn't actually put behind bars for his scurrilous offence.

Of course, the more extreme reports are from the USA, but even here in Ireland there are extraordinary stories to be heard: in the summer of 2013 a Galway father of two, aged five and three, was surprised to have the police called when he let his children go barefoot. After a long winter, there came an intense heatwave and one sunny morning, after a wet and dreary week of rain, the children enthusiastically took their shoes off and ran joyously onto the manicured green grass of the park, shrieking with joy. A concerned passer-by (another one!) said to the father that the children should have shoes on their feet for fear of hurting themselves. The father replied cheerily that it seemed a shame to ruin their fun. The passer-by paused for a few minutes and then again requested him, more forcefully this time, to put shoes on his children. The father, also more forcefully this time, answered that they were his children and therefore his concern. The passer-by huddled with a gang of other concerned parents and then, in a classic case of self-righteous group-think-gone-mad, a hapless policeman, who was until then enjoying an ice-cream and having a harmless stroll around the park, was asked to intervene in the situation. Thankfully, though much heated debate ensued, the father (my husband) wasn't carted away in a big Black Maria.

What was the worst that could have happened? They could have cut their feet on broken glass … he would have put a plaster on the cut. Is it right and proper to withdraw that oh, so special, heady exuberance and pure joy of childhood for fear of a cut toe?

Boy boils egg!

On a more comical note, in 2008 the columnist Lenore Skenazy earned the title of 'America's Worst Mom' when she wrote about allowing her nine-year-old son to ride the subway alone. Skenazy is evangelical about giving freedom back to the children:

> *Times are back to 1963 ... [alluding to reports that a child growing up in New York city is as safe today as s/he was in 1963] It's safe. It's a great time to be a kid in the city. The problem is that people read about children who are abducted and murdered and fear takes over ... Half the people I've told this episode to now want to turn me in for child abuse. As if keeping kids under lock and key and helmet and cell phone and nanny and surveillance is the right way to rear kids. It's not. It's debilitating – for us and for them ... We're brainwashed because of all the stories we hear that it isn't safe. But those are the exceptions. That's why they make it to the news. This is like, 'Boy boils egg.' He did something that any 9-year-old could do.*[40]

The story whipped up a media storm that was covered on the *Today* show and *Fox News*, and the incident led to the creation of Skenazy's 'Free-Range Kids' blog. In 2009 she published the book, *Free-Range Kids: How to Raise Safe, Self-Reliant Children (Without Going Nuts with Worry)* and has since proposed a day called 'Take Our Children to the Park & Leave Them There Day' as a day for children to learn how to play by themselves without constant supervision.[41] Skenazy comments, 'I just think about all the college kids who are still sending their essays home to be edited by their parents. I talked to one lady whose daughter sends her pictures when she's trying on clothes: "Mom, what do you think of this? What do you think of that?" At some point you have to let go and let them live their life.'[42]

Addressing this subject in her column, Skenazy said, 'These days, when a kid dies, the world – i.e. cable TV – blames the parents. It's simple as that [sic]. And yet, Trevor Butterworth, a spokesman for the research centre STATS.org, said, "The statistics show that this is an incredibly rare event, and you can't protect people from very rare events. It would be like trying to create a shield against being struck by lightning.'"[43] When Skenazy was asked how she would feel if one of those terrible and rare events happened to her son, she replied, 'It would be horrible. But you can't live your life that way; you could slip in the shower.'

2

Life is a Risky Business

A ship in harbour is safe, but that is not what ships are for.

John A. Shedd[1]

Cruising through the aisles of our local supermarket the other morning, my husband and I were discussing what we should buy for a late breakfast. Henry picked up a packet of rashers in one hand and a box of Frosties in the other hand: 'Heart disease or diabetes?' he inquired.

And this is how it is: we weigh up one dreadful risk against another, never really having a clue which one is worse. Are the children safer walking to school or being driven? Should I send the children out to play, risking all sorts, or should I allow them to stay in and play on their screens, risking obesity and other issues? Should I forbid my child to play the sicko computer games at his friend's house or will he become a freak in school if I ring his friend's parents to put a stop to it?

These questions are, of course, often unanswerable. As it is, we tend to pause for a moment and then make a quick choice based on our gut instinct. But, the problem with that decision process is that everything to do with children has become heightened in our society, with cautions and warnings everywhere we go; our brains have been infected by shocking images in the media or on our screens and so our decisions are often completely distorted by our alarmist and consumerist culture.

FEAR AND LOATHING IN PARENTHOOD

'Once she was born, I was never not afraid,' the American author Joan Didion said of her daughter Quintana.[2] Many parents will identify with Didion's worries: 'swimming pools, high tension wires, aspirin in the medicine cabinet, strangers who appeared at the door, unexplained fevers …' and on and on we go, inventing ever more unlikely scenarios that might harm our children. But worrying about risk is itself risky: while the odds of your child being abducted or dying in a terror attack are minuscule, the effects of chronic stress caused by such fears and worries are significant.

Studies have found that the more people were exposed to media portrayals of the 2001 twin tower attacks, the more anxious and depressed they became. Chronically raised stress levels harm our physiology, weakening our immune systems, impeding bone formation, impairing memory and increasing the likelihood of infertility, clinical depression, diabetes, cardiovascular damage and high blood pressure. Oh God, we'd better stop worrying!

> *FACT: After 9/11, 1.4 million people changed their holiday travel plans to avoid flying. The vast majority chose to drive instead. But driving is far more dangerous than flying, and the decision to switch caused roughly 1,000 additional auto fatalities that wouldn't have occurred had they flown.*[3]

JUDGING RISK

Humans tend to be much more confident in the face of slow-burning risks that creep up on us, such as obesity, diabetes and mental ill-health, than they are for immediate risks – and so they lose their heads if their little chicken falls off the slide and hurts him or herself, but they can be pretty casual if the same little chicken is becoming a fat little chicken from a slow and steady weight gain. This isn't particularly rational but it's human nature (and that's why diets don't work).

'Risk decisions are not about risk alone,' says Paul Slovic, president of Decision Research. 'People usually take risks to get a benefit.'[4] When we judge and evaluate risks, we place a certain value on our behaviour and so, despite what we tell ourselves, our decisions are rarely if ever made purely 'on the science'. We prefer our children to stay inside playing on screens than to go outside because parents have been told by society that they should keep an eye on their children all the time, and grown-ups often don't really want to hang around outside, mindlessly watching their children play. Consequently it suits us better to go for the risks associated with the children playing inside. This, of course, is a classic example of misguided risk assessment, as the statistical data tells us that these days a child is much more likely to be faced with vile images on the computer than to encounter real-life perverts.[5]

Equally, adults often prefer to use the car instead of walking and, because it suits us to drive, we prefer to ignore the fact that it is dangerous. (For the record, I'm not some crazy anti-car zealot – I've got a car and I couldn't survive without it.) Indeed, the current tendency to keep children under benevolent house arrest has created a whole new set of dangers for them to deal with. Physical ill-health, eating disorders, anxiety disorders, compulsive behaviour and addiction to technology are among the slow-burning risks associated with over-supervised, over-controlled, indoor children.[6] Which is why sitting quietly, eating a bag of crisps on the family couch while playing on the computer is now considered by most child psychologists a far more dangerous activity for your child today than to play outside.

Indeed, it is a little-known fact that our children are being polluted more from staying indoors than from going outside. As

Richard Louv, in his book *Last Child in the Woods: Saving Our Children from Nature-Deficit Disorder*, points out:

> *The Environmental Protection Agency now warns us that indoor air pollution is the nation's [USA's] number one environmental threat to health – and it's from two to ten times worse than outdoor air pollution. A child indoors is more susceptible to spores of toxic molds growing under that plush carpet; or bacteria or allergens carried by household vermin; or carbon monoxide, radon and lead dust. The allergen level of newer, sealed buildings can be as much as two hundred times greater than that of older structures.*[7]

EVIL INDIVIDUALS OR SOCIETY IN DECLINE?

In 2007 a study at Cardiff University analysed the coverage of abduction cases in the media in the twentieth century and noted that, prior to the 1990s, media coverage perceived cases of child abduction as the isolated behaviour of evil individuals; however, from the 1990s onwards such cases were viewed as an indication of a society in decline.[8] This is simply because 'society in decline' articles get a much stronger reaction from the public and ultimately sell more papers.

A deeply insidious blame culture has developed where almost as soon as a tragedy strikes, we endeavour to find someone to blame. Parents today are considerably more likely to be blamed by the media and by the public for 'allowing' their children to be abducted (as we saw in the Madeleine McCann tragedy) than in previous years. Nowadays the media wonders whether the parents might have been neglectful, or perhaps the police were inept? And the questions continue to be asked until we finally fix on someone to blame for the tragedy. But sometimes horrible people do horrible things, and as a society, united we stand and divided we fall. If we begin to insinuate that less-than-perfect decisions by loving parents mean that they deserve tragedies such as child abduction to fall on their shoulders, then we are simply going for the easy prey. In truth, the blame is to be placed on the evil psychopath, not on the fallible parents or police.

WHY ARE WE OBSESSED WITH GHOULISH STORIES?

A mixture of schadenfreude, relief and a desire to learn from tragedy compels us towards horrifying stories in the media. We all have a dark side, and reading ghoulish stories allows us the freedom to tap into that shadowed side without ourselves doing anything dark. It also allows us to breathe a sigh of relief that this tragic event is not happening to us (and perhaps even enjoy a feeling of grim satisfaction that it is happening to others and not to us). But while this is very human, it doesn't do us much good, which is perhaps why an overdose of reading the tabloids can leave a person with the same slightly sick aftertaste we get from overdosing on junk food.

Perhaps most significantly, many people experience the very natural desire to learn from such tragedies so that they can be prevented from happening to their own families. While this is only right and proper, once we have learned the lesson involved we need to move on and not obsess about the irrelevant minutiae provided by irresponsible tabloid journalism. For example, how often did the tabloids refer to Madeleine McCann's teddy 'Cuddle Cat' that her mother Kate carried around during the initial days of the family's heart-wrenching search? This was photographed and documented to an intense degree as a means of luring everyone deeper into the tragedy without serving any other discernible purpose.

Paul Slovic, the president of Decision Research in the USA, had this to say about the media's obsession with disaster:

Because fear strengthens memory, catastrophes such as earthquakes, plane crashes, and terrorist incidents completely capture our atten-

tion. *As a result, we overestimate the odds of dreadful but infrequent events and underestimate how risky ordinary events are. The drama and excitement of improbable events make them appear to be more common. The effect is amplified by the fact that media tend to cover what's dramatic and exciting. The more we see something, the more common we think it is, even if we are watching the same footage over and over.*[9]

The following excerpt from *Psychology Today* examines how our minds have become overwhelmed and bewildered in our attempts to weigh up one modern threat against another:

The human brain is exquisitely adapted to respond to risk – uncertainty about the outcome of actions. Faced with a precipice or a predator, the brain is biased to make certain decisions. Our biases reflect the choices that kept our ancestors alive. But we have yet to evolve similarly effective responses to statistics, media coverage, and fear-mongering politicians. For most of human existence, 24-hour news channels didn't exist, so we don't have cognitive shortcuts to deal with novel uncertainties. Still, uncertainty unbalances us, pitching us into anxiety and producing an array of cognitive distortions. Even minor dilemmas like deciding whether to get a cell phone (brain cancer vs. dying on the road because you can't call for help?) can be intolerable for some people. And though emotions are themselves critical to making rational decisions, they were designed for a world in which dangers took the form of predators, not pollutants. Our emotions push us to make snap judgments that once were sensible – but may not be anymore ... It's impossible to live a risk-free life: everything we do increases some risks while lowering other risks. But if we understand our innate biases in the way we manage risks, we can adjust for them and genuinely stay safer – without freaking out every ten minutes.[10]

Eliminating risk

In our increasingly risk-averse society, parents are now keenly motivated to attempt to control all risk in their children's lives. People these days don't embark on having children as lightly or as mindlessly as they did in the past, and consequently parents' increased emotional investment in their children means that all manner of risk has become distasteful. But it's impossible to live a risk-free life: as we decrease one risk, we increase another. For example, if you give your child a mobile phone so that he or she can call you if they feel threatened, they are then more likely to be attacked by thugs who wish to steal the phone. So, paradoxically, the child can be more at risk by your attempts to make him or her safer.

In years gone by the risk of accidents was an accepted part of life. However, nowadays we tend to think of accidents as being preventable. Organisations such as The Royal Society for the Prevention of Accidents (RoSPA) and the Child Accident Prevention Trust (CAPT) represent the popular paradoxical (and in my view laughable) view that accidents can and should be prevented. But they can't be – because they're accidents!

Facts and figures

We are now at the stage when a certain level of critical rigour is required in the study of risk and child safety. Unfortunately, it is difficult to gather clear information about child abduction in Ireland, but nevertheless, if we take the year 2012 as an example, according to Department of Justice and Equality figures there were 276 cases of inter-familial abduction, but there were no cases of stereotypical kidnapping by a stranger.[11]

In Ireland in 2012, approximately:

- 49 young people aged 25 and under died in road traffic accidents
- 57–77 young people aged 25 and under died by suicide
- 276 children were abducted within the family (e.g. parental child abduction)
- 0 recorded cases of stereotypical kidnapping*

* *Stereotypical kidnapping refers to a stranger abducting a child against their will and keeping him or her overnight.*

Sources: Road Safety Authority, National Office for Suicide Prevention & Dept of Justice.[12]

As the parenting expert, John McSharry, commented in *The Irish Times*:

> *In the last 20 years in Ireland and the UK, there has only been a handful of child abductions, yet in the same time many thousands of children have been killed or seriously injured in road traffic incidents, either as pedestrians or passengers. In simple terms, this means that children are thousands of times more likely to be harmed on the road than to be abducted and harmed by a stranger.*[13]

Because of the dearth of research on the tiny number of child abductions by strangers that have happened in Ireland, there are few meaningful trends to be studied, and so we need to go to a larger population such as the USA to be able to find trends.[14] The most extensive research available worldwide on child abduction is from

NISMART (National Incidence Studies of Missing, Abducted, Runaway and Thrownaway Children) in the USA, and from these studies we see that in 1999 (the year of the most extensive survey), out of approximately 72 million children, there were 115 stereotypical kidnappings in the USA.[15] Just like in Ireland (but perhaps more surprisingly) the US Department of Justice also reports that the number of stranger child abductions in the USA is very small and concludes that stereotypical kidnappings 'represent an extremely small portion of all missing children'.[16]

Out of an approximate figure of 72 million children, there are 800,000 children reported missing each year.* These approximate break down of the figures is:

- 358,000 are runaways or 'thrownaways'**
- 341,000 have a benign explanation to the story
- 62,000 get lost or injured
- 57,000 are abducted by family members
- 12,000 are abducted by friends or acquaintances
- 115 are 'stereotypical kidnappings' (meaning they involve a stranger taking a child overnight, transporting them at least 50 miles [80 km], demanding ransom or intentions to keep the child permanently or kill him or her) and only 90 of those were actually reported missing

* Some children have multiple episodes, which is why the numbers add up to more than 800,000.

** 'Thrownaway' means that the children have been thrown out of the family home.

Source: NISMART, US Dept of Justice.[17]

The US Department of Justice shows us that there is approximately one child abduction murder for every 10,000 reports of a missing child in the USA.[18] In comparison, a staggering 41,717 people were killed in car accidents in the USA that same year,[19] and to further compare, an average of 400 people are estimated to be struck by lightning every year in the USA.[20]

It is perhaps much more significant and more worrying that in the USA a reported one million people attempt suicide each year, and 35,000–40,000 people actually die by suicide each year.[21] And (just as in Ireland), in the USA today, suicide is actually a bigger killer than road accidents.[22] Indeed, unless you chose to dig deep and examine the statistics, you would never guess that in the United States suicide is a more frequent cause of death than homicide. As Sabrina Tavernise noted in *The New York Times*:

> *Nearly 20,000 of the 30,000 deaths from guns in the United States in 2010 were suicides, according to the most recent figures from the Centers for Disease Control and Prevention. The national suicide rate has climbed by 12 percent since 2003, and suicide is the third leading cause of death for teenagers.*[23]

PERCEPTIONS OF DANGER

Ultimately all this emphasis on stranger danger is worse than unhelpful; it is teaching children to be afraid of the wrong people. In truth, the devil you know is significantly more dangerous than the devil you don't, and teaching children not to talk to strangers merely frightens them without any proven benefit.

A culture of fear and a lack of reliable knowledge on the subject of child sexual abuse and abduction has given rise to misinformed hysteria around this subject. Even though the rates of stranger danger among the general population in the developed world is tiny and is not rising significantly, society as a whole perceives the risk of stranger danger to be increasing. According to research, the least likely event to happen – non-family child abduction – is the greatest fear among parents. As the sociologist Dr Frank Furedi points out:

> When the marketing organization System Three surveyed public opinion on the safety of children in Scotland for the BBC in 1998, the results suggested an overwhelming sense that children were far less safe than 20 years ago. Although the incidence of child murder by a stranger in Scotland is very low and has shown no change in the past 20 years, 76 per cent of respondents thought that there had been an increase in such tragedies, while 38 per cent believed that the increase had been 'dramatic'. A large majority – 83 per cent – also thought that more children were now being knocked down by traffic on the roads of Scotland. In fact the incidence of road injuries to children had decreased by 60 per cent during the previous 20 years.[24]

Perhaps most interestingly for parents is that current studies show the true risk of stranger danger is less of an issue than the parents' perceptions of the risk of stranger danger! And parents' perceptions of danger are having a significantly negative impact on children's lives. Put another way, it is not what you are worrying about that is harming your child, but *the fact* that you are worrying about it that is causing significant harm to your child.

CRIME RATE DOWN/PERCEPTION OF CRIME UP!

The peak for violent crime in the developed world was during the 1990s.[25] However, many of us have missed this good news as the media have learned that if they exaggerate and sensationalise tragic events (especially concerning children) their sales figures soar. Indeed, it's a little known fact that, even though 74 per cent of US citizens believe that the violent crime rate is getting worse, 99.5 per cent of Americans will never experience *any* violent crime.[26]

In the USA every year, the average:

- Number of children aged under 21 killed in car accidents: 5,000

- Number of children abducted in 'stereotypical kidnappings': 115

- Number of children killed by their abductor: 50

- Number of children killed each year by family members and acquaintances: 1,000

- Number of teenagers between 14–17 years dying by suicide: 5,000

- Number of teenagers between 14–17 years attempting suicide: 276,000

- Number of people struck by lightning: 400

Source: National Highway Traffic Safety Administration (NHTSA); Centers for Disease Control and Prevention (CDC); National Weather Service.[27]

The vast majority of children who go missing today are teenagers, but by its very nature it is difficult to discern what constitutes a case of stranger child abduction and what is a runaway case or a murder by someone known to the child. Fifteen-year-old Dubliner Amy Fitzpatrick went missing in Malaga on New Year's Day 2008 and, tragically, no one knows her whereabouts to this day; we can only look at the facts and wonder whether she went off with someone or could she have been murdered by someone known to her. Sadly, we may never know.

DECLINE IN THE RATES OF CHILD SEXUAL ABUSE

Thankfully, there is good news regarding the rates of child sexual abuse as the number of victims is declining rapidly every year. The director of the US Crimes Against Children Research Center (CCRC), David Finkelhor, the premier researcher on crimes against children in the Western World, reports that substantiated cases of child sexual abuse in the USA declined by a massive 62 per cent between 1990 and 2012.[28] This data shows that, of the approximately 74 million children in the USA in 2012, there were an estimated 62,700 cases of child sexual abuse, 122,600 cases of physical abuse and 525,900 cases of neglect.[29] And so we can see from this that neglect from parents and guardians is a much bigger issue for kids than is child sexual abuse.[30]

WHY ARE THE RATES OF CHILD SEXUAL ABUSE DECLINING?

Professor Finkelhor believes that the drop in the rates of child sexual abuse is primarily because of increased awareness in society and better treatment of offenders, and not, as many parents believe, because of supervision, stricter laws and harsher punishments. These days, children are much more likely to tell their parents if they have been exposed to unsavoury behaviour, and parents and children are more acutely sensitive to unhealthy behaviour than in the past – we have all moved far beyond the simple: 'Don't take sweets from strangers.'

Perhaps the most heartening news is that children these days are much more likely to recover from abuse because of parental awareness and education. It is reassuring to read in Andrew Solomon's recent book, *Far from the Tree*, that victims of child abuse are exposing the perpetrators much sooner – often as soon as the abuse happens – and because of concerned adults' sensitive handling of the situation, the impact on the victims is also considerably lessened.[31] The average six-year-old in Ireland today tells his or her parents if something uncomfortable has happened, and the average parent today puts an immediate stop to it. This is starkly different from even twenty years ago, when children felt such a terrible sense of shame and guilt that they kept their secret for many long years, and if they did work up the courage to speak out, they were often not believed. Victims of historic child abuse often report intense feelings of abandonment when they had disclosed abuse and their words went unheeded. Of course, there are exceptions to this and some children don't tell or aren't believed (especially if the child has been groomed for a long time), but in the main they do.

There is also better offender treatment. Abusers are now stopped earlier – because children are disclosing earlier – and so more children are saved from the cycle of shame, reducing the risk that they will be abusers themselves. Not only that, but researchers have identified effective treatment and therapies for teenagers who act in sexually predatory ways, helping them to change their behaviour before they become lifelong offenders. Professor Finkelhor points out that the drop in child sexual offences began in 1990, around the time that selective serotonin reuptake inhibitor (SSRI) antidepressants came on the market.[32] SSRIs are known to inhibit sexual impulses and, according to Finkelhor, Prozac is reducing child sexual abuse more effectively than education, awareness or progressive laws. Prozac has had a significant impact simply because the stranger is rarely the danger. The danger is often the depressed, impulsive uncle or the weird teenager next door.

Other reasons have been proposed to explain why the rates of child sexual abuse are declining. Better awareness is agreed to be a significant factor, as churches, sports teams and schools all now specify the rules of engagement for adults and children, and strict codes of conduct are now followed. Both adults and children are alert to the signs of abuse and know to report them immediately. Also, the stigma is now on the offender, not the victim, and we now know that offenders can be upstanding members of society, such as priests, teachers, fathers or uncles.

Who abuses our children?

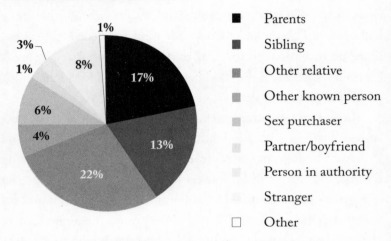

Figure 2.1: Percentage of total number of abuse cases (data in round figures).[33]

Notes: Parent 16.94%, sibling 13.11%, other relative 21.86%, other known person 29.51%, partner/ boyfriend 1.1%, person in authority 2.73%, stranger 7.65%, sex purchaser 6.01% (under-age prostitution), other 1.09%.

Source: Dublin Rape Crisis Centre Annual Report 2012, p. 28.

According to the data from the Dublin Rape Crisis Centre shown in Figure 2.1, the vast majority of child sexual abuse is perpetrated by someone known (on some level) to the child, and only 7.65 per cent is perpetrated by a stranger. Parents' perceptions of stranger danger need to be re-addressed, as they are missing a significant risk of child abuse when they focus their concerns on strangers.

So long as they can direct their concern about child sexual abuse towards an unknown stranger, parents can avoid the more distressing issue of how to handle the odd behaviour of the much-loved relative or the strange child next door; indeed, the Rape Crisis Network of Ireland reports that over a third of child sexual abuse cases (37 per cent) are carried out by other children.[34] (On that point, we all know that there are many problems with looking at the bare statistics without examining the details – for example, it might be surprising for many people to read that two young teenagers, aged sixteen and eighteen, who engage in consensual sex would be included in these statistics for sexual abuse, as are underage prostitutes who turn to prostitution to feed their drug habits.)

Because of the secrecy involved, sexual abuse is a crime that remains under-reported, and with the arrival of the Internet entire new avenues for cyber child sexual abuse have opened and we cannot be certain at what level this is impacting children – this is an area that has yet to be conclusively researched. What we do know is that one in five youths have received unwanted sexual solicitations online (mostly through chat rooms or instant messaging).[35] But half of these children don't tell their parents because they are embarrassed or are afraid that their online usage will then be restricted.

The following story, recounted to me by my friend Sylvia about her son Jamie, shows us how things can quickly go wrong for a child when using the Internet. Jamie was an innocent seven-year-old boy who accidentally typed in the word 'cam' into his computer instead of 'camp' and a whole slew of graphic cam-videos appeared on the screen that Jamie, in his (soon to be lost) innocence found both compelling and horrifying. A few days later his mother checked the Internet history and realised that her little boy had gone back on to the site again and again, looking for the porn at every opportunity in those unrestricted few days. It was only then she put in parental controls.

Our technological age has normalised paedophilia in many ways. Previously this was a lonely life, where perverted behaviour remained a dark secret, but now online paedophiles have access to unlimited fellow predator 'friends'. In 1990 there were an estimated 7,000 known images worldwide of child pornography in circulation in print, but in 2007 Interpol's child abuse database contained a staggering 500,000 unique images.[36] This is why it would be considerably more helpful if the media and society encouraged us to concentrate more of our efforts on the growing problem of children accessing Internet porn and being targeted by sexual predators on social media, than focusing on much rarer incidents of stranger sexual abuse.

THE CONSEQUENCE OF A PARANOID SOCIETY

Melanie is the mother of four children ranging in age from six months to ten years old. She is a very loving mother who enjoys the baby years but is finding the older children more challenging. Her two eldest boys, Jack and Sam, eight and ten years old, are pleading for more freedom, wanting to walk to school on their own instead of travelling by car, but Melanie can't trust either her boys or the world in general. 'To be honest the school run in the morning gives me nothing but grief, with the kids squabbling in the back and the baby crying. And then there is the annoying hour between 1.30 and 2.30 when my little girl gets out earlier than the boys. But I can't let them walk to school – there are two busy roads they have to cross and I dread to think what would happen to them. I know I probably should teach them road safety but I just can't trust that they would be safe and anyway, I'd be afraid some weirdo would spot them and pick them up.'

And this is the crux of the problem: as parents we are often vague and uncertain about what it is we are actually scared about, but are sure that there is something awful out there that we should be frightened of. As a result, we are often too burdened by fear to give our children the freedom and responsibility they need to grow up to become functioning members of society. We understandably prefer not to dwell on horrible, grisly images from the backs of our mind, and instead instinctively take the easy way out and keep the kids close to our sides. This would not be a problem if it wasn't harming our children's emotional well-being, but it is.

The following excerpt from the 'Free-Range Kids' website shows us how unchecked hysteria and paranoia can create a crazy world filled with suspicion and parenting madness:

I'm not a parent, only an uncle, but today a question presented itself at my niece's new school: When did picking up a kid from school turn into such a gruelling, hyper-orchestrated ordeal? When did fear of accident or abduction necessitate so many onerous rules? At my niece's school, the parents are required to stay in their cars, with a number on the windshield, which a volunteer messages inside to let the teacher know that a parent is here, and that it is 'safe' to 'release' the child from school.

Then the children are sent out one at a time, and a volunteer checks that every child goes into the car with the appropriate number. Meaning 600 parents are stuck in idling cars in a single-file line, slowly inching forward, picking up 600 kids, one at a time (virtually nobody walks). Meaning the kids don't hang out casually with each other after school, making new friends. Meaning each parent spends thirty minutes in a car, doing nothing, admonished if they attempt to get out and stretch. Meaning I was stuck with a toddler in the back seat screaming for juice or snacks – which of course I forgot – for half an hour. Meaning that parents, too, never mingle, and instead are just treated like anonymous chauffeurs, or eyed suspiciously as frothing kidnappers or vehicular maniacs bent on running down hordes of children.[37]

I couldn't live with myself if …

The sociologist, Dr Frank Furedi, points out that many parents know deep down that their children's lives are unhealthy but they allow these dull lives to continue, based on the phrase 'I couldn't live with myself if …'[38] They acknowledge that really they should allow their son to walk to school to give him some exercise instead of travelling with Mummy in the car, but again they relieve their feelings of guilt by alluding to their depth of love: 'I couldn't live with myself if he had an accident.'

And when the parent forbids their child to walk on a wall, climb a tree, go rollerskating, ride a bike unsupervised and any number of slightly risky actions, they then defend their over-protective style of parenting with the well-worn phrase, 'I couldn't live with myself if he hurt himself.' Tragically, as a consequence of a toxic culture which often encourages unhealthy behaviour, the parent can live with him/herself (probably because it has become so prevalent) if his/her child is diagnosed with emotional or behavioural problems as a by-product of our dysfunctional culture.

The big-thing point here is that this phrase refers neither to the vulnerability of the child nor to the likelihood of danger, but rather it reflects the parents' sense of insecurity in this age of anxiety. It's all about the parent – not the child – and the parent is primarily concerned with his or her own state of mind instead of the welfare of the child when s/he declares, 'I couldn't live with myself if …'

Childhood in Captivity

If you want total security, go to prison. There you're fed, clothed, given medical care and so on. The only thing lacking ... is freedom.

Dwight D. Eisenhower[1]

The Wild Child Survey conducted by The Heritage Council of Ireland in 2010 shows us that childhood in Ireland has been seriously impacted by irrational fears.[2] One thousand adults were asked to identify where they played when they were young. These adults included 492 parents, and the parents were then asked where their seven- to eleven-year-old children played now. Surprise, surprise, children today spend a great deal less time playing outside than their parents did:

- The number of children who play regularly in fields has fallen by 23 per cent, playing in wild spaces has fallen by 20 per cent, and playing in woodlands has declined by 19 per cent.

- There has been an overall increase in the level of supervision among children today, with notable increases in the level of supervision at home (31 per cent), school playing fields (19 per cent), outdoor playgrounds (35 per cent), gardens (29 per cent), indoor activity centres (43 per cent), fields (16 per cent) and wild spaces (14 per cent).

According to the Wild Child Survey, lack of neighbourhood safety – in particular, stranger danger and road traffic safety – are the key factors influencing parents' perceptions of childhood risk. Supervision was identified as the main reason why parents aren't allowing their children to play outdoors as much as they themselves did at the same ages. The Heritage Council's Chief Executive, Michael Starrett, pointed out:

> *What the research found is that the key barrier to children not spending time playing and exploring the real outdoors is supervision. Today children are spending the majority of their time playing at home or in playgrounds and indoor centres, all of which are closely supervised … The concern is that supervised areas such as playgrounds or indoor centres do not provide the same learning opportunities as the natural world.*[3]

The Wild Child Survey also shows that the level of supervision in playgrounds has increased dramatically.[4] In the past, children were allowed to play freely in the playground, as parents chatted on the benches. Nowadays the benches in the playground are usually empty, as many parents choose to follow their children around, always hovering, always supervising, driven by a fear that has been artificially exaggerated by commercial interests, and always ready to swoop in and save their little chickens for fear they will fall and bang their knees (on the rubber surface).

BENEVOLENT HOUSE ARREST

As a direct consequence of parents' tendency to hold their children under what has been described by the author Richard Louv as 'well-meaning, protective house-arrest',[5] free play is deserting neighbourhoods and becoming an increasingly restricted and formalised activity. Robin Moore, in an influential study on children's play, analysed how such play took place in a variety of environments with an array of imaginative outdoor activities. Subsequently Moore became very concerned by what he terms as the 'commercialization of play', where public money is now directed mainly towards organised sports instead of free play areas.[6] Richard Louv went even further in *Last Child in the Woods*, when he remarked that children's free play areas are becoming 'criminalised' as the adults attempt to bludgeon their grown-up version of children's play into a neat, organised and structured activity.[7] When my own children attempted to climb trees in a local park recently they were asked on two separate occasions to get down by adults who presumed that climbing trees is 'not allowed'.

PLANNING FOR CHILDREN

The National Trust in Britain and the Heritage Council in Ireland are both concerned about the way that free space for children to play is being reduced and limited – notice the open greens in the middle of the new estates, with perhaps three weedy little trees in a corner – very safe, but not much doing if you want to build a secret den there.[8] And research shows again and again that this is exactly what children want to do when they play: they want to build secret dens and pretend to be grown-ups; they want to be captains of their own ships, rulers of their own kingdoms – even if it is just until dinner time. As the author Jay Griffiths notes:

> *Where there are children there are dens and burrows and nests. Sometimes adults can overlook them; it might be just a scrap of mucky, muddy nothingness to a grown-up, but to a child it's the secret place they go to, their soul-making hideaway ... They used to have dens on the land. Now they have dens in their room, and it's not a good swap.*[9]

The Celtic Tiger housing boom in Ireland has a lot to answer for, and one major issue is the lack of creative town planning, with overpriced houses upon houses spread out all over the country and little attention being given to amenities for children. Cycle lanes are like a Paddy Irishman joke – they start randomly and end randomly, but with fewer than 1 per cent of children cycling to school in Ireland, the joke is on us. The national media seems to be obsessed with our obesity epidemic, constantly reminding us that one in four Irish children are either overweight or obese, but rather than wringing our hands in anguish about what can be done, the simple matter of cycle lanes and safe routes leading to and from every school in every town would quickly improve the situation. But it's not only the lack of safe routes; it is also a lack of imagination that is an obstacle to children's play. The parks are too boring, too sanitised and too small – probably because that is the cheapest approach. When a playground is stuck into a housing estate the children and parents cheer with delight but, even though playgrounds are great and very necessary, children need more than that: they need interesting layouts, they need nature and they need challenges.

Abandon rules all ye who enter here

The Swanson Primary School in New Zealand submitted itself to an interesting experiment in 2011 and radically agreed to suspend all playground rules. Children were suddenly allowed to run, climb trees, ride skateboards, slide down a muddy hill, jump off swings, and play in a 'loose-parts pit' (containing wood, tyres and an old fire hose). By easing the rules, the dull school yard suddenly turned into a mini adventure playground. The teachers weren't enthusiastic, as they predicted chaos and injury, but in fact what they got was a drop in serious injuries, vandalism and bullying – the principal said the kids became more responsible for their own physical safety, and they were too busy and engaged to cause trouble. They also reported better concentration during academic work.[10] When the experiment ended, the school was so pleased with the results, it made the changes permanent. Professor of Public Health, Grant Schofield, who worked on this research experiment, urges other schools to embrace risk-taking: 'It's a no brainer. As far as implementation, it's a zero-cost game in most cases. All you are doing is abandoning rules.'[11]

TOP TIP: Wu wei

Parents could do worse than learn to practise the ancient concept of wu wei; the effortless action of knowing when not to act, and achieving a result without making an effort. Previous generations seemed to understand instinctively that children can be left to figure things out for themselves sometimes, but our brains have been so distorted by the media and business interests in recent years that parents today leap into the fray at the slightest opportunity.

If your children are fighting among themselves, remind yourself that if you leave them alone to figure it out this can be a golden learning moment in your children's lives. Sometimes a touch of light bribery can work wonders: 'If you can become friends by yourselves in the next ten minutes then I won't punish you both/you can have a treat,' can encourage the peace process along. If one child always gets the better of the other, maybe the other sibling needs to learn how to navigate his/ her way around the top dog? Relying on Mammy to step in can cultivate feelings of weakness, an inability to cope and a tendency to victimhood.

IS THE OUTDOOR CHILD AN ENDANGERED SPECIES?

It is becoming increasingly uncommon to see children meeting friends on an informal basis or running errands for their mother. If children are outside playing, it is in the garden, or very close to the home. 'Cul de sac kids' are totally dependent on the quality of the estate where they live for their play environment, and sadly this is often reduced to a square of green grass. Peer-reviewed research from child psychologists doesn't provide us with any surprises when they show that the home is now the most frequent venue for children's play, and outdoor play now tends to be organised and supervised by adults.[12] The following excerpt from the National Trust study explores the current situation:

> *So are our children really prisoners in their own homes? The statistics would appear to support this view. In a single generation since the 1970s, children's 'radius of activity' – the area around their home where they are allowed to roam unsupervised – has declined by almost 90%. In 1971, 80% of seven- and eight-year-olds walked to school, often alone or with their friends, whereas two decades later fewer than 10% did so – almost all accompanied by their parents. Running errands used to be a way of life; yet today, two out of three ten-year-olds have never been to a shop or park by themselves.*[13]

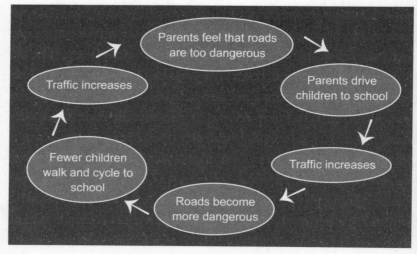

Figure 3.1: The social trap.[14]

TRAVELLING TO SCHOOL

Oliver and Gillian Schonrock, from the London suburb of

Dulwich, decided to allow their children (aged eight and five) to cycle to school less than a mile away without anticipating the national outcry that would ensue. The head teacher responded by threatening to report them to social services and the media soon became involved. The public outcry was intense about these 'reckless parents' and the 'How dare they' brigade came out in force over the social networking sites. Online comments such as 'the mother looks cold' echo the deep injustices done to Kate McCann, the mother of Madeleine McCann, when she didn't weep, wail or gnash her teeth adequately for the hungry media. Eventually, the Schonrocks felt forced to defend their decision to *The Sunday Times*, stating that they had enjoyed cycling to school as children and they wanted to give their children the same opportunities. They had cycled the route with the children many, many times and the children were both confident and eager to cycle unaccompanied. Chillingly, Gillian Schonrock said that she was more worried now than she had been previously, as she was nervous that, after all the publicity, some batty and sanctimonious mother might not give her children enough space on the road in a twisted bid to teach the parents a lesson. Oliver Schonrock said: 'These days children can do nothing unless it's planned. We are trying to let them enjoy their lives and teach them a little about the risks of life.'[15]

These days children's pursuits such as walking in the rain, playing alone in the park or cycling to school are generally viewed as parental neglect. When I appeared on the *Dave Fanning Show* on 2FM to speak about such issues, a caller rang in to say her child was almost the only child in the entire school who walked to school every day. Instead of supporting the parent in her bid to give regular exercise to her children, when it rained the school made their disapproval plain to the parent – the child should be driven in. But it rains in Ireland a lot.

Bearing in mind the serious implications that child obesity brings, the lack of children walking to school is astonishing, and when we consider that the RSA's Child Casualties Report 1997–2012 shows that while 43 per cent of children killed in this period were pedestrians, 42 per cent of children killed in the same period were car passengers, we realise that the safety argument is misguided.[16] In 2010 in Germany 67 per cent of eight-year-olds had permission to walk to school without supervision, while in England only 8 per cent were allowed to walk to school unaccompanied (see Figure 3.2). But as Sir Digby Jones, president of HTI (Heads, Teachers and Industry Ltd) points out: 'We do our children no favours by shielding them from every imagined danger when all the statistics show they are under no greater threat to life and limb than they were 30 years ago.'[17]

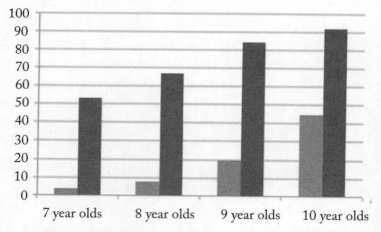

Figure 3.2: Permission to walk to school unaccompanied, England (light grey) and Germany (dark grey) (percentages).[18]

The *Growing Up in Ireland* study shows that the situation is equally unhealthy in Ireland. As can be seen in Figure 3.3, a hefty 60 per cent of nine-year-olds in Ireland travel to school by car, while a paltry 1 per cent get there by bicycle. Considering that a massive 70 per cent of children live within one and a half miles of their school we realise that, when it comes to the car, we've actually gone a bit mad.[19]

Travelling to School

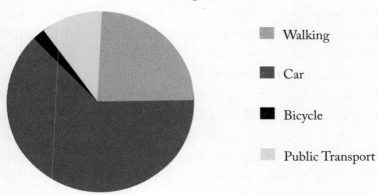

Walking

Car

Bicycle

Public Transport

Figure 3.3: Rate of nine-year-olds walking to school in Ireland.[20]

In Ireland:
- *39 per cent of children live within a half mile of the school*
- *70 per cent of children live within a mile and a half of school*

Question:
Why are 60 per cent travelling to school by car?

The experience of Caoimhe, a lively mother of four, who nearly caused a riot in her Dublin suburb when she allowed her nine-year-old and six-year-old children to walk to school, shows us that a general hysteria is overtaking our common sense. Her eldest child has ADHD (attention deficit hyperactivity disorder) and therefore benefited particularly from the forty-five-minute walk, but even though both the headmistress and the resource teacher thoroughly approved, society couldn't stand idly by and let such reckless parenting take place.

The attack began with ostensibly friendly texts, asking was Caoimhe *really* allowing her kids walk to school? All those roads!

Were the children safe?!! (The added exclamation marks tacitly replacing a thousand words.) 'What if some weirdo picks them up?' some neighbours wanted to know (the tone becoming slightly more aggressive) – 'It's a sick world out there! What then?'

'Well,' stuttered Caoimhe, 'they've been taught safety behaviour. And it's good for Róisín,' she protested. 'The resource teacher said it would help with her ADHD.'

It was a couple of days before the phone calls started to come in: 'I just saw Róisín and Conor on the main road and I thought I'd better check,' said one concerned friend. The next friend wasn't so subtle – she stopped her car and stuffed the two embarrassed and enraged kids into the back of the car (which was, in actuality, more dangerous than walking in the street) and drove them home, despite their protestations that they were allowed to walk home from school. In the end, three weeks into the experiment Caoimhe dropped the whole thing. 'It just wasn't worth it,' she said. 'I was becoming so nervous in the face of all the worries that I just felt I was flirting with danger. You can only face down worries about your children's safety so many times without feeling foolhardy. We might try again next year.'

And this is exactly what's gone wrong in our society – a crowd of misinformed and paranoid adults group-think a healthy and beneficial walk to school into a stroll through the valley of death. The mother, who merely wishes to give her children some much-needed exercise, doesn't feel strong enough to fight back against such strident mass disapproval and in the end backs down and throws the children back in the gas-guzzling, obesogenic car. Compared to society's hysteria, Caoimhe's response, though equally valid, sounds vague and feeble: 'it's good for their health' versus 'some weirdo might kidnap them' doesn't really wash with a worst-case scenario, crisis-obsessed public.

THE ELEPHANT IN THE COMPUTER ROOM!

While the computer is a magnificent addition to the world, we'd all be lost without it, yada, yada, yada, nevertheless the arrival of the computer in almost every home has heralded a raft of previously unheard-of problems. Cyber-predatory behaviour and cyber bullying, along with the graphic violence, early sexualisation, instant gratification, dissatisfaction and lack of empathy that are associated with playing computer games and using social media, are leading to many issues of grave concern to child psychologists. More often than not the child would be safer, and happier, climbing trees with his or her pals than being inside playing on the computer.

Tim Gill, a child play expert, comments:

Climbing a tree – working out how to start, testing for strength, feeling how the breeze in your face also sways the branches underfoot, glimpsing the changing vista through the leaves, dreaming about being king or queen of the jungle, shouting to your friends below once you've got as high as you dare – is an immersive, 360-degree experience that virtual or indoor settings simply cannot compare with.[21]

TV OR NOT TV?

Children's television illustrates just how much childhood has changed in recent years. When I was a child, children's television was so awful it drew very little interest among the children on my street. *The A-Team* and *Grange Hill* were good, *Diff'rent Strokes* was great, but frankly that was about it. Television in the 1980s was also limited to a couple of hours each day, if that. But in this era of twenty-four-hour cartoon channels there is always something for children to watch – even at 3.30 a.m. should they so wish (perhaps these kids are working night shifts?).

And so, because there was nothing on TV in my childhood,

I usually ended up going outside to play with my friends after school. Yes, we were sometimes bored playing outside, but from boredom springs creativity and, to be fair, mostly we had great fun. It is definitely the times spent outside that I remember with most pleasure from my young days, not the times spent watching TV.

Nowadays, as I gaze at my daughter who is gazing at the TV, the choice is simply stupendous. Children's television is brilliant – it is witty, exciting, interesting and educational; it has everything and it has become a very hard act to follow – mindlessly playing kerbs with dopey Dionna from next door is simply no match for staying in and being entertained by *The Simpsons*. The makers of children's television are so far ahead of us it would make your head spin. These days, many children's programmes are educational, so a child can feasibly spend the entire day zonked out on front of the screen watching an array of educational programmes.

However, even educational TV can dull the creative mind, and what's more, TV programming is often sustained from advertising sales and risks creating consumerist junkies out of our children. Walking through a supermarket with the kids the other day, on a mission to buy milk and bread and Absolutely Nothing Else, my daughter spotted the latest Barbie plastic pink castle and exclaimed, 'Oh, Mammy we need to get that – that's the place where dreams come true!' … Ugh!

And so we now need to ascertain how much TV is too much TV, and then, a more complicated question, is too much screen-based education 'a bad thing'? The following account from a client indicates the issues arising from too much TV watching:

My baby had been watching the Baby Einstein DVDs until one day I took her out to play in the grass and she didn't respond at all. She just looked like an uninterested lump. But when we got home, I put the TV on and suddenly she came to life and she was fighting to turn around and watch it. That was it. I turned the rubbish off and after a while she began to respond properly again, smiling, playing …

We are nervously aware that our kids are plonked in front of the electronic babysitter far too much, but we console ourselves that all the other kids are doing it; at least they are safe indoors and the programmes are educational. But all TV shows are educational these days!

Screen Time

- 66 per cent of nine-year-olds in Ireland watch one to three hours of TV every day and 10 per cent watch more than three hours per day.

- 74 per cent of nine-year-old boys and 54 per cent of nine-year-old girls spend additional time every day playing video games, with 30 per cent of boys and 12 per cent of girls spending more than an hour on them.

- 54 per cent of eleven- to fifteen-year-old Irish children watch more than two hours of TV a day.

- 'Electronic addictions' increase as children grow older, and eleven- to fifteen-year-olds spend about seven-and-a-half hours in front of a screen: half their waking lives.

- Older teenagers are spending more than twenty hours a week online (mainly on social networking sites).

- 25 per cent of twelve-year-old children have watched porn online.

Source: 'Growing Up in Ireland' Study; BBC News; National Trust in England.[22]

Children's television is just one aspect of the highly complex issues facing parents today, and because we are still unsure as to what is the long-term impact of many of these developments, we simply don't know what to do. Until recently, 'Internet addiction' was considered a derisory concept, with the naysayers asking mockingly, 'What's next? Microwave abuse and lip salve addiction?' But since the arrival of the smartphone, many of us have had our own mild brushes with 'connection addiction' and so have woken up to the insidious and compelling nature of some of the new technology (guilty!).

In the face of seismic changes in technology, parents feel rudderless as they try to figure out how to approach these advances. We may feel anxious and guilty about our children's overuse of technology, but believe we have no other choice.

Case Study

Mark, a single father of two teenagers, came to me for counselling when his wife left him. Though Mark was angry with his wife about the break-up, he was amazed to find that, in hindsight, he hadn't appreciated how much his ex-wife had had to deal with.

Mark was finding it hard to handle the teenage years. 'It's the heavy silences that kill me!' he exclaimed. 'David [his sixteen-year-old son] *hasn't spoken to me properly in years! All he ever does is play with his phone and ask for lifts to his friend's house. When his friends come over they just play computer games, they don't seem to talk about anything at all. They just comment on their scores from the damn games. And when I check his online history the porn he accesses is really weird. I don't know what to do!'*

Sue, his fourteen-year-old daughter was proving difficult

in a different way. 'Social media. That's all Sue and her friends do. They go from Snapchat to Twitter and over to Facebook, and it's all so horribly, self-absorbedly vain – and it's all she and her pals talk about, that and celebrities.' Mark and his ex-wife had provided their kids with the best of everything: music, dance, sports. Mark used to drive a 100-mile round trip to take them surfing every Saturday.

'When I think about all those wasted hours in my car taking the kids to all those activities! But what's the net result of all that effort? Grand Theft Auto, weird porn and feckin Snapchat!!'

Mark was disappointed in his children. He expected that, as they were sixteen and fourteen years old, respectively, they would begin to have an interest in the world around them. But instead all he found was apathy.

Eventually, Mark came to realise that he needed to retrieve his own life as he was simmering with rage and resentment over what he had lost. He had put too much effort into his children's lives and too little effort into his own. Mark decided to renew his interest in music and started playing with a local band. Instead of hoping fervently that his children would find a passion in life, he needed to re-find his own passions in life. Mark hoped that eventually his children would be influenced by his example. And even if they weren't, Mark would have regained his own life, which would help him to have a sense of perspective about his children's lives.

I'M BORRRRED!

In medieval times, according to Patricia Meyer Spacks, a Professor of English and the author of *Boredom: The Literary History of a State of Mind*, if someone displayed signs of being bored, the person was said to be committing 'acedia', which was considered 'a dangerous form of alienation'.[23] Perhaps in today's world simple boredom and frustration with their dull and restricted lives is leading many children to act out in frustration? Indeed, in a *Newsweek* article, Professor Ronald Dahl suggested that more doctors are prescribing Ritalin and other 'stimulants to deal with inattentiveness or antidepressants to help with the loss of interest and joy in their lives'.[24]

If used properly, boredom forces creativity, and constructively bored children will eventually find something entertaining to do; for example, they might pull out a book, take apart a radio, or create a game – certainly some of the best fun I had as a child started out when I was bored with my friends and we had to look for something to do.

The educational expert, Dr Teresa Belton, believes that cultural expectations that children should constantly be active and never bored hampers the development of their imaginations. In this age of play-dates and activity centres, children are rarely given the freedom to be bored. Over-entertained children lack resourcefulness; they have become reliant on their screens and on supervisors or parents jumping in to provide fun. Dr Belton advises that 'children should be allowed to get bored so they can develop their innate ability to be creative'.[25] She has also studied the impact of television on children and suggests that:

> *When children have nothing to do now, they immediately switch on the TV, the computer, the phone or some kind of screen. The time they spend on these things has increased. But children need to have stand-and-stare time, time imagining and pursuing their own thinking processes or assimilating their experiences through play or just observing the world around them.*[26]

TOP TIP: Pre-empt boredom!

- *Turn off the screens!*

  Children will not get the chance to be bored if screens are allowed to vaguely capture their attention as they while their lives away day after day … and as the Pink Floyd song goes, 'and then one day you find ten years have got behind you!'

- *Be patient.*

  Many children will yawn when their parents try to cultivate their enquiring minds. Patience and understanding are needed. These children have grown up in a culture that has provided entertainment for them since they were only weeks old; we're the ones who gave them the drugs, so we need to be understanding as we help them to recover from the addiction; a gentle weaning off can work as well as cold turkey.

- *Structure unstructured time.*

  A paradox I know, but if children are provided regularly with unstructured time, their natural ability to entertain themselves will resurrect itself.

- *Take some time out in the wild.*

  Remember that your children probably have a lot less of a connection to nature than you did when you were a child. Suggest some games you can play using nature as your playground. Silently back out when things are up and running (this may take time).

> • *Provide interesting things to play with in the garden.*
>
> *When we look at the Swanson Primary School in New Zealand, or 'The Land' in Wales (see excerpt from Hanna Rosin's article at the end of this book), a key element to the fun is that 'stuff' is left for the children to play with; an old chair, a mattress, a fire hose … And yes, you're right, your garden might resemble a junk heap (you could make a 'loose-parts section' in the garden if it really does your head in), but your kids will have great craic!*

THE DANGERS OF HEALTH AND SAFETY

We live in a litigious age where events are simply banned if there is even the tiniest chance of an accident. We have become so used to the 'health and safety' excuse that we no longer even argue with it, even though it is commonly accepted that this is, in truth, more often than not a 'fear of being sued or losing our insurance' than a true 'health and safety' issue. But these days a person only has to utter the infamous words 'health and safety' and that's it – argument over. Could it be time to begin the fight back against the 'elf and safety' brigade?

Might we be able to convince the health and safety extremists that some risk is not only inevitable but also necessary for children to learn to handle unexpected situations? The ability to live happily in an insecure world is arguably a key element to achieving contentment in this crazy world, and perhaps parents need to concentrate on helping their children to handle this challenge instead of attempting to avoid all risk in a risky world.

LIFE IS A RISKY BUSINESS

Evolutionary psychology shows us that children need to learn to negotiate risk in play so that they can practise these skills and learn to understand danger, how to manage fear, how to arrive at sound decisions and how to conquer challenges. In his book, *Brain Rules*, Dr John Medina points out that life itself is risky and children need to be challenged to practise their risk-taking skills in developmentally appropriate environments.

Children need to experience risk to be able to handle it. Experiences that offer children an exciting challenge to test their individual limits build independence, resilience, persistence and problem-solving skills. They also enable children to become confident, capable and creative thinkers who are prepared for life through learning how to judge risk, how to make appropriate decisions and how to take responsibility for their own actions. This cannot be overstated; in the appropriate environment, children thrive from learning how to handle risk.

TOP TIP: Expose children to risk
(and you will help them more)

When child's play becomes too simple and we become overly concerned with eliminating every potential bump or bruise in the playground, we also increase the risk of children indulging in destructive, mindless behaviour, and at the same time we eliminate the potential to reach their brain's potential and for healthy, lifelong developmental skills. Sometimes parents need to look the other way, so that their children realise that they are responsible for the outcome of their activities. Parents may choose to begin with baby steps in the playground and explain to their children that Mum or Dad won't be able to look out for them during this visit because they have to read something important in the paper. Then follow through on that and position yourself so you can't see them but they can see you. That way your children know you're there if they need you, but can't rely on you to assess their risks.

Ellen Sandseter, a Professor of Early-Childhood Education in Trondheim, Norway, had her first child in the mid-1990s, around the time that a law was passed in Norway requiring playgrounds to meet certain safety standards. Sandseter had previously researched the need for sensation and risk in the lives of young teenagers and had concluded that, if teenagers weren't exposed to the sensation of risk in a socially acceptable way, some would turn to more reckless and destructive behaviour. Sandseter then watched as, one by one, the playgrounds in her area were transformed into sterile, manicured, safe and boring places, and she wondered whether there might be a similar response among younger kids if they became less exposed to risk. And so she began studying children's behaviour in playgrounds.[27]

In 2011 Sandseter published a paper entitled 'Children's Risky Play from an Evolutionary Perspective: The Anti-Phobic Effects of Thrilling Experiences'.[28] In the paper she noted that children have a sensory need to taste danger and excitement (this doesn't mean that they need to experience danger, but that they need to feel they are taking a great risk). Sandseter identified six kinds of risky play that children need to experience for their brains to develop properly:

1. *Exploring heights* – Sandseter notes it has to be 'high enough to evoke the sensation of fear'.

2. *Handling dangerous tools* – and yes, sharp scissors, knives, heavy hammers are all included. They need at first to seem unmanageable so that kids can learn to master them.

3. *Being near dangerous elements* – experiencing large bodies of fire or water teaches kids the reality of danger and the genuine need to behave responsibly.

4. *Rough-and-tumble play* – wrestling and play-fighting teaches kids the limits of aggression and co-operation.

5. *Speed* – cycling or rolling down a hill at a pace that feels too fast – this teaches children their individual outer limits. They learn to understand themselves better.

6. *Exploring on one's own* – this gives children the space needed to figure out who they are and what they like.

According to Sandseter, the last one listed is the most important: 'When they are left alone and can take full responsibility for their actions, and the consequences of their decisions, it's a thrilling experience.'[29]

A sign in Albert Einstein's office at Princeton University read 'Not everything that counts can be counted, and not everything that can be counted counts'; another benefit that unsupervised outdoor play can provide to children is immeasurable nourishment for the soul, the inner being, the self, whatever you wish to call it;[30] children need time to themselves to give them the opportunity to connect with their deepest selves. Like all of us, children need time alone, to discover who they are, what they enjoy and how they are feeling. Without this solitary time, children become over-dependent on others, never learning the ability to tune into their feelings, their wishes or their inner self. And it is exactly this that concerns practising psychologists in Ireland today – the unique identity crisis the Millennial Generation faces – a fear of growing up, a feeling of disconnectedness and an inability to think for themselves.

Throughout history, human beings have always had rituals to ensure that they are in touch with nature. Children need to be introduced to nature so that in times of trouble they can access the special type of peace that only nature will provide. Anne Frank was a child who knew a thing or two about living without freedom or nature, and here's what she had to say about it:

> *The best remedy for those who are afraid, lonely, or unhappy is to go outside, somewhere where they can be quite alone with the heavens, nature and God ... As long as this exists, and it certainly always will, I know that then there will always be comfort for every sorrow ... I firmly believe that nature brings solace in all troubles.*[31]

If a child has never been touched by nature, where can he or she turn in times of crisis? When teenagers get a knock, as they all do, they need to be able to draw on their inner resources to make them resilient enough to cope. We all have moments in life when we lose faith in ourselves, in other people, in the world in general, but if children have never had the opportunity to build their inner resources, then the well is dry, they have nothing to draw on from within and, if they have never been touched by nature, there is also little emotional sustenance available from outside. In this culture of instant gratification, teenagers can quickly become consumed by hopelessness if they have little connection with the world on a deeper level. The feelings of existential alienation so often reported by teenagers today need to be taken seriously and handled sensitively, because, if left unchecked, they might eventually give rise to suicidal thoughts.

Every twenty minutes, a teenager in Britain attempts suicide, and sadly, in December 2013, Lily Cleal, aged eighteen, was one of those who succeeded. She had seen her ex-boyfriend with another girl in school, so she went home early, sent farewell texts to four friends, then rang the ambulance service and told them she planned to harm herself. When the paramedics arrived they found her hanging from a tree in the garden. It was described as an impulsive act and the inquest found that Lily was a 'victim of the digital age'. 'It sounds dismissive now, but with Lily I thought it was just the teenage ups and downs,' said her mother, Kate. 'She wrote a beautiful suicide note, saying we'd given her everything and she couldn't have wished for a more idyllic childhood. I think she somehow thought that would make it OK.'[32]

The detrimental impact that modern life has on our children has not gone unnoticed; in Britain, Baroness Susan Greenfield established an all-party committee to examine the effects of contemporary culture on the well-being of twenty-first-century children.[33] And an open letter signed by more than a hundred leading British paediatricians and academics published in *The Daily Telegraph* identified how the contemporary style of parenting is damaging children and causing subsequent emotional and social damage.[34]

Parents today presume that providing their children with every opportunity is ideal, but in truth it is more beneficial for parents to teach their children how to handle the 'slings and arrows of outrageous fortune' so that they are properly equipped for life. Similarly, it is presumed that total supervision is the ideal goal, but this doesn't actually eliminate risk – it merely creates a whole new set of dangers for parents to deal with. For example, according to research, the constantly supervised child is more likely to fall prey to disordered food patterns, anxiety disorders, compulsive behaviour and addiction to technology than the less supervised child (as we shall examine in Chapter 5).[35]

EXPLORING UNSUPERVISED OUTDOOR PLAY

Table 3.1 (overleaf) is a synthesis of current research documenting the benefits of unsupervised outdoor play for children (of course, this is for children in middle childhood – nobody's proposing you throw your two-year-old out to play in the traffic!).[36]

Developmental	The child learns to ascertain, judge, evaluate and cope with risk.
Cognitive	The child's brain thrives on conquering challenges, adapting problems, overcoming risks and using his or her imagination.
Social	When playing with other children away from an adult's gaze, children learn to trust others, and about the limits involved. Close friendships are established and an understanding of human nature is developed.
Character building	Resilience, persistence, independence, emotional strength, personal responsibility and problem-solving skills are fostered.
Physical	Dexterity, strength and fitness are improved.

Table 3.1: The benefits of unsupervised outdoor play.

In 2011 the Children's Society in the UK released a report stating that parents' fears about young people's safety outside the home are exaggerated.[37] 'Children must be safeguarded, but this should also be balanced with the freedom to be themselves and to take some risks,' said Bob Reitemeier, the Children's Society's chief executive. 'It is a question of balance. Young people consistently tell us that they need to be able to develop friendships, have fun and to play without adult supervision.'[38] And actually, science says that they're right!

Despite all the evidence that children are far more likely to be hurt in a domestic setting than outside the home, parents continue to cling to the notion that, so long as the child is inside, he/she is safe. This disconnect among parents between perceptions of safety and the actual dangers cause them to look for danger in the garden, on the green and in the wild spaces, while the true dangers are inside, in the sitting-room, in indoor play centres (where the risk of cross-infection is sky high) and in other so-called safe areas.

TOP TIP: How to get your kids to play outside when they prefer their screens

Until very recently children pretty much always wanted to go out to play, but nowadays many children haven't been introduced to the delights of outdoor play and 60 per cent of children prefer to play on their electronic devices than to play outside.[39] Children often don't want to go out because there are no other children out playing, and because the electronic amusement indoors is better. Children today don't actually realise how much fun they're missing out on. This situation has mostly come about as a result of adults' misguided beliefs that they need to constantly supervise children's play – adults aren't so keen to go out to play and so they subtly urge children to stay indoors.

But we now know it is damaging for children if parents supervise every moment of their children's lives, and so, in truth, in our bid to raise happy children, we parents can have more breaks from relentless, sweatshop parenting, and children can go out to play on their own more often – everybody wins!

To get your kids outside you will need to be firm, compassionate and creative. You will need to figure out whether your child needs a focus, such as an errand – to go to the shop or post a letter – or perhaps your child would enjoy having a picnic outside. A more timid child may still may need you to go outside with them at first. Keep your eyes on the prize and hold on – if you have patience with this project, a whole new way of living will unfold as it dawns on your children that they can make their own fun in life.

Articles, such as that in the *Irish Independent* about 'Why more "helicopter parents" hover in their children's college life', journalist Philip Howard's article 'Why safe kids are becoming fat kids' in *The Wall Street Journal*, and Eleanor Mills' piece 'Slave mothers wield a love that smothers' in *The Sunday Times*, explore how over-parenting is a very real phenomenon we must pay heed to in our own lives – just because your child is performing best in his or her class does not suggest that he or she is the happiest or best-adjusted.[40] According to Robert Epstein, visiting scholar at the University of California in San Diego, and West Coast editor of *Psychology Today*, 'Parents' most important task is to help young people to become independent and autonomous. When we infantilise our young, we stifle their development.'[41]

And yet many parents today are less concerned with encouraging independence and instead strive to make their children's lives easier and easier. The concern that child psychologists have with this is that parents are 'disabling' their children and at the same time sending them the message, 'You can't do it properly; it's a disaster if you do it wrong. Here, let me, I'll do it better', which is, of course, another way of saying: 'You aren't doing it well enough, life will fall apart if you make mistakes, watch out, you must improve; you are not good enough as you are' and so the children's confidence is impeded and they grow up with the belief that they are at some level inadequate. If children get the message that they shouldn't make mistakes, they end up fearing mistakes and believing that what they do should be perfect. Being willing to make a mistake is an integral element of the creative process, and the child who fears mistakes becomes a neurotic and stifled child.

TOP TIP: Hang back!

An easy way to follow the experts' advice is simply to do a lot less for our children. Allow them to make mistakes, and hang back when you have the urge to fix up their sloppiness – in fact, put your feet up, take out your magazine and have a coffee instead! And when they come looking for help, as they inevitably will if they've always been aided and abetted until now, offer them a reassuring, 'Sure try it your own way, I'm sure it'll be fine.' (Warning: this will take practice!)

RISK-TAKING + PLAY = GROWTH

One of Britain's leading thinkers on childhood, Tim Gill, points out that the progressive view now is that play equipment should be as safe as *necessary* but not as safe as *possible*, to allow children to engage in experiences that offer challenge and excitement.[42] As the former Minister of State and HTI president, Sir Digby Jones, remarked:

If we never took a risk our children would not learn to walk, climb stairs, ride a bicycle or swim; businesses would not develop innovative new products, move into new markets and create wealth for all; scientists would not experiment and discover; we would not have great art, literature, music and architecture.[43]

4

Education and Performance Anxiety

How to begin to educate a child. First rule: leave him alone.
Second rule: leave him alone. Third rule: leave him alone.
That is the whole beginning.

D. H. Lawrence[1]

Yes, yes, yes, we all know education is good. In fact, education
can be great! But is society's obsession with education, ability and
performance making us lose sight of our common sense? Are we
over-educating our children to the point that they know everything
except how to be happy?

The leading educationalist, Ken Robinson, is noted for his pioneering approach to learning – and he is scathing about formal education in the developed world today: 'We have sold ourselves into a
fast food model of education, and it's impoverishing our spirit and
our energies as much as fast food is depleting our physical bodies.'[2]
Two hundred academics and writers, among them Britain's Poet
Laureate, Carol Ann Duffy, also complained about the current approach to education, in an open letter to *The Times*, stating that in-
cessant testing and labelling of results was damaging for children.[3]
The 'all education is good' approach is not serving us well; and these
days, when craftsmen such as carpenters require paper qualifications,
hotel managers require degrees, and nurses more often than not require a master's degree to be successful in their field, perhaps we have
forgotten that it's the ability to do the job that is key – not the ability

to study successfully. But where will this stop? Is there such a thing as too much education if it is gained at the expense of other goals?

ALL GOD'S CREATURES HAVE A PLACE IN THE CHOIR

The academic route doesn't suit everyone, and many potentially superb nurses are being lost to the profession because of the ultra-high points required to even *begin* to study nursing. Yet again, just as parents know intuitively that children's lives are boring and over-scheduled, they also know deep down that the current obsession with qualifications is inappropriate. Yet again, however, we seem to believe that there is nothing we can do. 'At least it's equally unfair to everyone' is the common argument for the Leaving Cert. *Er? Really?*

We all know we need the more physical people to do the more physical work, we need the person-centred and kind people to do the work that requires sensitivity and kindness, and, equally, we need educated people to pioneer the concept and theories that work best for society; the key point here is that education, although important, is no more important than other work. Yet today, in our education-obsessed society, not many among us will dare to argue that perhaps education isn't the be all and end all of life, and that perhaps some people needn't reach the stellar heights of education ... but maybe it's time to fight back against a culture that is obsessed with qualifications. Because these days it seems that all children are expected to be academic – and that's not fair.

PARENTS LOOKING FOR 'THE EDGE'

We live in an age of anxiety and insecurity, where financial insecurity, job insecurity and status insecurity have created intense feelings of competition and worry among adults. Parents are reacting to this sense of anxiety by ensuring that their children have 'the edge' on other children and can get ahead of the competition. The

problem is that this winner-takes-all mentality creates an enormously selfish and individualistic attitude towards our children
– we feel that so long as our own child is thriving then we don't
need to worry about how the system is failing others.

Of course, the government is delighted with 'eager beaver'
parents, because if it weren't for the parents' intense efforts
then the state would be required to offer more help. Intellectual
development has been deemed to have infinitely more value today
than social, emotional or physical development – as could be seen
in Dáil Éireann in March 2011, when the rather overwrought
then Minister for Education, Ruairí Quinn, announced that a
child not read to when going to bed at night was an abused child.[4]
Oh, how I wish I had been there that fine day so I could have
stood up in the Dáil and asked him very slowly, but very clearly,
'Minister, are you for real?'

FROM SAFETY TO EDUCATION

When the children of over-involved parents move from the
trenches of the early years to the front-line of middle childhood,
the parents often find that the focus of their anxiety has been
re-directed *by commercial interests* from being obsessed with
the child's safety to being fixated on the child's future. External
pressures are so heightened and doom-laden that no sooner does
the child begin school that the parents begin to worry about his
or her education and future prospects.

I personally have endured innumerable conversations defending my lack of a college fund for my children (who are aged four
and six!): 'Have you any idea how expensive third level is, Stella?
You really should be saving now!' Good gracious, is it not enough
that I give them love and comfort, a cosy house, healthy food, music lessons, dance lessons, etc.? I wonder should I begin a savings
account to put a down-payment on their first house while I'm at

it? The media, of course, adds to these fears: How well does your child's school perform in the school league tables? How effective is your tutor? Which is the best university? Which is the best course? Educate, educate, educate! Improve, improve, improve! Even though, if truth be told, there is little use in cutting yourself and your family to ribbons in a bid for future success; the advantages gained by attending Kumon (a specialist study group) classes can be lost very quickly because of the stress surrounding actually getting to the class (and the subsequent strain of listening to the rampantly competitive parents bleating on about their gifted children).

PROGRESS, IMPROVE, DEVELOP, ADVANCE, EDUCATE ...

Carl Honoré is the author of *Under Pressure: Rescuing Our Children from the Culture of Hyper-Parenting* and he established the Slow Parenting movement as a backlash against parents putting excessive pressure on their children.[5] Sometimes (and often as a consequence of our hysterical education system) parents can become intensely aware of their children's potential and believe it is their duty to ensure that every ounce of it is capitalised on. Honoré himself understands how parents can tip into this hyper-parenting madness, as his own epiphany came when his seven-year-old son was described as 'gifted' at art by his teacher. According to Honoré the word 'gifted' is the Holy Grail for all pushy parents. Just like any proud parent, Honoré's head was turned by the teacher's words and that night he asked his son if he would like to be enrolled in an art clinic. The unimpressed son looked at his father as if he was from outer space and asked: 'Why do grown-ups always have to take over everything?'[6]

CRAMMING CLASSES IN THE WOMB

Commercial interests have, of course, begun to realise that they can make a lot of money from parents' anxieties. The baby-care industry is making ever increasing profits by creating a culture where parents are not only expected to cultivate their children's intelligence during the early years, but – get this – apparently we should also be adding IQ points when the baby is in the womb, and even before he or she is conceived! Magazines such as *Prima Baby*, *Mother & Baby* etc. regularly urge expectant mothers to add to their babies' brainpower when they are still not much more than a twinkle in their daddy's eye. The mother-to-be is advised to eat certain foods and avoid others; in addition, she must also sing, talk and play music to her unborn child in order to boost the baby's IQ.

This would all be well and good if earnest parents were merely adding to their knowledge base about babies; however, a more insidious message is implied: the good mother follows this advice and the bad mother ignores it. And so the plumply expectant new mother is happily taking a coffee break, eating a scone with butter and flicking through a magazine when she comes across an article about unborn babies' IQ levels and suddenly she is seized with shame and throws a dark look at her coffee cup: 'I shouldn't be drinking that latté! I should be doing my Pilates! Oh no, I'm going to be a bad mother!'

Daisy Waugh's recently acclaimed book *I Don't Know Why She Bothers* rather hilariously gives a list over more than two pages of the 'bottomless trough of impractical and officious precautions' a mother is advised to take.[7] It is difficult to enjoy something that you feel you are consistently failing at, and the uptight message from the baby magazines (which are enjoying unprecedented levels of sales) makes it almost impossible for parents to feel they are succeeding in the mammoth task of parenting – there are simply too many tasks to do: eat nuts and blueberries, drink mango juice, listen to Mozart, undertake courses of Pilates and Reiki, and read Shakespeare aloud. And all this before the baby is even born.

THE REIGN OF THE KIDDIE-KING

From their baby's first days, parents are expected to devote their time to enriching, monitoring and developing the kiddie-king (or queen) – often before the child can even walk or talk. A lead article in *Newsweek* claimed that, in the newborn baby, 'Every lullaby, every giggle and peek-a-boo, triggers a crackling in his neural pathways, laying the groundwork for what someday could be a love of art or a talent for soccer or a gift for making and keeping friends.[8] 'Oh great,' remarked one mother, 'not only do I have to breastfeed on demand all day, feed the other kids, get them to school with clean clothes, lunches packed and homework done, but I also have to become a home-school tutor to my ten-week-old baby.'

In recent years there has been a massive upsurge in baby sign language lessons, with franchises like tinytalk.co.uk providing more than 500 baby signing classes a week,[9] and books with titles such as *Brain Foods for Kids: Over 100 Recipes to Boost Your Child's Intelligence* all urge us to add extra points to our kids' IQ in as many ways as possible.[10]

Loving parents are nowadays encouraged to expect too much of themselves. And many of us react to these expectations by valiantly upping our game, turning ourselves inside out by trying to be the all-singing, all-dancing Mary Poppins and *Dead Poets Society* inspirational teacher all rolled into one. And, of course, we fail miserably and end up yelling at the kids because they don't appreciate our intense efforts.

A good example of how many parents have (water-) painted themselves into a corner is illustrated in the case study overleaf. Today, the child is king, and parents (whether they agree to it or not) have been given the designated roles of eager courtiers to the tyrant in the nursery.

Case Study

Marianne is a successful lawyer who found her life turned upside down when she had her first child, Reuben, when she was thirty-eight years old. After so many years trying to have a baby, Marianne decided that she should stay home and enjoy raising her child herself, and so she decided to work part-time from home.

Almost immediately, however, she found being a stay-at-home mother incredibly difficult: 'I haven't a minute to myself! It's unbelievable, Reuben needs so much stimulation and is simply always asking for my time – it's a bottomless well!' Marianne spent the day cultivating and stimulating her son. She did arts and crafts, she played creative number games with him, she used flash cards to progress his reading skills, and online aids to teach him sign language and she also sang vocabulary-building rhymes to him at bedtime. Marianne tried to limit 'screen time' but often admitted defeat and parked him on front of the TV – 'We're all for "edutainment" in this house as I only let Reuben watch educational programmes and really they are very beneficial to him, so I shouldn't feel as guilty as I do.'

At first Marianne couldn't conceive how she could take the pressure off herself – 'I'm really suffering but Reuben is thriving, I don't know what to do! He loves all the games and stuff but I'm exhausted constantly. I try to work when he goes to bed; however, I'm so drained I usually get mangled on red wine instead.'

After beginning counselling, Marianne began to calm down and trust herself. She slowly came to realise that she needed to reduce the pressure on her, and began to chase the pleasure and not the pain.

'We just hung out in the garden today,' declared Marianne some time later, 'it was great crack ... I read my book and Reuben hunted for insects. What the hell was I at? Killing myself with those dratted

> *brain developing games? I hated them. I used to want to chew my*
> *arm off with boredom. What on earth was I trying to achieve?*
> *He's a perfectly happy little toddler; he doesn't need to learn to read*
> *and write before he's four – there's more to life.'*

A simple and beautiful film called *Babies*, which chronicles the first year of four babies' lives from Mongolia, Tokyo, San Francisco and Namibia, compares the addled over-parenting of the West with the more relaxed approach to parenting that 'primitive' cultures enjoy.[11] The Japanese and American babies are surrounded by expensive toys and live a strikingly busy lifestyle in contrast to the Namibian and Mongolian babies. The American baby attends baby yoga, while the Namibian baby is quietly enthralled by a fly. It is remarkable how the super-stimulated babies are significantly more prone to crying tantrums, while the babies from Mongolia and Namibia seem more content.

PARENTS AS GODS – YOU CAN MAKE OR BREAK YOUR CHILD!

Parental determinism alludes to the theory that parental behaviour determines the child's future outcomes; that is, effective parents produce effective kids. To an extent this is true, but there are many other factors that shape children's lives. According to Noam Shpancer in *Psychology Today*: 'The role early experience may play in shaping adult outcome is heavily dependent on subsequent experiences and conditions, many of which cannot be predicted from (or controlled by) early experience.'[12] While the child of an anxious mother may in turn become an anxious adult, nonetheless there are many other significant factors that impact the child: childcare, friends, classroom environment, Granny or Grandpa, the culture in which the child grows up, the lifestyle he or she lives, physiology and many other elements all contribute positively or negatively to the child's overall sense of anxiety.

The current 'bio-psychosocial' model argues that the reason why any of us are how we are has much more to do with a combination of forces that have gathered to influence our personalities, rather than simply our parents. If parents had such a powerful impact on their children, then parents would, of course, be more successful in producing the serious academic, the doctor, the dancer, the footballer or whatever you're having yourself; but we're not able to do that – we parents are just not that influential.

And this is why the message that parents have the ability to mould, shape and make their children is burdening mothers and fathers with unreasonable expectations, and, worse still, leaving the children feeling as though they are disappointing their parents.

Indeed, society has performed a horrible little trick on parents in recent years: it has inflated the importance of parenting while simultaneously undermining parents' abilities. Dr Frank Furedi is a leading sociologist with a particular interest in parenting and families.[13] He argues that the actions of parents are less decisive than others claim, and that the theory of parental determinism is causing serious harm in our modern world as parents throughout the land are silently seething, 'I ate the blasted blueberries, I bought the baby Mozart CD, I sang the stupid songs, and I did the tedious homework with him every single day … so why the hell is he getting only mediocre grades in school?'

The pressurising message is that the parent is a mini-god who creates and develops the little prince or princess; but are these claims true? The answer is simply: Who knows? Who can tell? Andrew Solomon's remarkable book *Far from the Tree* devotes an entire chapter to the parents and children of rapists and he describes some parents of serial killers as remarkably kind, thoughtful, educated and considerate.[14] From Solomon's comprehensive work it soon becomes clear that parents are not necessarily the only factors in the creation of an individual; the combination of biology and culture also play a significant role.

'The Mozart effect' is perhaps a salutary tale for parents. This multi-million-pound industry was built on claims that parents could boost babies' brainpower by exposing the baby to classical music. Companies marketed products such as 'Baby Einstein' that warned mothers to buy these products immediately, before their opportunity for improving their child's brain was irrevocably lost. The brand expanded to include 'Baby Mozart', 'Baby Bach' and 'Baby Shakespeare'(!) and the state of Georgia in the USA enthusiastically supplied every new mother with the CD entitled 'Build Your Baby's Brain Through the Power of Music'. However, the claims of 'The Mozart effect' have since been disproved by researchers. Consequently, the Walt Disney Company (extending a refund policy that was already in existence) felt forced to offer a full refund with no receipt required for 'Baby Einstein' products to every customer who bought their so-called brain-building CD between June 2004 and September 2009.[15]

It is now accepted that 'Baby Einstein' products have little or no long-term impact (apart from the fact that TV for under-two-year-olds may be harmful) and the company now declares that they were never intended to be educational – rather, they were supposed to be entertaining (that must be why they called the products 'Baby Einstein'– after all, apparently Albert Einstein, just like Crusty the Clown, was a well-known children's entertainer!). Similarly, a $200 learning programme called *Your Baby Can Read* has recently been censured by US consumer watchdogs for falsely inflating parents' expectations.[16] Thankfully, such exposés allow many parents to breathe a huge sigh of relief as they are freed to go back to being mothers and fathers rather than home-school tutors to their six-week-old babies.

TOP TIP: Loving your kids is enough

It is generally agreed among psychologists that babies are actually good at getting the information they need, and all this extra effort from adults is unnecessary. And so the relentless advice from everywhere is merely inciting an unnecessary sense of guilt and creating needless excess pressure on parents and expectation on children. The principal pioneers in the field of cognitive sciences point out that babies thrive and develop 'most of all by playing with the people who love them'.[17] *Everything else is debatable. The pressurising message that children need to be constantly monitored, taught and stimulated is simply a creation of salespeople who are profiteering from parents' guilt and anxiety.*

HOMEWORK FOR PARENTS

'What fresh hell is this?' Niamh wondered as she scanned her four-year-old's homework sheet. 'Oh God! Not more wretched homework.' Niamh is not a natural teacher. She is a good mother and she also works three days a week as a designer. And while she is a very successful designer, in many ways it is the traits that make her successful at work that make her a pretty useless teacher. She is creative, quick-minded, urgent and impatient. She is restless, gets bored easily and hurries her child along as she laboriously spells out the phonetics of the wuh-uh-rrr-duh. Niamh and her daughter usually have a wonderful relationship; they have great fun hiking in the woods and they love singing and dancing together, but every single homework session, every single schoolday ends in tears.

Niamh is not alone, as many Irish parents these days are

quietly appalled by the level of parental involvement necessary for their children's homework. And while there are some worthy exceptions, many parents are not particularly good at actually teaching their children how to read, write and do 'take-aways'. A now famous YouTube hit from the United States is a 911 call from a four-year-old pre-schooler who needed help with his 'take-away' homework. The boy asks the person on duty to help him with his maths – though considering the little boy then asked what is 16 take away 8, it was evidently very difficult for a four-year-old, and so someone had to help him!

Homework was first devised in the days of rote learning, when the child would have poems or facts to learn off by heart. However, nowadays homework has become a very different animal, with harried parents being required to help their children complete elaborate projects to enhance their learning. Homework is no longer considered an opportunity for the child to practise what he or she learned in school – instead, it is work for the parent and child to do together. And so yet another duty is created for the parent (or the parent has the option of ignoring this duty and feeling a familiar sense of failure at parenting).

Brendan O'Connor, the successful journalist and TV presenter, recently predicted in the *Sunday Independent* that 'The next big book in childcare will be the one that says we are too involved as parents these days, and that we are raising a generation of what my mother would call Mollies.'[18] O'Connor bemoaned his five-year-old receiving homework every day. Homework is now given to all children from Junior Infants onwards, which means that my enthusiastic little six-year-old is forced to do her homework every day. And I, as the so-called 'involved' parent, am expected to oversee every detail of her task. But I don't want to. You see, I've done my homework: I did it from 1979 until 1992 and I hated every minute of it!

Interestingly Seán O'Connor, on *The Marian Finucane Show* on RTÉ Radio 1, had an unusual take on educating children. He doesn't believe in sitting down with kids and doing their homework, and he didn't check on his own children's homework, as he believed they would learn and develop for themselves. And they did. Considering that Seán O'Connor is the father of the singer Sinéad and the writer Joseph, we should probably sit up and listen to this bit; O'Connor instead thinks it's more beneficial for parents to 'see a little glimmer of talent and put your hands around it and not let the flame go out. But you do it subliminally … sing to them going to bed and read them poetry when you feel like it yourself.'[19]

Now, isn't that much nicer than dragging yourself through your child's homework every day? It is generally accepted that parents today will make up for the shortfall in the system – we're expected to get our children extra tutoring in the form of grinds classes if the maths teacher or the Irish teacher is useless (we all know a complaint will merely mark us down as troublemakers instead of marking the card of the incompetent teacher). Parents must also dig deep to fund the 'voluntary' contribution for the school and contribute to fund-raising efforts for improved facilities. Parents of children who need extra help are often required to carry out the bulk of the intensive, specialised work that is needed for children with special needs. Society won't provide it adequately and hey, parents these days are supposed to be super-parents – so get with the programme, qualify as a speech therapist and improve your child's speech impediment before it's too late!

Is it no longer enough that we provide a warm and loving home with a positive attitude towards 'book-learning'? No, so they tell us, apparently it's not. Today parents are expected to be almost as good as the experts. And we have to do homework. Again.

TOP TIP: Fail is the new succeed!

The author Lenore Skenazy coined this phrase to remind parents that we need to allow our children to fail if they are ever to learn anything. If a parent refuses to take their hands off the handlebars when teaching their child to ride a bike, that child will never learn to ride a bike. Equally, if parents, in a bid to show the child how to 'do it right', pretty much do the children's homework for them, then the children will never learn to do their own homework. Let your children fail, regularly. Then teach them, à la Samuel Beckett, to 'fail better'.

WORK TOO MUCH AND THEN YOU DIE

According to the philosopher Allan Bloom, 'education is the movement from darkness to light'. However, not many Leaving Cert students today feel as though they are moving towards the light – in fact, their only opportunity to enjoy the light is by peering out of the window and looking wistfully at the sky during one of their tightly scheduled study breaks. Whether we look east towards the Chinese system, where teenagers are forced to spend twelve-hour days shackled to their desks during the summer holidays, or we turn towards the American model, where standardised testing has dulled creativity and originality among their brightest brains, education has changed from being a worthy pursuit to being the only way to get a job.

Parents today are frequently shocked by the intense focus on performance and ability in their teenagers' lives. But is there an intrinsic value in learning to do something you dislike every day? Is this nourishing the soul? Promoting well-being or happiness? Or is it simply buying into a culture that encourages us to work too much and then die?

The creativity crisis

The most systematic assessment of creativity globally is widely considered to be the Torrance Tests of Creative Thinking. This is a highly regarded test of creativity that focuses on skills such as divergent thinking, problem solving, fluency, flexibility, originality and elaboration. According to the data recorded in these tests, in the past decade or so, American children have become:

- less emotionally expressive
- less energetic
- less talkative and verbally expressive
- less humorous
- less imaginative
- less unconventional
- less lively and passionate
- less perceptive
- less apt to connect seemingly irrelevant things
- less synthesizing
- less likely to see things from a different angle
- less able to expand upon ideas in an original way.

Source: Creativity Research Journal.[20]

TOP TIP: Less is more!

Kids raised with the intensity of battery hens, their minds similar to a veal calf, dulled and filled to bursting, are shown to have little room for creativity or fun. Creativity and independent thought is overlooked today, even though it is these very traits that may be most valuable to the child in his or her future. But the good news is that it is relatively easy for parents to encourage creativity and independence; no need to take them to creativity class or to employ an independence tutor – all we need to do is to take our foot off the pedal, cool the jets, and allow our kids make their own fun and do their own homework. Hooray!

CONTINUOUS ASSESSMENT

Of course, this continuous competitive pressure on children to perform in frequent examinations and other performance-based projects discourages many of them and turns them *away* from real education. We know this. Just as we know that often children are so intent on scoring highly to get into their college of choice that their creative minds have been stifled – there is no room for originality if you're spending all your time busily improving, developing and memorising. Our culture today encourages children to follow the strictly laid-down criteria for exam success and learn vast tracts of information to be repeated verbatim in exams. Over the last couple of decades the amount of students who memorise essays and even their entire exams has massively increased from previous times. And so, in a weird way, as the children are educating-up, they are simultaneously dumbing-down.

By pushing our children towards intensive study as the only means to long-term success in life (which is measured by financial success), we are encouraging them to buy into a future that will involve long working hours, costly childcare and little opportunity for freedom or fun with their family or friends. By buying into this they will continue the horrible cycle of children working too hard so they will be able to pay for future classes and future childcare for their future children.

EXTREME EFFORTS LEADING TO EXTREME EXPECTATIONS

Unfortunately a direct result of parents' extreme efforts is extreme expectations. Parents try too hard and then unconsciously expect their children to give a good return on the emotional investment by being intelligent, popular, musical, sporty, good-looking, creative or whatever floats their particular boat.

Some parents who, for one reason or another, haven't achieved the job satisfaction that they could have, can become highly motivated to help their children reach the starry heights of achievement. This Type A personality can be ambitious, hard-working and meticulous, and they put their considerable energy into fostering their children's potential. Yet, when too much focus is on a child's performance, the child can end up feeling harassed and pressurised, while the parents feel tense and anxious. After all, what will happen if this child, who has been given (whether he or she wanted it or not) every single possible privilege, wants to marry early and work in the local factory because he or she is in love, not very ambitious, and the hours are handy? This will please Mommy darling, no?

Children do not like disappointing their parents but they also try to balance this with choosing a life path that suits them. The deep disappointment parents can feel if they believe their children are not benefiting wildly from their intense effort is heartbreaking. The parents can think, 'We spent hour upon hour teaching Theo the Suzuki method and now all he wants to do with his ability, his education, his talent for music, his proficiency in languages … is manufacture cardboard boxes in the local factory!' The intensive parent has given everything into the project of parenthood but often the child doesn't appreciate, or even desire, the effort.

TOP TIP: Take the emphasis off performance, and put it on effort instead

Research has shown that children will thrive best if their effort is recognised, but not as much if their performance is congratulated. If a parent focuses on the results of an activity by saying something like 'Johnny, you came first in the race! Well done, I'm so proud of you', the child will learn that what matters most in life is results. Many children will then tend only to choose areas in which they will succeed, because that is the main point, and their lives will be narrower and more fearful as a result.

On the other hand, if a parent learns to praise the effort involved, 'Johnny, you really tried very hard. Well done, I'm so proud of you', then the child will learn that it is the spirit of the effort that counts. The child will then be more likely to try and enjoy life, from a standpoint of curiosity and interest rather than being driven by a desire for success.

THE RISE AND RISE OF THE ULTRA-PARENT

Modern parents have become over-involved as a consequence of being warned constantly that if they don't develop, expand and exploit every ounce of their children's potential, they are neglecting to provide their kids with the tools to survive in this competitive world. 'It's survival of the fittest,' argued one of my clients. 'You have to do what you can to get your children ahead of the pack.'

Over-parenting, intensive parenting, hyper-parenting, hot-housing, over-protective parents, ultra parents, helicopter dads, black hawk moms, snow plough dads, tiger moms: the list goes on, endlessly; however, the all-inclusive term 'over-involved' neatly sums up this style of parenting. Larry Sanger, co-founder of Wikipedia, evidently is all for hyper-parenting as he speaks of using PowerPoint presentations to teach his son to read before he was two.[21] But the eminent psychologist, David Elkind, the author of the ground-breaking books *The Hurried Child, The Power of Play* and *Miseducation,* argues that development works best in a balanced way and it is more appropriate for children to develop socially, cognitively and physically in tune.[22] We all know the children who are 'brainboxes' in school but who don't seem to have even the tiniest piece of common sense outside the classroom. There is little point in hurrying one aspect of your child's development, because the rest of the child will simply have to catch up with the over-developed trait in a discordant manner.

THE TIGER MOM

Yale law professor Amy Chua is better known in parenting circles by the nickname 'Tiger Mom'. Chua's book, *Battle Hymn of the Tiger Mother*, stoked a major parenting debate that could be described as being representative of the zeitgeist. Chua describes hyper-parenting her daughters from babyhood so that they became excellent at music, sports and academic subjects.[23] Chua, a funny, self-deprecating woman, is a strict disciplinarian and she readily admits that she is an over-involved and controlling mother. In this extract, Chua describes how she got her daughter to learn a piano piece:

> *I hauled Lulu's dollhouse to the car and told her I'd donate it to the Salvation Army piece by piece if she didn't have* The Little White Donkey *perfect by the next day ... I threatened her with no lunch, no dinner, no Christmas or Hanukkah presents, no birthday parties for two, three, four years. When she still kept playing it wrong, I told her she was purposely working herself into a frenzy because she was secretly afraid she couldn't do it. I told her to stop being lazy, cowardly, self-indulgent and pathetic.*[24]

They then 'work[ed] right through dinner' without letting Lulu 'get up, not for water, not even for bathroom breaks' (and in case you're wondering, yes, Lulu did eventually master *The Little White Donkey*).

Chua appeared regularly on TV and other media, defending her extreme style of parenting. Chua herself seems to be aware that she is driven by fear, as she addresses why she believes the book has struck such a chord with parents: 'We parents, including me, are all so anxious about whether we're doing the right thing. You can never know the results. It's this latent anxiety.'[25] While critics claimed that she was damaging her kids emotionally by implementing such harsh rules, Chua maintained that she was merely grooming the girls for success and pointed out that she wouldn't really burn their stuffed animals and donate their doll's house to charity if they neglected their music. Oh phew, so that's all right then.

Chua has been called a cross between Leopold Mozart (the ultimate stage father) and Joan Crawford (made infamous in the book *Mommie Dearest*). As Chua notes in her book:

> *Here are some things my daughters, Sophia and Louisa, were never allowed to do: attend a sleepover; have a playdate; be in a school play; complain about not being in a school play; watch TV or play computer games; choose their own extracurricular activities; get any grade less than an A; not be the No. 1 student in every subject except gym and drama; play any instrument other than the piano or violin; not play the piano or violin.*[26]

On 17 January 2011 the *New York Post* published an open letter written by Chua's older daughter, Sophia, to her mother. In this letter Sophia defends her parent's child-rearing methods and ends the letter saying, 'If I died tomorrow, I would die feeling

I've lived my whole life at 110 percent. And for that, Tiger Mom, thank you.'[27] Evidently her daughters feel perfectly happy with 110 percent living. From reading the book, readers soon see that Chua's wry and self-deprecating sense of humour saves the day – I have no doubt she is a loving and kind mother – but the question still remains; will a childhood so focused on performance lead to contentment or anxiety? Can we truly live a happy life with 110 per cent effort, or is dissatisfaction and burn-out inevitable?

SUPERKIDS BUILDING SUPER CVs

Along with her husband, Jed Rubenfeld, Chua has recently written another book, called *The Triple Package: How Three Unlikely Traits Explain the Rise and Fall of Cultural Groups in America.*[28] Apparently the 'triple package' to succeed in America is to be driven by a sense of superiority, feelings of insecurity and impulse control. Yay!

From a psychological point of view Chua is right – people motivated by these traits are often outwardly successful. But they are rarely nice people – Walter Isaacson's best-selling biography of Steve Jobs showed us a brilliant innovator who could also be petulant, spiteful, rude and ruthless – and a well-known study shows that more psychopaths are CEOs than any other profession.[29] What's more, these traits are pretty much the opposite of the traits that will make a person feel satisfied, and so people shaped by these traits are almost never happy.

OVER-COMPENSATION TACTICS FROM WORKING MUMS

'Killing with kindness' is a phrase used again and again by psychologists as a way to describe the problems involved in parenting today. Parents are driven by the hysterical message that if they don't fulfil every ounce of their children's potential, they have failed in the 'most important job in the world'. And that's how parents are treating their children – as a job, a project rather than a relationship, and a project in which the parents are challenged to squeeze every last drop of potential out of their children. But, as we shall see in Chapter 5, all this effort merely serves to add to both children's and parents' stress and strain.

Non-parental childcare is increasing in the developed world, and some experts believe that the rise of over-parenting is a direct consequence of the increase of the numbers of mothers returning to the workplace and their efforts to assuage the subsequent guilt. Michelle, the mother of an eight-year-old boy, was referred to me for counselling as she was suffering from obsessive compulsive disorder (OCD). Michelle's situation perfectly illustrates the conflict that can arise within a working mother in the twenty-first century:

I'm incredibly aware of how little I help James with his homework but he is really very bright; and so I try to make up for my lack of attention by ensuring he is taken to an array of educational activities so that he remains ahead of the class. I take him to Mandarin class on Saturday mornings and he attends CoderDojo (a computer coding class) on Wednesday evenings, and Kumon on Thursdays. Of course, he is learning the violin as well – Suzuki method – and he himself has requested to attend karate classes. I am nervous that it is too much for a small boy, but what can I do? If I was at home I would ensure that he was keeping up with his class through homework etc., but I'm not – I work full-time – and the crèche, although they're great, they can't give him enough one on one time for his homework.

Thus the working mother can over-compensate by over-parenting her child – even though she is not actually spending many hours a day with him or her. This type of mother is akin to a project manager; she makes all the decisions and ensures they are carried out, thereby maintaining her control of the situation. This also calms her harried mind as she feels guilty for working too much, but she justifies this by thinking about all the extra-curricular 'opportunities' for which her money pays. Michelle can tell you at any time of the day exactly where James is and what he is likely to be doing, and this provides her with a pleasant feeling of reassurance and motherliness.

CHILDREN DRIVEN BY A FEAR OF FAILURE

Living in an era fixated on performance and ability can affect children in different ways, but one thing these children have in common is a deep and abiding fear of failure. On the one hand, some children respond to the focus on performance by becoming neurotic and perfectionist. These high-functioning children tend to avoid subjects in which they are not experts as they don't like new or different challenges.[30] They become narrow-minded, highly anxious over-achievers who are terrified of failure, terrified of not ending up with a highly prestigious job, and terrified of their deep and secret fear that they are not as good as people think they are.

However, perfectionism is not always manifested in the uptight 'Duracell bunny' bouncing from one fabulous project to the next; sometimes children can react to this pressure to perform by developing a persona of laziness and lack of interest. Such children prefer to stay out of the game rather than run the risk of not coming first. They can become paralysed, learning to avoid challenges and procrastinate endlessly (as one client memorably said, 'I love the smell of self-sabotage in the morning!'). A fear of failure can become so oppressive that they tend to put off doing anything in their adult life, forever enrolling on course after course; anything to delay making a significant decision about their life.

Other children react to their parents' obsession with qualifications and performance by deciding to kick against the pricks, either passive-aggressively or downright aggressively. They become rebel children, troublesome and unpredictable, prone to attention-seeking behaviour, disorganised, unpunctual and unreliable; these children simply will not be told what to do. Rebel children often go on to grow up to be adults who cannot handle authority and end up moving from one career to another, always seeking something better and always dissatisfied.

Increasingly I meet young clients who come for counselling as a consequence of their destabilising fear of failure. Pressure about exam success and choosing the correct college course combine to push them over the precipice. They are petrified that they will choose badly and their peers will get the edge on them. Many children today cannot cope with the tension involved in the possibility of making the wrong decision and so choose not to choose: 'paralysis by analysis' hits and they can become dreadfully stuck.

As parents, we mostly seek for our children to be happy more than anything else, and so it is important that we do not mindlessly yield to the over-the-top work ethic that is rampant in our highly pressurised society today. Working too much, trying too hard and always chasing the next achievement is not the royal road to happiness; instead parents can kick back and enjoy their family life with the kids – and do less homework!

TOP TIP: Just don't hit them over the head with a frying pan!

Parenting styles and the intensity of parental involvement continues to be a matter of vigorous debate when discussing how to tap into children's potential. But Dr Steve Petersen, head of neuropsychology at Washington University, St Louis, USA, has perhaps the most interesting take on parenting: 'development really wants to happen. It takes very impoverished environments to interfere with development ... [just] don't raise your child in a closet, starve them, or hit them on the head with a frying pan'.[31] Quite.

5

The Impact of the Age of Anxiety on Parents and Children

Our anxiety does not empty tomorrow of its sorrows, but only empties today of its strengths.

Charles H. Spurgeon[1]

When I was nine months pregnant with my first child I was sitting reading in a café when a complete stranger came up to me and said, 'I hope you're enjoying that, because you won't get the chance to read another book for eighteen years. Ha, ha!' A chill of total terror went through me – I had read all the pregnancy books, they had told me how difficult it was all going to be – and now I wasn't going to be able to read a book for the next eighteen years? Me, who needed reading almost as much as I needed to breathe? Oh, my God, what on earth had I got myself into? I began to hyperventilate. Ha, ha, indeed ... 'Eh, excuse me, hello? I've changed my mind – er, can the baby be recalled?!'

The complete stranger was speaking utter rubbish, of course, but I wasn't to know that – and this is exactly what we're up against: a culture that spreads the word that parenting is a horrendous ordeal that must be endured. The language of dread, fear, guilt and worry that is habitually used in association with parenting reflects a dysfunctional culture that needs a revolution ... yes, reader, a revolution.

PARENTS UNDER SIEGE

The phenomenal growth in the numbers of women suffering from postnatal depression shows us one of the many reasons why we need a revolution: mothers are simply crumbling under the burden of society's expectations. In October 2012 I attended the launch of 'Nurture', a nationwide charity set up to help mothers suffering from postnatal depression and post-traumatic stress disorder (PTSD). Many of the experts present, among them Senator Jillian van Turnhout, Dr Anthony McCarthy and Senator Feargal Quinn, pointed out that parenting has simply become too hard on parents – these days the demands are too great. At the launch meeting for the charity, the latest statistics were shown:

- 10,000 mothers will experience depression during their pregnancy
- 12,000 mothers will experience postnatal depression
- 9,000 mothers will experience post-traumatic stress disorder
- 1 in 1,000 mothers will experience post-partum psychosis

But those numbers are probably underestimating the prevalence of postnatal depression – in my experience it is a rare mother these days who *doesn't* believe she experienced some form of mild depression in the early months after her child was born. We hear talk about postnatal depression everywhere; on the radio, in magazines – it's even explored in the soaps – nevertheless, despite extensive consideration and research, we're still not sure why exactly the rates of the condition are increasing. And yet, if we look at some of the main symptoms of postnatal depression we can see immediately the link between pressure from our culture and stress for new parents:

- Low self-esteem – because the general message is that we're fools who will harm our kids.

- Guilt – feelings of failure – natural birth anyone? Breastfeeding? Working mother? Organic food?

- Low or no energy – never mind about that, get the waterpaints out, baby needs stimulation!

- A feeling of being overwhelmed – parent, parent, parent; no breaks! Never stop parenting!

- Exhaustion – hah! Who on earth wouldn't be exhausted with all the demands?

- Becoming easily frustrated – because the children don't appreciate our crazy efforts.

- Feeling inadequate in taking care of the baby – too many expectations from society.

- Spells of anger towards others – murderous rage often comes out of sheer frustration.

- Social withdrawal – feelings of inadequacy often lead to withdrawal.

- Increased anxiety or panic attacks – from all the stress and pressures.

- Sleep and eating disturbances – anxiety induced.

AN EPIDEMIC OF MISERY?

For the record, scary research about the impact of intensive parenting practices within hi-tech contemporary lifestyles is not presented here with the intention of frightening parents or adding to their woes; rather, it is included to highlight the true issues – emotional distress – with the intention that parents will then feel able to take their shoulder *away* from the wheel and raise their families in a more pleasant and enjoyable manner.

The negative impact that contemporary culture is having on the emotional well-being of our children can be seen in the *Growing Up in Ireland* study by the Department of Children and Youth Affairs. This study was based on interviews with 8,500 Irish children and their families, and the results show that 19 per cent of nine-year-old children have significant emotional or behavioural problems.[2] Mental health disorders, eating disorders and compulsive disorders such as OCD are an increasingly common feature among children in the present day, with an estimated increase of 70 per cent in emotional problems among young people over the last thirty years.[3] The World Health Organization (WHO) predicts that by 2020 unipolar depression will be the second leading cause of global disability.[4]

Suicide is the tenth most common cause of death globally,[5] and Ireland ranks fourth-highest in youth suicide in the European Union (EU) for under-twenty-four-year-olds.[6] When we examine the figures it seems that the developed world in general is experiencing an epidemic of misery; for example, about 35,000 children in England are prescribed antidepressants every year, and approximately 8 million children in the USA suffer from mental disorders.[7]

Yet, with relative wealth and political stability in Western society, is it not astonishing that we are so miserable? Regular reporting of schoolchildren driven to suicide by their peers terrifies parents and children as we wonder what on earth is going wrong? Cyber bullying is inciting suicide among young people, with heartrending pleas from grieving parents for 'something to change' striking terror into our hearts. We shake our heads and wonder what's going on, and yet we all seem to know deep down what is going on: our contemporary lifestyle is making us miserable and we need to change it.

My neighbours, Marie and John, work all the hours they can

to try to provide their children with an acceptable standard of living. But standards have been raised so much that an acceptable standard of living is now incredibly expensive: the huge mortgages, the cars we drive, the clothes we wear, our gorgeous kitchens – everything costs money, lots of money. This means that Marie and John have little time to spend with their children, and any time they do have is often fraught with tension as they are permanently over-worked and 'under-slept' – there are not enough hours in the day to do everything. So what can we do? Could we lower the bar and live more cheaply, and happily?

There are about 1.15 million children in Ireland. Every year, approximately:

- 1 in 5 nine-year-old children have emotional or behavioural issues.

- 8,000 troubled teenagers contact Teenline.

- 12,000 people present to hospital with cases of deliberate self-harm.*

- 1 in 8 teens aged between fifteen and seventeen engage in deliberate self-harm.

- 1 in 5 teens aged between seventeen and twenty-five engage in deliberate self-harm.

- 140–200 young people aged under twenty-four die by suicide.

*The rate of deliberate self-harm is highest among the young. Some of the self-harm is suicide attempts and/or repeat episodes.

Sources: Growing Up in Ireland; National Office of Suicide Prevention; My World Survey; National Study of Mental Health.[8]

In his book, *Affluenza*, leading psychologist Oliver James explored whether it is possible to be successful and stay sane in this mad world.[9] James asks why so many people are unhappy when we are experiencing unprecedented wealth, and concludes that comparing ourselves to others is often to blame. But our pursuit of a great life is in truth leaving us with a poor life and, according to James, the foot must come off the pedal if we are to be happy and relaxed.

The continued rise in the number of prescriptions for anti-depressants and medication for anxiety shows us that our contemporary lifestyle isn't working. Even though suicide is vastly under-reported, it still remains the leading cause of death in the USA.[10]

FACT: *Every year, approximately:*

- *35,000–40,000 people die by suicide in the USA*
- *1 million people attempt suicide in the USA*
- *450–700 people die by suicide in Ireland*
- *1 million people die by suicide every year worldwide (3,000 people every day)*

Source: WHO; CDC; NOSP.[11]

A GENERATION OF WEAKLINGS?

However, it is not only misery and suicide that parents have to contend with; the never-ending quest for perfection, which has put parents under sustained pressure to over-parent, has paradoxically produced a generation of children who have unhealthy lifestyles. Parents simply haven't the time to create the organic, home-cooked meals that they know they should be cooking and wish they could provide. Instead parents feel so pressurised to improve and develop every other part of their children's lives, the lure of convenience food is simply too great to withstand, which is why, despite the widespread availability of cheap quality food, children's health is often compromised as a consequence of their poor diets. And so, with a reported major decline in children's heart and lung fitness, we're not only miserable, but we're also at serious risk of producing 'a generation of weaklings' who may not as live as long as their parents did.[12] Already, it is predicted that Irish children will be the fattest in Europe by the year 2030.[13] As we all know, children raised indoors miss many opportunities for physical activity, which in turn gives rise to whole swathes of health problems.

The governments of developed countries have already recognised this problem and issued guidelines recommending physical activity of moderate-to-vigorous intensity for children for at least one hour every day. However, the recent *Growing Up in Ireland* study reported that a massive 75 per cent of nine-year-old children in Ireland today don't reach the recommended level of activity,[14] and a simply enormous 88 per cent of Irish eleven- to fifteen-year-olds also fail to meet these targets.[15] (And, for the record, the majority of those children attend GAA, dancing classes and so on.)

WHAT'S EATING OUR CHILDREN?
When I read that teenage girls in Ireland spend on average nineteen hours a day sitting or lying down, thus putting their hearts at risk, I didn't believe it, but having checked it out, it's true![16]

Many of us are aware that one in four Irish children is overweight or obese.[17] But this statistic doesn't take into account all the other, more worrying ways that children are showing disordered eating patterns – there are food refusers, fussy eaters, bulimics and anorexics, to name but a few. For example, on the one hand there is Abby, a cheerful but slightly bored nine-year-old child who spends her days grazing in front of the TV. Abby lives with her mother and little brother; she loves school but beyond that life is rather boring, so she eats to stave off feelings of boredom and listlessness. Then there is Susie, an intense and focused teenager, who has become focused on the one thing she can excel at – not eating.

The eating disorder websites are full of insecure young people striving to gain a sense of control and power in their over-controlled lives. It is frightening to see the exultation that follows a day when Susie has managed to eat just an apple, and that sense of achievement is enough to carry her through the hunger pangs. The definitive clarity of the weighing scales gives intense children such as Susie a beguiling sense of power and a hook to hold on to in a bewildering and insecure world. Whereas previously Susie was considered extremely good at her schoolwork and was showing a serious talent for English, now she believes she is 'best' at losing weight – and can see the steadily decreasing numbers to back it up each time she weighs herself.

CHILDHOOD OBESITY

It is not an exaggeration to say that children are becoming physically addicted to junk food. The psychologist Deanna Jade, founder of the National Centre for Eating Disorders in Britain, points out that food highly flavoured with salt, and containing fat and food additives, works in the same way as drugs: 'It changes our mood and it impacts on the chemicals and neurotransmitters in the brain in a similar way to alcohol, nicotine and cocaine'.[18] In addition, according to nutritionist Dr Susan Jebb, 'Children develop very strong learned preferences – junk food can become a psychological addiction.'[19] This epidemic has become heightened in the last decade as frazzled and time-stretched parents don't have time to cook and don't have the energy to argue when their kids pester for the food they want instead of the food they need.

As many of us know from bitter experience, the more junk

food we eat, the more we want, and that's why kids now dive straight for crisps or a bar of chocolate as a response to the slightest feeling of distress. Jamie Oliver's valiant efforts to change the eating habits of schoolchildren had a significant impact in the UK, but this has not been an easy path to travel and his campaigning even caused a backlash, with parents arguing for their right to choose to feed their children junk! As children become more accustomed to the taste of processed food they are less likely to be thrilled with the rare event of Mammy's home-cooked stew and are more at home with the comfort of the habitual – which is often highly processed rubbish.[20]

In the obesogenic environment in which we live, parents are right to worry about their children's food consumption, because our screen-based, junk-food lifestyle means that the path of least resistance is to become obese. The nutritionist Patrick Holford remarked, 'We're seeing outrageous imbalances in brain chemistry caused simply by eating the kinds of food that, sadly, millions of kids are eating.'[21] Moreover, a multitude of studies has proved links between children with ADHD and an excess of certain foods combined with a lack of specific vitamins and minerals.[22]

Case Study

Ruth came to me for counselling because she hoped that she could learn some techniques to help her manage her increasingly uncontrollable life. There could be no doubt that Ruth had a deep and abiding love for her three children, aged six, seven and nine; however, she was finding the stress of coping with the children and working full-time overwhelming. Ruth's husband also worked very long hours so there was little support available from him.

Every evening she dashed out of work to collect her children from the after-care facility by 4.30 p.m. She had permission to leave work at 4.15 p.m. but her boss didn't like it and so she always felt on the back foot at work. Then she had to get home, get the homework done and the kids fed by 5.45 p.m., because then she had to pile them into the car again to drop them to the GAA and other activities, which usually started at 6 p.m. The schedule was just too tight and Ruth said she pretty much lost her temper every day as a result of her frustration.

Homework was a constant source of argument and what the children were eating was a source of constant guilt: 'I'm afraid I'm forced to feed them convenience food nearly every day. There is simply no time to peel the vegetables etc. I just throw things in the microwave while I'm helping with the reading and the homework and everything.' This was particularly distressing for Ruth as she really enjoyed cooking and when first pregnant had looked forward to leisurely days cooking with the children. This hadn't happened. Her middle child, Sally, was overweight, and this caused Ruth deep shame and embarrassment. 'I know the food I give her isn't ideal, but it's not that bad, and she get loads of exercise – she loves her GAA. I don't know what I'm doing wrong – nothing is working out!'

I explained to Ruth about children's need for free play and independence, and while she smiled wryly at some of the examples I gave, she was adamant that she couldn't risk her children playing unsupervised – she couldn't live with herself if anything happened to them. Nor could she countenance the children walking home alone – that was out of the question.

As the weeks rolled by and our sessions continued, Ruth and I began to collaborate to work out what was working and what wasn't in her family's lifestyle. Ultimately, Saturdays and Sundays were great, but the other five days of the week were a disaster.

> *Ruth began to realise that something had to give. First she reduced the number of activities the children went to, then she found a lift to take the eldest girl to dance class. Then she stopped helping with the children's homework so much, and instead put more time into making the children's dinners. Finally, after a few months of counselling, she decided to allow the children to walk home from school. This meant that she could leave work at the proper time of 4.30 p.m. She got home at about the same time as the kids and saved herself a significant amount of stress from driving in traffic as the school was at the other end of the town. These were all small changes, but they ended up making a big difference. Life went from being unmanageable to being manageable.*

BIG BUSINESS IS MAKING CHILDREN FAT

In a quick-fix world, the fastest and most accessible way to satisfy hunger is to turn towards highly processed junk food. Canny manufacturers know this and their profits are often created by targeting stressed parents and gullible kids. More and more children are becoming fussy eaters as their palates have remained undeveloped because of the high quantities of fat, salt, sugar and food additives in processed food and the snacks that are available everywhere. (Even at the chemist's – what's that all about?!)

It is no coincidence that the rise of the fussy eater has coincided with the rise of junk food cynically marketed towards children. Again, the media puts the frighteners inconsistently on parents, with articles dedicated to the dangers of sugar highs and junk food, while at the same time selling lucrative advertisement space to the marketing industries who devote themselves entirely to junk food, pester power and couch potato kids. Gaah!

In the past, the child often knew exactly what he or she was having for dinner that day: a roast on a Sunday, stew on a Monday, shepherd's pie on a Tuesday and so on. These days, if the parent is in a hurry (and let's face it, we often are) the food advertisers are ready and waiting to pounce like alligators in a milk-chocolate-flavoured swampland. They have all manner of ready-made meals for children, with words such as 'healthy and nutritious' emblazoned ubiquitously somewhere on the label to soothe our tortured consciences. As a stressed client sighed to me, 'I know I shouldn't give them so many pizzas and oven chips, but since the baby came I'm always fire-fighting and it is simply the easiest option.'

DINNER, INTERRUPTED

The technological age has, among other things, hurried the decline of the family meal, and our new way of grazing constantly throughout the day means that many of us, children and parents alike, never feel fully hungry, and equally, never feel fully satisfied. But how can the family sit down to an evening meal if the parents are busy working to provide a perfect childhood and the children are spending vast amounts of time on schoolwork and extracurricular activities? When exactly can we have the famous family meal? At ten o'clock at night?

Gone are the days of breakfast, dinner and tea; rather, we now eat anywhere and everywhere: at our laptops, in our beds, on the couch – even dashboard dining is on the rise. A UK survey of 2,000 families showed that 20 per cent of them never sit down to a meal together, and 75 per cent eat while watching TV.[23] The journalist Sheila Pell neatly encapsulates how family life is structured these days:

Like much of the nation, everyone in the family is so busy that we long ago became used to eating in shifts. Dining has become dinner, interrupted. It is often a staggered affair, where people wander in following

their own schedules, gaze into the refrigerator as if it were a 1950s
automat, and make a selection. Even our seating arrangements have
evolved out of this moveable feast.[24]

ANXIOUS PARENTS, FUSSY EATERS

The psychotherapist Susie Orbach first made the connection
between anxious parents and 'fussy eaters', and indeed, working in
private practice as a psychotherapist myself, it is remarkable how
many anxious parents have children who are fussy eaters.[25]

All children need a certain amount of power in their lives and
sometimes the only power a young child can assert is either in
eating food or in eliminating it; otherwise, the infant is prey to
the whims of his mother or father: strapped into the car, put down
unwillingly to sleep, strapped into a buggy, taken to nursery, etc.
This is, of course, understandable – we have to do what we have
to do, and yet if a child is over-controlled by his or her over-
anxious parents (often through excessive attention) he or she will
frequently either have difficulties in eating or in toilet training.

The overly controlled child may become incredibly picky
regarding which food he or she will eat as a way to assert a sense of
control in his/her life, or another child may become constipated,
again as an unconscious method of retaining a vestige of control.
The 'fussy eater' can create intense feelings of panic in anxious
parents as the child either spits the food out or won't open his or
her mouth. This is the last frontier of control and the child often
wins.

Parents driven to distraction by the fussy child's eating habits
often engage in lengthy battles with the child. The parent is aware
that the child needs nutrition in one form or another, and the
child realises that finally he or she has some cards to play with
and uses his/her trump card to the max. Extravagant promises
of treats or threats of punishment fly around, but many children

unconsciously enjoy the sweet feeling of power and have no desire to relinquish it. The longer the situation continues, the more likely it is that the child will begin to dictate the menu. Many parents decide that any food is preferable to no food at all, and this heralds the arrival of the 'turkey twizzler' and 'chicken popcorn' into the house.

And yet parents are missing the true problem – the link between control and food – and instead become fixated on getting the child to eat … eat anything, anywhere and at any time. This is perhaps a prime example of our eye being on the wrong ball, as very few children in the developed world suffer from starvation while many, many children suffer from problems with their teeth, their bowels and other conditions arising as a consequence of eating too much junk food. The number of children and young people being admitted to hospitals with inflammatory bowel diseases (IBD) has trebled in recent years, and this has been linked to the consumption of junk food and antibiotics. This is a lifelong chronic condition that has a devastating impact on people's lives and can't be cured but only managed. Seamus Hussey, consultant at Our Lady's Children's Hospital, Dublin, has pointed out that between the years 2000 and 2010, 400 children were diagnosed with IBD in Ireland, but since then, in just two years, a further 196 children have been diagnosed with the condition.[26]

Studies showing us the long-term impact of a diet of junk food have not caused a return to home-cooked meals, but rather an upsurge in spending on food supplements for children, which are advertised to parents as IQ enhancers or brain food for kids. The manufacturers prey on the anxieties of the parents, and the parents, driven by anxiety that the child won't eat the right things, yield to the pressure to buy junk food, and then, driven by guilt, they also buy food supplements. And the fussy eater is taught the dubious lesson that complex issues can be solved by taking a pill.

TOP TIP: Take control of the what, where and when of food

The highly respected nutritionist, Ellyn Satter, has a rule of thumb to help stressed parents with their children's eating habits: adults should decide what, where and when to eat, and children should be allowed to decide whether to eat and how much.

This can calm parents as they begin to free themselves from mealtime war. It can also help to improve the situation for children as they will eat less junk food if the parents alone have control of the what, where and when.

HEALTH-DAMAGING JUNK FOOD

Less wary customers aren't aware of the cunning tricks and clever plans the manufacturers hatch to make money from them. I saw this myself when I had to employ a new childminder. On the first day I explained to her that there were just three main rules that myself and my husband considered vital – keep the children playing outside, no TV and no junk food. We had a trial day where the childminder took me into the kitchen and proudly showed me the array of 'healthy' food she had bought in for my kids. I literally could not believe my eyes, as laid out before me were cheese strings, cheesy crackers, turkey twizzlers, milk shakes, sweetened yogurts, yogurt pops, chicken fingers, chicken popcorn, chicken nuggets, chicken bites, chicken crap (oops, I made that last one up) … It was insane – did this caring, kind and engaged woman seriously think that this was healthy food? Yes, actually, she did.

When I questioned her, she showed me the 'added vitamins … healthy and nutritious … full of vitamins and proteins' labels on the food packs that made them healthy in her mind. At this point, I could not believe my ears. I quickly said no, that the kids had a lunchbox of fruit, and that would do for any snacks they needed. And, in fact, what was I thinking? They had had their lunch and they didn't need any additional snacks at all – they could eat at dinnertime. The childminder then showed me the SunnyD she had got for the kids to drink – full of vitamins and minerals! 'Just milk or water – that will do them,' I squeaked.

Sadly this childminder isn't the only one to fall for this false advertising and it is worrying how many parents who truly believe they are giving their kids healthy snacks are in fact unwittingly feeding them high-sugar, high-fat junk.

WHY DO WE NEED SNACKS ANYWAY?

Manufacturers are constantly dreaming up ever more ingenious snacks that will be attractive to children. But really, what is this obsession with snacks? Is breakfast, dinner and tea not enough for us? The concept of the 'snack' came into being in the 1970s as food manufacturers realised that certain foods were 'expandable' while others weren't – if you buy more chicken than usual this week, you will buy less other meat; however, if you buy more crisps, you won't necessarily buy less of anything else: this item is expandable! Yay! … And so are our waistlines! Not yay!

Manufacturers focus on hard-selling the more expandable items on the shopping list – they don't care if we expand and get fat – all they care about is that the shopping list is expandable. It is for this reason that the 'buy one, get one free' items are very often junk food – we won't reduce our shopping list if we get freebies with junk food – the more the merrier. Ha, ha, ha.

The snacks in the 1970s and 1980s were small treats such as a Milky Way or a 'finger of fudge', which back then was 'just enough to give your kids a treat' (and don't forget 'it's full of

Cadbury's goodness'); however, the amount of snacks consumed has increased to form a large part of some children's entire diet for the day. Canny marketing managers put words such as 'healthy and nutritious' somewhere on the label and parents heave a sigh of relief as they pop these handy snacks into lunchboxes.

Don't mind the tasty sandwiches, give her Tuc biscuits!

I was chatting with some mothers at the school gate recently about how annoying it was that my daughter wasn't eating the school lunches lovingly prepared for her, and the response was startling. Give her Tuc biscuits, Rice Krispie bars and Cheese Strings, I was told, the child mustn't go hungry. Apparently, it was unconscionable that she would go through the school day without eating much more than the fruit we provided. But, I argued, she eats a huge breakfast at 8 a.m. and a huge dinner at 2 p.m.; maybe all she needs are light snacks in between? 'No, no, no,' I was told, 'the child must eat.'

'But my husband gives her tasty sandwiches every day,' I bleated, 'and he's a great cook!'

The reply was swift –

'Don't mind the tasty sandwiches, kids never eat them nowadays, give her Tuc biscuits; she'll eat them.'

Sophisticated marketing campaigns use colourful packaging, toys in packets and product placement in movies to lead children to see certain foods as 'fun' and 'cool' – and it works, as even two-year-olds can recognise and ask for specific branded products. The impact of marketing and subliminal messages such as product placement means that even if the parents are diligent in cooking healthy meals and snacks for their children, other adults such as caregivers, grandparents, friends and relatives will often 'treat' the children with 'goodies'. Certain food quickly becomes associated with love, comfort and reward, and so begins an unhealthy attitude towards food in general. Research has proved that, for many Americans, the sight of a can of Coca-Cola imbues the person with feelings of self-image, memory and cultural identity … yes, Coca-Cola, one of the richest global organisations in the world, has had such a trickle-down impact into the nation's consciousness, that Americans feel warm, fuzzy and at home with the drink. It's no wonder so many of us are fat!

TOP TIP: Teach your children to be savvy!

Some of the most depressing moments of my life have been when walking the aisles of my local supermarket. (It's true!) But there are ways we could cut the tedious hours endured by parents squinting at tiny print on the side of packages, attempting to ascertain whether the food is reasonably healthy or pure junk. In years to come we will undoubtedly look aghast at the way junk food is peddled to children these days, just as tobacco was once peddled to an unsuspecting public in the 1950s.

But what are busy parents supposed to do? Are we supposed to get a degree in nutrition? Or perhaps even better, get a qualification in business and marketing so that we can see through the marketing ploys?

Perhaps we should demand more from regulation bodies? If food could be separated into standardised 'healthy, neutral or treat' sections in each aisle, then harried parents could quickly assess if the food they were buying was 'healthy' or 'junk-food-pretending-to-be-healthy'. This could be arranged using the already popular traffic light system: with the green section of the aisle for healthy food to be lower down, at the height of children, the amber section for neutral food at mid-height, and the red section for food that should be consumed strictly as a treat, on the high shelves (along with the vodka), so the parents wouldn't be pester-powered to death so easily during every single shopping trip.

As it is today, parents need to teach their children about the concept of marketing and how the canny marketeers are busily trying to swipe Mammy and Daddy's money by luring children with their bright colours and false promises. Your children will then become savvier individuals, more adept at the ways of the modern world, and also become aware of how to handle being constantly subjected to sly tricks to get our money.

PATHOLOGISING DIFFERENCE

Though the rise in childhood depression, youth suicide and the rates of disordered eating patterns are startling, nevertheless few would argue that the most worrying change compared to previous generations is the rise in the number of children with behavioural and learning difficulties. There has been an explosion in the rates of children being found to have special needs, and an alarming number of children have been diagnosed with a behavioural or learning difficulty of some sort – many of which hadn't even entered the public consciousness before the twenty-first century.[27]

The reasons for this explosion are manifold: earlier diagnosis, improved detection, higher expectations and narrower standards of behaviour, to name just a few. Though increased knowledge and better understanding of special educational needs has led to conditions that were undiagnosed in the past now being recognised routinely, it is also accepted that on many levels we are pathologising childhood and over-diagnosing; for example, extreme shyness has controversially become a syndrome in *The Diagnostic and Statistical Manual of Mental Disorders*, 5th edition (DSM-5), considered to be a universal authority for psychiatric diagnosis.

Children with emotional problems are presenting at a younger age every year and, while it is great that specialists are becoming more expert at early diagnosis, many child specialists are concerned that the phenomenal growth in the rate of learning and behavioural difficulties is linked with current favoured parenting practices and the tendency for experts and parents to pathologise difference.[28] The pain and anguish suffered by children previously left undiagnosed is intense, but on the other hand, the complicated stress of inappropriate expectations on a child also causes great pain.

Some disorders now found in DSM-5 are increasingly being used to pathologise misbehaviour, leading parents to believe that their child can't help his or her bad behaviour. In one episode of 'Supernanny' I saw (bizarrely enough, it's the only programme the kids and I will agree to watch together), the mother was finding the behaviour of her three-year-old child increasingly uncontrollable and she said that she had sent the child for assessment – 'They think he may have a behavioural disorder, but it's not definite. To be honest, I don't know what I'll do if they *don't* diagnose him with something – I know there's something wrong!' After the family spent some time with Supernanny and learned some effective behavioural techniques, all talk of disorders had vanished and the offender was transformed into a happy, healthy and well-functioning child.

This matter is now a source of heated debate among experts as it is becoming apparent that some parents these days may prefer to label their children's problems instead of labelling the family's lifestyle as problematic. Critics of the growth in sales of mind-altering drugs such as Ritalin to treat ADHD often argue that parents prefer their children to pop a pill to enable them to settle into our rigid and ambitious expectations of what is deemed appropriate behaviour (in the past, many children in these situations would simply have been whacked – not a recommended route, but another demonstration of how parenting these days has become so much more demanding).

But perhaps what is being asked of some children is completely inappropriate? Children certainly need boundaries, but excessive use of discipline in a dull and strict atmosphere is too hard on them; kids need to be able to run around, yell, sing, laugh etc. Just today as I was yelling at my five-year-old to come in to the sitting room and do his homework, I found him in the kitchen where he was trying very hard to go all around the kitchen without letting his feet touch the ground (as you do). I paused before yelling and thought for a second; for this task he needed to be resourceful, creative and agile. Now this little boy already has a deep aversion to homework – he loves school but he dislikes doing his homework. And so I left him to it – learning how to re-write an 'o' seemed to pale in comparison to the difficult challenge he had set for himself. (By the way, after many attempts, he eventually pulled this off and we all gave him a great, big cheer.) If I had dragged him in to write the letter 'o' ten times I would have had a frustrated and disgruntled child on my hands, who disliked homework even more; as it was I had a very proud little boy (who didn't quite finish his homework).

The intensive current school system doesn't suit some children, the lack of free time on their own frustrates many other children, and the focus on what you aren't good at can have a deeply negative impact on still other children. If what we ask of some children is misguided, then of course a lot of them will act out, which of course leads to problem children. While all the time perhaps it is the environment and not the children who are at fault.

Many parents are simply following the path laid down by society. They often don't have the time to discipline their children – they are too busy trying to hold down a job while at the same time attempting to improve their children's performance with extra-curricular activities and keep them supervised at all times, so that by the time some creative 'outside the box' thinking is necessary for your child's individual needs, the parents just don't have the energy to think of a solution and, even then, they don't have the confidence to enact their solution – which can often be as simple as allowing them to miss some of their homework. As Justine Roberts, CEO of Mumsnet, says, 'It's impossible to do everything – you just fall over'.[29]

In addition, there is such an extreme emphasis on performance that parents are led to believe that their children may have significant problems if they are 'under-performing' compared to their schoolmates; but perhaps they aren't 'under-performing' – maybe that's not the way their brain works?

DRUGGED CHILDREN

ADHD affects the individual's ability to concentrate and control behaviour, causing stress and pressure on both the child and the family of the child affected. A recent international study led by NUI Maynooth showed that as many as one in twenty children in Ireland (mainly boys) are considered by experts to be at risk of the disorder (one in ten American children have been diagnosed with ADHD)[30] and there has been a staggering 62 per cent increase in prescriptions for ADHD drugs over the six years between 2007 and 2013 in Ireland.[31] As we can see from the graph in Figure 5.1 (overleaf), there has been a similar sharp rise in the use of drugs for ADHD in the UK.[32]

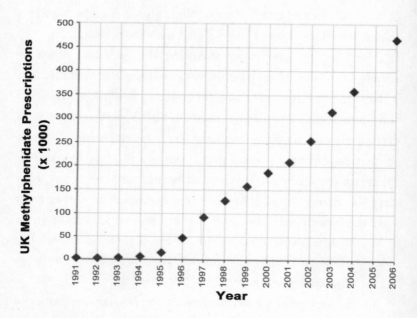

Figure 5.1: Increase in methylphenidate (Ritalin) prescriptions between 1991 and 2006, United Kingdom. *Source:* Futuremind, UK.[33]

The Quality Care Commission's report in Britain shows that doctors believe many more people are buying drugs online. A recent Cambridge University survey shows that the pill-popping continues into the third level, with the report also describing a 'smart-drug craze', with many students turning to cognitive-enhancing drugs to improve their performance.[34]

In the UK in just two years, 2000 to 2002, there was an astounding 68 per cent rise in prescriptions for mind-altering drugs for children.[35] And, while it is evident that this staggering rate of increase has snowballed since 2000, equally, it is clear that this epidemic is still largely unexplained – though experts tend to speak vaguely about contemporary culture being one of the many culprits.

Case Study

Bernie was a working mother of three children, who came to me for help in dealing with the issues involved in being a single parent to unruly teenagers. Her son Thomas was fifteen years old and had been diagnosed with ADHD when he was eight years old. During the holidays Thomas stopped taking his medication as he functioned very well in the free space of the farm where they lived. However, when he returned to school he had to go back on the medication again as he wouldn't sit still in school and needed the drugs to enable him to behave as the school required; when Thomas was taking Ritalin he was easier to manage in school.

Thomas hated school, but he loved working on the farm, which he would one day inherit. Still, according to the diktat from society, Thomas had to continue to go to school; and even on to third level education if he wanted to be a successful farmer, and so he continued to take the drugs.

As a single parent, Bernie had very little time to spare, but when things went from bad to worse for Thomas at school she decided to allow him leave school and attend Youthreach, a training and work experience programme for early school leavers, instead. In time Thomas reduced his dosage of medication and eventually stopped taking it completely.

AUTISM SPECTRUM DISORDER

The astonishing 600 per cent rise in the number of children diagnosed with an autism spectrum disorder (ASD) since the mid-1990s in the USA has caused a huge amount of speculation in recent years (with an estimated one in fifty American children diagnosed with ASD at the time of writing).[36] Experts say changes in diagnostic practices account for a rise of 200 per cent in ASD, but this doesn't even get close to the 600–700 per cent rise in diagnosed ASD cases since 1990.[37] While this is in the USA, other post-industrial counties are experiencing a similar trend of rising ASD incidence rates – for example, in 2012 in Britain there was a reported increase of 56 per cent of children diagnosed with autism in the previous five years.[38]

The rise of ASD

In the US:

- in 2000 1 in 150 children was diagnosed with ASD.
- in 2010 1 in 68 children was diagnosed with ASD.
- in 2013 1 in 50 children was diagnosed with ASD.

Source: Based on biennial numbers from the CDC (Centers for Disease Control and Prevention).[39]

Figure 5.2: Autism Today.

The rate of autism changes depending on where you live!

- In Ireland 1 in 166 children has ASD.
- In South Korea 1 in 38 children has ASD.
- In areas of New Jersey in the US 1 in 45 children has ASD.
- In areas of Alabama in the US 1 in 175 children has ASD.
- In Cuba 1 in 60,000 children has ASD.

Source: These are approximate figures from Autism Ireland, Autism Speaks and the CDC.[40]

Figure 5.3: Rates of Autism around the World.

Autism spectrum disorder affects children's ability to relate to the world and to communicate with others, with 'high functioning' children at one end of the scale and severely autistic children at the other. Though we have no real idea why autism is increasing, the pace of the increase in autism suggests to many that our lifestyle is influencing the rates of this disorder. In many ways this is good news: if something is causing autism, then as soon as we figure it out, we can work to reverse these increases.

SOME SING LOW, SOME SING HIGHER

Louis Theroux's documentary *America's Medicated Kids* examined the 'pill for every ill' approach that many contemporary Americans are choosing to use.[41] This made for shocking TV, showing us that in one household everyone, even the dog, was taking medication for depression. The American Academy of Pediatrics tells us that one in six children is diagnosed with a developmental disorder,[42] implying that one in six children in the USA is either educationally and/or socially dysfunctional. This causes many ripples within society, and within the classroom – if one in six children has different needs, then should the teaching be standardised for the other five, or is this percentage too high for such standardisation?

If the commonality of behaviour is one in six, then could it be argued that our contemporary culture simply doesn't suit these children? Maybe they have different needs and a different way of approaching life? In the past left-handed children were forced to write with their right hands; perhaps we are doing something similar today and forcing some children to behave in a manner that simply doesn't suit them? For example, the autistic rights movement is a global movement run by some highly functioning and breathtakingly impressive people who have been diagnosed with autism. These activists, some of whom are doubly incontinent and without speech, are now forcing society to re-think standardised behaviour as they reject the term 'autism' and prefer to use the term 'neurodiverse' – just as they use the term 'neurotypical' for the so-called 'normal' people.

When you study the data on learning and behaviour difficulties among children in Ireland it quickly becomes clear that our patterns of diagnosis are similar to those of the USA – we in Ireland are generally just a few years behind the USA in adopting new techniques. It is still unclear how many of these issues are behaviourally based, a result of our families and culture, and how many can be attributed to genetic inheritance. According to a study from NUI Maynooth, as many as 85 per cent of Irish children with ADHD have received some kind of medication to treat their symptoms, even though findings show that children whose parents underwent the twenty-week 'Incredible Years' training programme made 'significant gains' in reduced hyperactivity and inattentiveness – it also found these parents used notably improved parental interaction.[43]

The Incredible Years programme targets parents, teachers and children with an aim of promoting positive behaviour and reducing and treating challenging behaviour. One reason why parents aren't using these strategies continuously is that they are often difficult, time-consuming and need a tremendous amount of energy; another reason is that the parents often privately think that their child is a little bit different, and on some level it's the system that is causing the problems, not the child (and they could well be right on that one).[44]

I have counselled countless young people who don't suit the school system, but with the current emphasis on education and performance that is everywhere today, such 'square peg' children are being forced to fit into a round hole. And it isn't working.

Currently, children within our school system are required to maintain a certain standard of behaviour: they are asked to sit still, when that doesn't come naturally to them; they are asked to keep quiet when that is entirely unnatural to their way of being; and they are asked to learn with words and numbers, when that is incredibly frustrating and goes against their nature. Instead of working *with* their personalities, we are asking their personalities to fall in with the style of the majority. But if we look at some very successful people, such as Jamie Oliver, Richard Branson, Jim Carrey, Jay Leno and Eddie Izzard (to name but a few), we can see that people with dyslexia, ADHD and other learning and behavioural difficulties, can grow up to be very successful people – once they stop trying to fall into step with the rest of us neurotypicals. And yet more and more parents are falling into the trap of believing that the rigid learning system promoted by the current system of education is the only way for their kids to succeed and learn (and the current culture of providing children with a series of over-supervised, after-school activities further adds to the problem).

Another argument offered about methods of dealing with learning and behavioural difficulties is that children have fallen out of touch with nature and that this has a particular impact on children with ADHD. In Richard Louv's *cri de coeur* for the loss of nature in children's lives, *Last Child in the Woods*, he argues that 'An environment-based education movement – at all levels of education – will help students realize that school isn't supposed to be a polite form of incarceration, but a portal to the wider world.' Louv has a different take on ADHD, and in his book he outlines his version of 'nature deficit disorder' – which is described as 'the human costs of alienation from nature, among them: diminished use of the senses, attention difficulties, and higher rates of physical and emotional illnesses'.[45] According to Louv, it is not enough to ensure children with ADHD get enough exercise; it is also imperative that these children have enough nature in their lives, as a connection with nature soothes and calms the soul in ways we cannot fathom. And when we read in a 2008 National Trust survey that 33 per cent of school-going children could not identify a magpie; and 50 per cent could not tell the difference between a bee and a wasp, yet 90 per cent were able to recognise a Dalek, we soon realise that nature is indeed being bypassed by many contemporary children and perhaps this is part of the problem.[46]

Troubled rock stars Courtney Love and Kurt Cobain were both on Ritalin as children, and both became addicted to heroin as adults, with Kurt Cobain eventually taking his own life. I am not suggesting that if children take mind-altering and mood-changing drugs they will therefore become drug addicts in the future; used with care and consideration they can make the difference between an unhappy and exhausted family and a thriving, well-adjusted one. Yet Courtney Love has a penetrating point to make about drugging children: 'When you're a kid and you get this drug that makes you feel that feeling, where else are you going to turn when you're an adult? It was euphoric when you were a child – isn't that memory going to stick with you?'[47]

6

Bring on the Professionals

One thing I had learned from watching chimpanzees with their infants is that having a child should be fun.

Jane Goodall[1]

Like many new parents, when I first became pregnant I overdosed on the baby books and attempted to read nearly every publication available. Yet the baby books didn't calm me down, instead the worry and the tension became even worse – because the overriding message was that an untold amount of future grief would ensue if I didn't follow their advice … But I had to follow the right advice – the problem was that I couldn't figure out which *was* the right advice!!

According to one guru, if I picked my baby up every time it cried I would create a needy, attention-seeking monster. Another book told me that if I didn't pick the baby up when it cried I would create an insecure and depressed child. Which would I prefer, I thought to myself pensively: needy and attention-seeking, or insecure and depressed?

An experienced parent might find this laughable, but not many of us forget the special terror created by the arrival of our firstborn. Often parents under such pressure rashly change horses in mid-stream and jump from one drastic method to another (causing, of course, a whole new set of problems).

And so what advice are the hallowed professionals giving to new parents these days? The answer, I'm afraid, is that the advice is as varied as to how to make a good 'spag bol' – add lots of tomatoes, add very few tomatoes, heavy on the olive oil, light on the olive oil, garlic, no garlic – we need to agree to disagree on this one, as the so-called baby experts are in total disagreement with each other. *What to Expect When You're Expecting*, *The Contented Little Baby Book*, *The Baby Whisperer* and many more babycare manuals are all best-sellers as they *sell* their preferred method of parenting. Websites like 'Mumsnet' also dish out advice (and, all too often, judgement) on the 'hardest job in the world'. Parenting gurus sell their methods and parents are pretty much asked to join one religion over another when deciding on their style of parenting, which, of course, causes even more anxiety and distress as the embattled parent consults 'The Book', praying that they have chosen the right book.

So how did this obsession with baby books evolve? Our own parents probably used to consult a book for advice on specific childhood ailments, but it would have been almost unheard of in Ireland for parents to seek advice from a book on general parenting issues. However, over time, the baby book has developed from being an academic treatise at the time of Freud to creating an entire lifestyle approach à la Penelope Leach today.

CHILDHOOD IN HISTORY

Although it is difficult to believe, until relatively recently parents killed their children in their billions. Not only that, but children were routinely 'starved, mutilated, raped, neglected and beaten'.[2] Without a shadow of a doubt, the most disturbing book I read while researching for this book was *The Emotional Life of Nations*, by the leading psycho-historian Lloyd DeMause.[3] Child abandonment was commonplace, and children were frequently sent to extremely neglectful wet-nurses, tied up in painfully tight swaddling bandages and hung on pegs. This enormously abusive pattern moved DeMause to offer a prize to any scholar who could find even one 'good mother' prior to the eighteenth century – the definition being one who would not today be imprisoned for child abuse.

Children in the past were largely viewed as screaming, needy little fiends, requiring strict and constant discipline. If the little wretch grew up to be a 'bad un', the parents decried their bad luck to have a child that brought shame on their family, without feeling any guilt or responsibility for the behaviour. It seems hard to believe, but in not much more than a hundred years we have gone from cruelty to children to cruelty to parents. It is pretty much the polar opposite of the view that is rampant in society today, and if a person turns out to be a bad 'un these days the parenting is immediately called into question and the parents are usually named, shamed and blamed.

WHEN DID WE FIRST START BLAMING THE PARENTS?

With the advent of psychoanalysis and 'talk therapy' in the nineteenth century, a laser-like focus was suddenly shone on hapless parents. Out went the wet-nurse, beatings and abandonment, and in came the fashion to treat kids with, well, kid gloves. Society has gone from being focused on pre-supposing that children were blights on their parents' lives until they grew up, to believing that parents are blights on their children's lives, and children need help to escape unscathed from the inept methods of their foolish parents. This new-found belief that children are in fact emotionally fragile blank slates, and that parents are the real villains of the piece, has resulted in a proliferation of complex theories and heavy-handed advice. This began with highly qualified psychologists such as Freud and John Bowlby, but in a modern society obsessed with short, easy-to-understand soundbites, we are now more inclined to take advice from the latest media savvy pop psychologist than a more complicated message emerging from a respected psychologist.

SIGMUND FREUD: IF IT'S NOT ONE THING, IT'S YOUR MOTHER

To simplify wildly, Freud's psychoanalysis was focused mainly on the unconscious and fantasies, and he argued that the personality is largely formed if not by your upbringing, then by your view of your upbringing. Freud believed that the first six years of a person's life were vitally important in shaping the person's disposition. He divided the psychosexual development of the person into five stages: the oral stage, the anal stage, the phallic stage, the latency stage and the genital stage.[4] If there was too much or too little emphasis on any particular stage, this would emerge in the person's disposition. For example, if the mother breastfed too much, too little or not at all, the adult child could eventually become orally fixated, needing to chew gum or smoke constantly. And so, according to Freud, your oral fixation that is manifested in smoking cigarettes or eating too much could be a direct consequence of your mother weaning you off the breast too early ... or too late ... or not breastfeeding you at all!

Of course, the vagueness of cause and effect made many parents tear their hair out as they tried to decipher the situation. Nonetheless, Freud could always be relied on to emphasise the parents' behaviour as the cause of the client's distress, and ever since that time parents have been in the direct line of fire for mental health practitioners.

DR BOWLBY: ATTACHMENT THEORY

A key figure in the theory of raising kids is Dr John Bowlby (1907–90), famed for his theories on the fundamental importance of attachment from birth for human development.

During the Second World War, young children were separated for extended periods from their parents, and Dr Bowlby, a Freudian psychoanalyst, became interested in the development of children who were affected by this separation. He developed his 'attachment theory' largely because he was dissatisfied with traditional theories, in particular rejecting the dominant 'cupboard love' theory of attachment prevailing in Freudian psychoanalysis in the 1940s and 1950s (that is, whoever was in charge of the food cupboard was the object of the child's affections).

In 1952 Bowlby and a film-maker, James Robertson, excitedly presented their film *A Two-Year-Old Goes to Hospital* to the British Psychoanalytical Society, but the Society was unimpressed and did not accept Bowlby's theories.[5] According to Bowlby, when the two-year-old in the film was distressed by her mother's absence, it was because she was mourning the separation from her mother. However, the psychoanalysts had an altogether different take on the child's distress. Unfortunately, the waters were muddied as the child's mother was pregnant in the film and the psychoanalysts viewed this as a key element of the child's grief. They took the view that the child's pain was caused by unconscious fantasies about the mother and the impending birth – nothing at all to do with the mother leaving the two-year-old on her own in a scary place … and so the educated experts began to argue … and so the concerned parents began to puzzle.

Bowlby's views that children were responding to real-life events and not unconscious fantasies were rejected completely by psychoanalysts and he was effectively ostracised by the psychoanalytic community. Nonetheless, his theories took hold, and this film was instrumental in a campaign to alter hospital restrictions on visiting by parents. Before that point, many children were abandoned in hospital until they recovered (and to this day adult children of that generation speak of the trauma they suffered as they were left to recover from TB in hospitals for months and even years without visitors).

Bowlby's main conclusions on childcare were that 'the infant and young child should experience a warm, intimate, and continuous relationship with his mother (or permanent mother substitute) in which both find satisfaction and enjoyment' and that not to do so may have significant and irreversible mental health consequences.[6] Then, as the toddler grows and develops, he or she uses the at-. tachment figure or figures as a secure base from which to explore.[7] This theory was both controversial and influential as it caused widespread changes in childcare practices. Nowadays attachment theory (though sometimes criticised) is the dominant modern approach to early social development.

A by-product of Bowlby's attachment theories today is that women who work long hours often feel uneasy and guilty about their children spending large amounts of time in childcare. Attachment disorder is a serious condition, which usually manifests in destructive behaviour. However, it is worth bearing in mind that attachment disorder theory was originally based on children who had suffered severe abandonment and so it is in many ways incomparable to coddled kids in crèches. Some childcare experts foresee a grim future for the 'crèche kids' and predict that children who were abandoned to childcare will in turn abandon their parents to state care in their later years. In truth, we have no real idea what impact large amounts of time spent in childcare will have on the child, and we don't yet know whether such children will be absolutely fine or will tend to form weak attachments to their parents.

Case Study

Olive had undergone many cycles of IVF before she gave birth to her son, Jack. She was a highly successful merchant banker and loved her job. She came to counselling ashamed and guilty because she was determined to retain her ambitions even though her longed-for baby had finally arrived. When Jack was six months old she had enrolled him into full-

time childcare without guessing that he would let his feelings be known as soon as he was physically able to protest – at nine months old Jack was cold towards her when she arrived to collect him from childcare each evening; at thirteen months he would run away when Olive arrived and it would take thirty minutes before he would let her cuddle him. Jack was evidently punishing his mother for leaving him. From then on Jack's behaviour around the crèche was difficult and Olive sank into a trough of guilt and anxiety.

Olive loved her work, she found it fascinating, she loved the status her job gave her and she enjoyed having money to spend. Yet she could see that her precious boy would prefer his mammy not to work. Olive didn't know what to do. She arrived in therapy on a mission to discover whether she was damaging her baby by working. She was keenly interested in attachment theory and spent a lot of her time in therapy trying to discover my views on attachment theory and on whether she was the worst mother in the world for leaving her child in childcare. As therapy progressed, Olive realised that my views on the subject weren't at all important – what mattered most in this dynamic was her and Jack's views.

Over the course of many sessions, Olive and I spent time exploring what were likely to be the many factors that would influence Jack. Eventually, Olive realised that while she was an important element in Jack's life, she was not the only influence. She realised that she simply couldn't be the nurturing, bustling motherly figure, baking cookies and making home-made soup, that she had for so many years fantasised about being, and that Jack seemed to want.

Instead, Olive came to accept that she was a conflicted, nervous person who was very driven and had a deep and overpowering need to succeed in her professional life – a need that was just as powerful as her need to become a mother. And that was the mother she would be in Jack's life – a flawed but loving mother – and the sooner she accepted herself, the sooner Jack and Olive could have an authentic and loving relationship. If Olive tried to be another type of mother it would simply lead to a false existence full of bitterness and resentment.

Olive began to examine the possibility that perhaps it was sending Jack to the crèche that was at fault? She busied herself in researching different forms of childcare, and decided that a childminder based in her own home was a better option for her child. Jack is now three years old and Olive has relaxed her firm grip on her career: 'Jack needs to be in my company and after all those years of waiting for him to arrive, I can't in all decency ignore his needs. Jack needs me more than I would prefer, and for the moment I am working a four-day week so as to meet those needs. My career is impacted but I'm happier because Jack and I are so strong together now. I plan to resume working at full throttle when Jack is settled in school.'

BRING ON THE BABY EXPERTS

Before the advent of the Baby Expert, the old style of parenting was that each family had its own approach to parenting, which the new mother tended to accept, with amendments. And that was that. Society believed that the child's character was the bloodline coming out in each family unit, and indeed enjoyed spotting the more unusual shared traits among family members.

Nowadays, however, there is a very different pervading attitude; today, there are simply thousands of theories and theorists to choose from as a guide, and so parenting has become a hotly debated topic. Not only that, but since the beginning of the suffragette movement each generation of women has tended to have a higher level of education than its mothers', and new mothers in the last hundred years or so are more likely to have dismissed their own mothers' knowledge as old-fashioned – as one client memorably said to me, 'I wouldn't touch my mother's method of child-rearing with a wooden spoon!'

Today, each family is viewed as a self-contained family unit – an independent kingdom with its own methods of governance. There is little overall consensus, and friends and family tend to agree to disagree about almost every aspect of raising kids. This means that each family is weaker, and more insecure, defensive and paranoid about disapproval from others, and more vulnerable to any troubles that might strike – when parents and children fall at any given hurdle, from toilet training to schoolwork to adolescent rebellion, other parents nod knowingly but think silently, 'Well, what would you expect with the way you allow them to go to bed anytime they like/feed them junk food/are so strict with them?' And so the parents feel even more stressed, judged, insecure and isolated.

GODLIKE PARENTS AREN'T GOOD ENOUGH

Society has moved on from serious analysis of the impact of parenting to a perhaps more cynical attitude that seeks to make money from parents' desires to raise happy children. More money is being made than ever before by capitalising on parental worries, and there appears to be a complicated negative message emerging: parents are being viewed as gods with total influence over their children's lives, while at the same time they are being told that they are emotionally illiterate beings who are pretty useless at parenting and need professional help from the baby experts, from parenting training programmes, and from the baby book, in order to perform properly.

Because parents today feel more insecure in their roles as parents, they tend to bow to the seniority of the experts, distrusting their own instincts and increasingly consulting childcare manuals. Insecurity breeds competition, and parents regard their friends' advice as unreliable because of the competitive instinct – often friends can't resist showing off about how their little Johnny was sleeping through the night at two weeks old. In addition, parents are also unsure about friends' advice as it all depends on which stable of parenting they subscribe to – are they a child-whispering mother, or do they adhere to the attachment school of mothering?

These days many a good friendship is seriously affected because one friend is secretly horrified by their friend 'breaking' their child by parenting in the strict mode as advocated by authors such as Gina Ford. Parents, of course, usually learn to agree to disagree over parenting methods, but as the children grow up, gatherings can become more difficult as the rules are different and the parents have to navigate the outcry if one set of parents forbids its children to eat junk, play inappropriate video games or go to bed at any time they like, and the other set of parents turns a blind eye. If the gatherings are few and far between, there is no problem, but if the families are meeting every week these issues can become fraught with tension and the fun can go out of the day.

This lack of agreement among parents can cause further feelings of insecurity as they worry endlessly, 'Have we got it right or have they got it right? Because we're approaching parenting so differently we couldn't both be right ... and so one of us is totally wrong ... yikes! Is it us or them?' Increasingly, there is no middle ground; you are either rigidly following the famous 'routine' or you are fervently feeding 'on demand', or else you are determinedly saying 'you can't learn parenting from a book, we just have to muddle through'.

The 'just muddling through' approach is probably the most popular among Irish parents – and this would be well and good but for the fact (as we saw in Chapter 2) that our behaviour is shaped significantly by the twenty-four-hour-news culture. The media, and society in general, encourages over-parenting, and so if you think you are 'just muddling through', in reality you are probably over-parenting according to the diktats of society.

To ask Supernanny or to ask my mammy?

Perhaps surprisingly, the arrival of the 'baby expert' has actually *increased* parents' feelings of doubt and insecurity – the lack of consensus means that nervous parents can't confidently turn their power over to the gurus. Previously, parents who were interested in their children's emotional well-being would have to be very committed and prepared to sit down with the more academic tomes of Freud *et al.*, but today the 'baby experts' are easy to read and provide lots of clear rules so that parents can dip in and out of the books as they please. However, first and foremost, these books are commodities to be sold and so the sales pitch behind them is often heightened and doom-laden, along the lines of 'If you want to raise happy children you simply *have* to read this book!' The hysterical tone of many publications means that the worry is ratcheted up several notches, leading parents to believe that they have more power over their children than they really do: 'If I get this right, my baby could well turn out to be a world leader – Nelson Mandela, how are ya? But if I get this wrong, goodbye Mandela and hello Jack the Ripper! After all, this is the most important job in the world!' And so it is in this miasma of insecurity, guilt and anxiety that feelings of inadequacy, isolation and depression are quick to take hold among parents.

If we look at the following summaries of the big names in parenting since the 1960s, we can see more clearly how the publications have become progressively less academic and more populist, with increasing emphasis on polarised views being cynically peddled to parents (with a view to making money, if nothing else).

Dr Benjamin Spock (1903–98)

Before Dr Benjamin Spock, parents tended to look at babycare manuals as ways to resolve specific problems, but when *The Common Sense Book of Baby and Child Care* was published in 1946 it sold a more general approach to parents. Dr Spock was considered a radical for suggesting that infants could be cuddled, praised and should be fed when hungry, rather than on a schedule. Previously, the likes of John Watson, author of *Psychological Care of Infant and Child* in 1928, advised mothers to:

> *Treat them as though they were young adults … Never hug and kiss them, never let them sit on your lap. If you must, kiss them once on the forehead when they say goodnight. Shake hands with them in the morning. Give them a pat on the head if they have made an extraordinarily good job of a difficult task.*[8]

Nowadays, Spock's more tender approach has become a societal norm and he is considered the grandfather of the boom in baby experts. Spock's publications also reflected a seismic shift in family culture, when for the first time more mothers turned to childcare manuals than to their own mothers for advice. Few of us would disagree with the inspiring opening lines of *Baby and Child Care*: 'Trust yourself. You know more than you think you do.'[9] By the year 2000, sales of this parenting manual had passed fifty million, so evidently millions of parents feel that it is Spock we should trust, and that the good doctor knows a lot more than most. Dr

Spock was clearly in tune with the concept of 'mother knows best' as he wrote: 'Don't take too seriously all that the neighbors say. Don't be overawed by what the experts say. Don't be afraid to trust your own common sense.'[10] However, Spock himself was one of the experts he mentions, and he dished out masses of prescriptive advice.

When we examine the different editions of Spock's seminal book it soon becomes clear that Spock's advice is a moveable feast that was easily swayed by contemporary society's views and trends at any given moment. A good example are the changes that took place in the numerous editions of *Baby and Child Care* that perfectly reflected society's shifts in attitude towards working mothers.[11] In the 1960s Spock's manual disapproved of working mothers; in the 1976 edition it had become slightly more positive about them; and by 2004 it was completely positive about them.

While Spock encouraged parents to see their children as individuals and not to apply a one-size-fits-all philosophy to them, he also issued some fairly prescriptive advice. For example, in 1958 Spock advocated that infants should not be placed on their backs when sleeping, stating that 'if [an infant] vomits, he's more likely to choke on the vomitus'.[12] This advice was extremely influential on healthcare providers, with nearly unanimous support through to the 1990s. However, later empirical studies found that there is an increased risk of sudden infant death syndrome (SIDS) associated with infants sleeping face-down, and a major 'back to sleep' campaign has been recommending the opposite position for sleeping babies.[13]

Another example of changeable, dubious and authoritarian advice from Dr Spock is in a revised edition of *Baby and Child Care* from 1998, where he recommended that all children should switch to a vegan diet after the age of two.[14] Spock himself had switched to an all-plant diet in 1991 after a debilitating illness, subsequently lost fifty pounds in weight and regained his ability to walk. So, based on this improvement in his health, he decided that everybody should switch to veganism. The seventh revised edition of *Baby and Child Care* stated that children on an all-plant diet would have a reduced risk of developing heart disease, obesity, high blood pressure, diabetes and certain diet-related cancers.[15] However, this approach to childhood nutrition has, not surprisingly, been severely criticised since that time. Nonetheless, in 2011, *TIME* magazine named Spock's manual as one of the most influential non-fiction books of all time.

WHATEVER HAPPENED TO 'THE GOOD ENOUGH MOTHER'?

The British child psychiatrist D. W. Winnicott caused mothers worldwide to breathe a massive sigh of relief when he first coined the term 'the good enough mother'.[16] Winnicott was ahead of the game when he warned about the dangers of allowing experts to override parental instincts and argued that disregarding parental intuition would have a harmful effect on the core of society. Dr Winnicott believed that professionals were undermining parents' confidence with 'petty regulations, legal restrictions, and all manner of stupidities' and he was concerned about a new cohort of experts, who patronisingly assumed that parents were blithering idiots.[17] Unfortunately, as we now know, in the twenty-first century there is a good deal less concern about parents' confidence and much more focus on parents' inadequacies.

THE CULT OF THE BABY BOOK

There has also been a striking change in the tone of childcare publications, and nowadays parents get less guidance and more pressure from baby books. In the past, child-rearing manuals provided advice for the mother to help her cope with the challenges involved in mothering, always assuming that the mother was fine and with some sensible advice would be able to get over a particular hurdle and continue, secure in her role as the mother who knows best. Nowadays, childcare experts assume that parents are in bits, on their hands and knees, crawling over the wreckage of their lives, overwhelmed in the face of child-rearing and that they need (and are advised to seek) the sage advice of the experts as they are failing miserably and cannot cope alone. The reason for this is simple: to sell more of their products. If parents believed they were doing fine, really, then they wouldn't feel compelled to buy the latest product promising happy, healthy, laughing and good-natured children.

Previously, childcare publications served primarily to help parents, but nowadays they are more often than not written primarily in the hope of making money. While I have no doubt that Supernanny has helped thousands of families, nevertheless a huge industry is now capitalising on her work. And the quickest way for companies to sell more baby books is to transmit the message that parents are causing damage to their children and need to improve, upskill and buy their book!

Parent's Report Card

Shows potential

Easily distracted

Doesn't do enough homework!

Could do better!!!!

Stamped, approved and accredited by POOPI
(the Professional Organisation of Over-Parenting in Ireland)

This message that parents are like broken-down old bangers, ignorant to the needs of their children and inadequate in every sense, transmits a sense of unease and uncertainty in modern parents as they internalise the belief that only the experts know how to parent properly.

THE CONTINUUM CONCEPT

When Jean Liedloff originally published *The Continuum Concept* in 1975 it was intended to be a manifesto on human nature. However, prospective mothers became so inspired by it that it is now known primarily as a baby book.[18] Liedloff (1926–2011) was born into an elite New York family, but an austere childhood left her bereft of a connection with her mother. Before she became an intrepid explorer among aboriginal tribes in Venezuela, Liedloff enjoyed high society in Europe and on the French Riviera. She wasn't qualified in psychology and perhaps led the way for experience to be considered equal to academic knowledge. When her research was published, experts questioned her credentials with phrases such as 'blonde goes up the Amazon', but her rigorous and enquiring mind soon saw off the begrudgers.

Liedloff wrote this book after spending some time living with the indigenous Yequana and Sanema on the banks of the Amazon, and she particularly championed the 'in-arms phase' to secure the infant's sense of being worthy, welcome and connected. She was unapologetic that she didn't have a college degree, and argued that it freed her mind to see the Indians as they really were, without prejudice. Liedloff studied how the mothers in the Amazon simply carried their babies in slings until the baby was able to toddle off on his or her own. These babies apparently rarely cried because their needs were constantly attended to. The babies were also taught at a very early age to handle knives and other materials with respect.

The difficulty with the continuum concept is that most of the mothers who follow Liedloff's teaching aren't living on the banks of the Amazon – in fact they are often living a notably hi-tech life, rushing from one appointment to the next. This means that each parent who follows the continuum concept of parenting tends to interpret the method to fit their own lifestyle, and these interpretations often differ significantly from the original ethos, leading mothers and fathers to argue over what is the right thing to do in each situation, which again causes insecurity and anxiety.

Case Study

'Sleep, that is the start, middle and end of the problem,' said Jenny when she arrived in my office. A tall, good-looking mother of four-year-old Labhaoise and two-year-old Sorcha, Jenny arrived at my clinic in a state of nervous exhaustion. She and her husband, Robbie, strongly believed in the continuum concept but while it had worked well initially, it wasn't working now Jenny had returned to work as a teacher. 'Both the kids end up in our bed every night; they've never got used to sleeping alone, but it's killing my sleep and since I've gone back to work I'm just not coping. When the kids come in, Robbie abandons the marital bed and goes into the guest room, but if I do that, the kids just follow me!' Jenny then proceeded to relay the comical tale of musical beds the family played every night, with the kids stalking their mother as she wandered from one bed to another.

Jenny's exhaustion had impacted everything in the family's lives; she was short-tempered and tearful, and Robbie had retreated behind his computer screen. The children had become increasingly demanding as they noticed *a severe drop in attention when their mother returned to work. Eventually, Jenny accepted that she needed to teach her children to sleep. It was a lifelong habit that was essential for good health. Everyone is different and so we had to figure out different solutions to ensure that each child learned to sleep throughout the night. Jenny and I became forensic in our efforts to establish what was and wasn't working and it soon became clear that once one child moved beds, chaos ensued. Jenny offered significant rewards if a child managed to stay in their own bed; she also went shopping and allowed the children to choose a bed for themselves in the hope they would begin to identify with their own beds. Lastly, she went mad in IKEA and redecorated the girls' rooms so as to change the atmosphere in the rooms. After some time and a lot of perseverance, sleep was finally restored.*

ATTACHMENT PARENTING

It was Dr Bill Sears who first coined the term 'attachment parenting', and he and Martha Sears first published *The Baby Book* in the early 1990s to promote a style of parenting that encourages a strong and early attachment between parent and child.[19] This philosophy stems from the continuum concept and is based on the principles of John Bowlby's attachment theory, but it is often argued that many modern interpretations of attachment parenting transform mothers into full-time servants to their children – 'attached' mothers respond to every cry, co-sleep with the baby in the marital bed, carry the baby in a sling everywhere they go, and so on.

According to this theory, the emotional bonds that a child forms with caregivers have lifelong consequences, and many parents hold that attachment parenting cultivates self-confidence in children (I certainly hope it does something significantly positive, because 'wearing' your child all day every day is no picnic). Physical punishment is avoided; instead, a holistic, sensitive understanding of the child is encouraged, with close contact and child–parent bonding being heavily recommended.

Attachment parenting focuses on responses that support secure attachments, with many attachment parents choosing to live a natural lifestyle. Natural childbirth, home birth, stay-at-home parenting, co-sleeping, breastfeeding, 'babywearing', home schooling, unschooling, natural health, co-operative movements, Paleolithic lifestyle, naturism, support of organic and local foods, and whatever you're having yourself, can all be considered part of the attachment parenting project. Evidently this approach to parenting, though well-considered, is not for the faint-hearted. It requires absolute commitment to the children and is often considered exhausting for the parents, especially the mother. (And this immediately begs the question, if you are continuously exhausted, can this be good for the family?)

Case Study

When Emer first came for counselling she was a stressed, beaten and exhausted woman. Her eleven-month-old child seemed to be thriving, but Emer wasn't. 'Motherhood is exhausting, hard and pretty much horrific 90 per cent of the time,' she stated bleakly. 'I cry more than the baby does these days.'

It turned out that Emer had read many books on parenting and was a firm advocate of attachment parenting. This would be fine if it were not for the fact that she needed a lot of quiet time on her own if she was to maintain her balance in life, and the attachment parenting approach didn't give her much time for herself. I'm going mad entirely! I look at my pals who are following "the routine" and I envy their freedom and peace. But deep down I think they are damaging their babies profoundly and I would never do it to my child. I might be killing myself but at least I know my baby is happy,' she added defiantly.

During the counselling process we explored Emer's firm parenting views and she was adamant that her baby needed this attention. She had read The Continuum Concept *and* The Baby Book *when she was pregnant and they had influenced her profoundly. So what to do?*

Eventually, after months of counselling, and through cognitive behavioural therapy (CBT) techniques such as 'guided discovery', Emer became less entrenched in her style of mothering and realised that for her child to be happy, she too needed to be happy, and without Emer's mental health everything would fall apart.

She was reminded of the advice given to passengers in the event of a loss of pressure in an aeroplane – the mother must put on her oxygen mask first before she can be ready to attend to her children. She realised that she needed certain breaks during the day or she would become depressed or sick; she needed to 'put on her oxygen mask' so that she was fit to mother her child.

PENELOPE LEACH (1937–)

Dr Penelope J. Leach is a British psychologist who writes extensively on parenting issues from a child development perspective. She is considered to be the softer, more indulgent end of parenting, where everything can be solved with love and affection, and her best-known book, *Your Baby and Child: From Birth to Age Five*, first published in 1977, has sold over two million copies to date. Leach notes in its introduction: 'Whatever you are doing, however you are coping, if you listen to your child and to your own feelings, there will be something you can actually do to put things right or make the best of those that are wrong.'[20]

Of course, another way of saying that is, 'whatever you are doing, however you are coping, you could be doing better, and here's how …' Dr Leach warns that the mother can help or hinder the child's development depending on the effort she puts into parenting, 'You can help him develop and learn or you can hinder him by holding yourself aloof. You can keep him happy and busy and learning fast, or leave him discontented, bored and learning more slowly.'[21] The message is stark: parents have to keep their nose to the grindstone of parenting – it's a full-time job and there are no breaks! So what are you doing, reader? You are either part of the problem or part of the solution: stop idling, throw down the book, you must parent, parent, parent! I'll see you in eighteen years.

TOP TIP: Scrutinise the impact of the baby books on your family

Personally (believe it or not), I am on my hands and knees in grateful thanks to the baby books – they were a great help to my family. They were practical, insightful and I would have been lost without them … BUT, if reading a book merely succeeds in making you work ten times harder and increases your anxiety levels, then, on some level, it is not working. If, on the other hand, reading a baby book succeeds in showing you how to get the baby to sleep, or to eat, or improves the quality of life in the family in some way, then it has been beneficial.

GINA FORD (1960–)

In striking contrast to the warmth of attachment parenting and to Penelope Leach's gentle but worthy approach, Gina Ford advocates a strict daily routine for both the baby and the parents, with the day divided up into very precise slots. Ford is a former maternity nurse, without children of her own, but one who has cared for over 300 babies during her career.

Ford's 1999 book *The Contented Little Baby Book* drew criticism that her methods are like 'training animals' and many say that the 'The Contented Little Parent Book' would be a more accurate title.[22] (Interestingly, Ford's own childhood was characterised by ultra-permissive parenting and she slept in the same bed as her mother until she was eleven!) In stark contrast to her own childhood, Ford's advice is characterised by strict discipline, whereby the parent wakes the baby on the dot of 7 a.m., changes its nappy and proceeds to play with him/her for fifteen minutes. Hard cheese if you would like to just hang out with your baby for a bit, as we go onward and upward to different fifteen-minute slots for breakfast time, chill-out time, another nappy change and then nap time from 8.30 to 9 a.m. During nap time the parent can do as he or she pleases for thirty minutes (though it could be recommended that the parent has a healthy snack such as a green apple and a glass of low-fat milk). The day continues with intensive time-management right up to the point that the baby goes to bed exactly twelve hours since it was first woken, at 7 p.m., when the parent can finally retire, perhaps to get legless on vodka from the strain of it all. (Though others, obviously a different species from me, would argue that in fact this is a real life-saver for parents, and that the regime, in a curious way, frees them up a lot more.)

In response to criticism levied against her, Ford suggests that the 25 per cent market share of childcare books that her publications enjoy is proof that her methods do not harm children. In reality, all this proves is that a lot of people buy her books and does not, in fact, prove anything about the relative success or failure of her methods.

In an article in *The Guardian* newspaper, Gina Ford certainly made a good case for her routine:

> *I don't think that three nights of 20-minute bursts of crying is psychologically damaging. What I think is more damaging is that four out of ten marriages are ending in divorce: people can't cope any more – and why can't they cope? Parents don't have any time to themselves in the evening and they're exhausted.*[23]

TO SLEEP, PERCHANCE TO DREAM ...

The starkly different advice that is offered to the new parent today about how to coax his or her child to sleep illustrates how bewildering it is for parents who are anxious to 'do it right'. On the one hand, we are told that we must be very careful to do no harm, as our child's future is in our amateur hands, yet on the other, the advice is completely contradictory!

In the 1980s paediatrician Richard Ferber became famous for his prescribed method of allowing babies to cry themselves to sleep, which he outlined in the best-selling book *Solve Your Child's Sleep Problems*.[24] Critics have argued, however, that 'Ferberising' (aka controlled crying) is emotionally damaging to infants. While Gina Ford also advocates a firm approach, where the child is put down to sleep and left alone for the set amount of hours and then woken up, whether they like it or not, Dr Sears and Jean Liedloff would be horrified by such practices and recommend a softer approach, allowing the child to sleep in the marital bed if it so wishes, right up until the child is ten years old and beyond. Supernanny suggests a complicated and difficult method in that the parent stays in the room with the child so it doesn't feel abandoned, sitting on the ground near the cot, keeping his or her head down and not uttering a word. Yes, for as long as it takes, the parent forgets about *Coronation Street*, forgets about dinner, about a glass of wine, adult life; instead he or she simply sits silent and expressionless on the ground in the dark, head bent. The net result is that each parent tends to follow a modified version of some of the methods advised, with often chaotic results – it's all a long way from 'this worked for my Mum, and anyway crying is good for their lungs'.

The truth is that the need for us to continue to live our lives infringes on our current idealised approach to parenting. We have other commitments – we care about our mothers, fathers, sisters, brothers, friends, neighbours and the wider community as well – and so we can't give our entire selves to parenting our children. Gina Ford, who grew up in a single-parent family, in particular seems to understand this and she paints a grim picture of what can happen after the arrival of a baby:

> *Father comes home from work; he has had a stressful day at the bank or the building society; the kid's screaming its head off; the wife looks a mess; he thinks, 'My God, what happened to that sexy, bubbly woman I married three years ago? Look at this old hag: she's got droopy tits, she's got wrinkles.' She throws the six-month-old at him and all she can go on about is what a rotten day she's had. Do you not think that scenario is a worse one? Because it goes on for months and months and months, and people reach cracking point. Look at the epidemic of postnatal depression and marriages going wrong. I'm sorry, but there are already enough strains on the family unit without a sleepless child.*[25]

Ford makes a very valid point here, as many experts agree that parents should worry less about their children and more about their partners – because it's very damaging for your kids to grow up in an unhappy marriage. We often fall into the trap of thinking we are raising a happy family by doing everything for our children, but if we neglect our partners or ourselves our marriages will suffer. And if our marriages suffer, our children suffer.

So – top tip – go mad, go out with your partner, eat some fine food, drink some fine wine and have a good laugh … and have more rampant sex – lie back and do it for the family!

PROFESSIONALISING PARENTING

Parenting has become professionalised and the emphasis has shifted from being child-centred to focusing on how to combat the impact of the ditzy, foolish adults. Parents are, somewhat bizarrely, often compared negatively to professional care-givers and, because so many children are placed in childcare, stay-at-home parents can feel inadequate in comparison to the professional care-givers. But the calm and consistent care that a child receives in childcare is a very different animal to the loving (but often volatile) warmth of a flawed mother or father. With the arrival of the baby books has come heightened expectations, and many parents now presume that they should be as good as the professional care-givers. Of course, in many ways we're not nearly as good at it. And this is why when many of us consider going back to work, we quickly reason that the children will be more stimulated and socialised if we place them in childcare.

The 'Swedish model' is often referred to as the byword for progressive parenting. However, there has been a growing backlash against the professionalisation of parenting in Sweden. As Swedish sociologist Jonas Himmelstrand has pointed out:

Sweden has offered a comprehensive daycare system since 1975; since the early '90s, negative outcomes for children and adolescents are on the rise in areas of health and behaviour. While direct causation has been difficult to prove, many Swedish health-care professionals point to the lack of parent involvement beyond the first 16 months as a primary contributing factor. Psychosomatic disorders and mild psychological problems are escalating among Swedish youth at a faster rate than in any of 11 comparable European countries. Such disorders have tripled among girls over the last 25 years. Education outcomes in Swedish schools have fallen from the top position 30 years ago, to merely average amongst OECD nations today. Behaviour problems in Swedish classrooms are among the worst in Europe.[26]

And so, while I dearly wish that childcare was much cheaper in Ireland, we can see that cheap childcare isn't necessarily the cure-all for parents' problems.

Not only has professional daycare put pressure on stay-at-home parents, but a power struggle is emerging between state and family about who has the ultimate care of the child. The insecurity of the parents' position was illustrated in *The Washington Post* in the USA by the story of the Chang household in Maryland, when Caleb and Ann Chang lost their bid to keep their eleven-year-old autistic daughter Jessica at home because social workers argued that she would be safer in a group home.[27] The Taiwanese parents totally disagreed with the state about what would be the best treatment for their severely disabled child; they argued that she had twice been placed in a group home and that she had been poorly cared for and had reacted very badly – in an eight-month stay in a residential home Jessica had rubbed the skin on her face raw, scratched her hands and torn at her underwear and shoes. Also their child, who had difficulty communicating, could speak better in Mandarin than with her few words of English. The judge agreed that the parents had 'done nothing wrong', but nevertheless Jessica was placed into a group home.

PARENTING AS ENTERTAINMENT

And so, from the starting point of Freud, who began the search to understand the impact of parenting on children, this subject has now become an entire industry, with whole sections of bookshops now devoted to parenting. The proliferation of advice from everywhere on every detail of the child's life continuously undermines the confidence of parents and promotes the authority of the experts. TV programmes such as *Supernanny, Nanny 911, The Three Day Nanny* and *The House of Tiny Tearaways*, though very helpful to parents, also remind them that they are not 'good enough' parents and are probably damaging their children (how else would the companies sell their product if they didn't suggest this?).

An interesting by-product of these shows is that they have turned parenting into entertainment, with viewers being invited to judge each other's techniques. These programmes invite us to feed into the competitive parenting 'psyche' and make the judging of other parents both acceptable and the norm. The shows often generate significant online debate on parenting forums, with parents pitted against each other, defending or criticising the methods involved. The media knows that parents are curious about how others approach raising their children, so they choose extreme examples to stir up controversy, generate debate and obtain better viewing figures.

It is remarkable how often parents make self-deprecatory and defensive remarks about their so-called dubious parenting skills, but a serious consequence of all this judgement is that parents have lost confidence, they've lost their nerve and they refuse to take a chance any more – even though, in truth, most parents *are* generally good enough. As a consequence of this insecurity, some parents tend to err on the side of caution by keeping their children in structured and supervised environments where they think, misguidedly, that little can go wrong.

TOP TIP: Re-consider your expectations

The advice from the different baby books often contrasts incredibly; however, one central message that all baby experts appear to agree on is that parents need to upskill. But is this right? Do parents really need to upskill? Should society instead downgrade its expectations? Are parents underachieving, or is society over-reaching in its expectations?

Meanwhile, perhaps society as a whole should upskill and begin to cater more for children. More safe routes to play areas. More exciting nature spaces for children. Easier access to childcare. Safe cycle routes to school. I could go on, endlessly ...

From Under-Parenting to Over-Parenting – How Childhood Has Changed in One Generation

Feckless or pushy: parents just can't win.

Sarah Evans[1]

All too often I meet mothers in my counselling practice wringing their hands in bewilderment at how easy their own mothers found child-rearing and wailing, 'How can rearing two children in 2014 be so much more demanding and difficult than rearing five children in 1984?' The answer is, of course, that parents in 1984 asked much less of themselves as parents – they weren't 'parenting', they were 'raising children'.

Before the 1990s Mother always knew best and she tended to assume that she was raising her children very well, thank you very much. Blithe, over-confident, authoritarian parenting was the order of the day. Parents in those days were often uninterested in their children's 'little problems' and, looking back, though children of the time enjoyed the freedom, they are now often slightly regretful about the lack of emotional engagement within the family. Children were frequently dismissed as unimportant, and not only that but childhood was often shrouded in mystery and half-truths, as society tended to try to 'protect' children from the truth.

Dr Patricia Somers, an associate professor at the University of Texas in Austin, has made an in-depth study of 'helicopter parenting' and cotton wool kids and she believes that many over-involved parents' behaviour today is a rejection of the less attentive child-rearing style of the baby-boomers and Generation X's own parents: 'Many of them were latchkey children who don't want to replicate that same level of removal from their own kids' lives.'[2] (Latchkey children refers to the common phenomenon in the past of kids being left to fend for themselves after school because their parents were at work.) Many parents today also feel that when their families experienced turbulent times, the children were often neglected emotionally, and these parents are determined not to allow their own kids to undergo the emotional neglect, loneliness and isolation they suffered as children.

Too far east is west

But thankfully, times have changed. We now listen to our children's worries, we anticipate their distress at every juncture – from their first day at school to their first competition to their first date we monitor the situation, foreseeing every obstacle and worrying sensitively about any disruption to their precious routine.

Parenting or childhood has never been, and will never be, perfect. Today's parents are much more empathic; the only problem is that we have moved swiftly from under-parenting to over-parenting, without pausing to enjoy simple, bog-standard, ordinary parenting! This complete reversal means that we now consider our children's problems to be *more* important than our own. But the pendulum has swung too far and perhaps we need to rebalance the equation. Could we instead meet in the middle and give the children the freedom we enjoyed while at the same time listening to their worries and validating their concerns?

Under-parenting in the last generation

Dr Andrea O'Reilly, author of several books on motherhood, and an associate professor of women's studies in Toronto's York University, believes that the 1970s was a pivotal decade for women and children, when the concept of the 'perfect wife' was collapsing but the concept of the 'perfect childhood' hadn't yet taken a firm hold. Dr O'Reilly recalls that, when she was a toddler:

> ... *my mother would have me in the playpen, my sister in the pram and my brother tied to the front tree. She'd be down doing laundry, as she was supposed to do as a good housekeeper, and we would be outside 'airing.' ... I don't think you air children on the front porch any more. If somebody walked past and saw three kids in such a situation today, the police would be called.*[3]

Ms Shar Lynn, a sixty-five-year-old former teacher, who now operates a childcare facility in Winnipeg, USA, has a unique perspective on motherhood. Ms Lynn raised three children in the 1970s with her former husband, and then, more than thirty years later, she adopted a baby girl whose birth mother could no longer care for her. 'It's quite a bit different,' she remarks with a laugh. '[Back in the 1970s] I assume my kids had homework ... I assume they did it, and if they didn't I assumed [*sic*] they got in trouble for it at school.'[4] (Oh God! Just imagine! These days I am so involved with the homework I can not only rattle off all the names of my children's schoolbooks – I can even tell you what page 'we' are on!) This time around, Ms Lynn, just like any other loving mother of our era, is totally immersed in her child's schoolwork and she sits down and does homework with her child every single day without fail.

Motherhood today, according to Ms Lynn, is 'more overwhelming, as if I am totally responsible for [the child's] social and psychological life. There's incredible pressure to make sure she has certain experiences every week.'[5] Back then, when mothers socialised with other mothers, they talked, bonded and made great friends. Nowadays, parents meeting other parents are no longer meeting for a 'cup of coffee and a chat', instead we are meeting for 'playdates' – it's all about the kids, and the adults' concerns are irrelevant. Indeed, adult conversation is rare; instead, it consists of quips about how demanding it all is and then, like exploited workers without a union, the parents turn back to the grindstone of attending to the babies in some sort of hysterical, fun-crazed sweatshop. After six months, maternity leave is over and many mothers are surprised to find that they are overjoyed to return to work – adult conversation! Lunch breaks! Going to the loo without constant interruptions! Wey hey – partay!

When I had my first baby, I recalled my mother chatting with her friends during my own childhood and (little realising that there had been seismic changes in expectations for parents in the intervening thirty years) I had warm and fuzzy notions of meeting other mothers in the area, gassing about the trials and tribulations of family life and bonding over everlasting cups of coffee.

But, oh, what a disappointment was in store for me! Whenever I managed to pack the car with the thousand pseudo-necessary things needed to take the baby anywhere, I would arrive red-faced and harassed, only to find that the other mothers spent the entire visit attending to their babies. We mothers (I would feel silently pressurised into it) would act like highly paid children's entertainers on a cocktail of speed and ecstasy for an hour or two, and then we would stuff everything back in the car and go home for the all-important nap. I would then flop, exhausted, on the couch and wonder why it was all so horribly hard.

Lesson from the past No. 1: If you are not enjoying parenting, your family will suffer

The single most helpful thing a parent can do for a child is to absorb their children into a life that fulfils both parents and children. If the children are thriving but the parents are unhappy, then the family is not working, and vice versa.

ARE YOU MOM ENOUGH?[6]

Many mothers appear to regard childbirth as the first test in which they can show their love for their child, and following closely at its messy heels, is breastfeeding. Even though women today often experience childbirth and breastfeeding as an opportunity to flex their mothering muscles, historically mothers were always ingesting various substances to try to ease the pains of childbirth. As Toby Young remarks in this excerpt, the gung-ho attitude of some mothers towards parenting today can really be quite startling:

> *I was amazed by how macho the atmosphere was in the antenatal classes. I attended these sessions under duress, expecting them to be a bit girly, but I couldn't have been more wrong. Virtually the sole topic of conversation was whether or not to have an epidural and woe betide the expectant mother who said she was considering it. Testosterone, not oestrogen, was coursing through these women's veins. Their unacknowledged role model was Rambo in* First Blood. *If he could stitch up his own leg without an anaesthetic they could jolly well give birth without any pain relief.*[7]

Breastfeeding is another bone of contention among mothers, and these days many mothers can go into paroxysms of guilt about it; 'It's a natural process, it's been practised down through the ages, so why am I so crap at it?' wailed Carol, an enthusiastic young mother. Yet wet nursing has also been practised in all societies, from Europe to Asia, down through the ages. According to Lloyd DeMause, a leading psychohistorian who wrote the seminal *The Emotional Life of Nations* in 2002, upper-class mothers almost never nursed their babies. DeMause quotes one mother as saying, 'Nourish an infant! Indeed, Indeed! ... I must have my sleep o'nights ... And a new gown to wear at the Opera ... What! Must the brat have my paps too?'[8] You won't hear many mothers say such a thing these days (no matter how many are thinking it!). Instead, mothers say that they tried breastfeeding but they 'hadn't enough milk' or the 'baby preferred formula' or any other excuse that faces down society's determination to expose them as 'bad mothers'.

Countless mothers report tears and guilt if they want to stop breastfeeding and they worry endlessly about the impact this will have on their little one. Social media websites such as Mumsnet buzz with breathless excitement when the subject of breastfeeding is mentioned. Sanctimonious mothers name and shame 'celeb' mothers who choose not to breastfeed. The vehement judgement is shocking: 'Shallow bitches, I managed to breastfeed my child until the age of two, *and* hold down a full-time job. What is wrong with these lightweights?'

This is all well and good for the kiddie-king (and to be honest I am entirely positive about breastfeeding and natural birth myself). However, if mothers are choosing to take the traditional route for these early days, they will probably end up looking, well, traditional. The difference between 'natural mothers' of this generation compared to the last one is that the 'natural mothers' were expected to look natural and traditional (with a corresponding naturally messy house too) but the natural mothers since the noughties have read the celeb magazines, where apparently the celebrity mothers have natural births, breastfeed and never use a nanny and they always look immaculate. Hmmmm. Then they go on Facebook and all their long-lost friends are shoving up photos of their immaculate lives, with their immaculate children in their immaculate houses! Double hmmmm. And so the 'natural mothers' of this generation strive to achieve a much higher standard than previous generations.

But we can't have it all – if we go through natural childbirth, full-time breastfeeding, making organic home-cooked food for baby to spit out for months on end, we won't look like Victoria Beckham as she struts through airports looking glam with a child on her shoulder and a fab designer nappy bag as an accessory. It's like not wearing make-up or not dying your hair; we can go natural all we want – but if we do, very few of us can go natural and still expect to look like a Yummy Mummy.

Lesson from the past No. 2: Something has to give – perfection isn't natural!

It can take a lot more commitment than many people are prepared to give to go the natural route in life, and then there is always the fight with the more 'convenient' method being sold to you by the doctors, the nurses, other mothers and, of course, the loathsome advertising moguls. (Indeed, perhaps mothers should sometimes simply say, 'What! Must the brats have my paps too?') On the other hand, some mothers may believe that the benefits of living a more natural life pays off, but if so, something else has to give.

If you breastfeed maybe someone will have to help you with your other children, or maybe the house won't be very tidy, or maybe the kids won't be perfectly turned out. On some level, we must learn to accept that in most families, if the mother is breastfeeding, or if the family is choosing the natural route in general, standards on another level will slip. Something has to give.

CHILDCARE, THEN AND NOW

Many parents today worry constantly about their children being reared in a crèche as they work long hours trying to cope with an ever-higher standard of living. We have become obsessed with quality time, but many of us are unaware that parents today spend much, much more time with their children than ever before – for example, a famous study showed that working mothers today spend more time with their children compared to what stay-at-home mothers did in the 1960s.[9]

The small, intense family unit as we see it today was almost never seen formerly, and when we realise how much the raising of children was spread out across the community in the past we can easily understand why parents today feel so overwhelmed. The entire responsibility of raising children is now on the parents: society is largely let off the hook, and the extended family is considered a bonus without any duty of care.

But can we ever know what is best for children? Though there is no movement entitled 'Leave the kids alone' (perhaps there should be!), nevertheless, as far back as 1918 the esteemed writer D. H. Lawrence had a very different take on childcare. He believed that mothers should:

> *Take all due care of him, materially; give him all the care and tenderness and wrath which the spontaneous soul emits: but always, always, at the very quick, leave him alone. Leave him alone. He is not you and you are not he. He is never to be merged into you nor you into him ... down with exalted mothers, and down with the exaltation of motherhood, for it threatens the sanity of our race ... [Babies should be given] to stupid fat women who can't be bothered with them ... leave the children alone. Pitch them into the street or the playgrounds, and take no notice of them.*[10]

THE EYES ON THE STREET

Previously, the whole community raised the children. If a child was in trouble, the nearest adult would assume the responsibility of care towards the child. They wouldn't search furiously for the useless parent, instead they would step in and try to help the child in the presumption that we should all pitch in and help the younger community to thrive and prosper.

Recently, British police left a five-year-old alone in a shopping centre and told her to look lost to see how long it would be before an adult came to her aid; 600 people walked by.[11] And so it is, sadly, that these days pioneering parents who wish to provide a freer lifestyle for their children are forced to proceed with more caution than they should naturally as the culture of the 'eyes on the street' (whereby neighbours would keep an eye on other children's safety) has diminished significantly in recent times. I remember when I was a child of about ten and getting up to no good in a phone box with my pal Martha, a distant neighbour spotted us, dragged us out of the phone box, ticked us off and sent us home feeling mortified, and rightly so – I salute you Mrs Toomey! Evidently, this neighbour felt a moral duty towards us that I can only respect.

Sadly, this loss of 'the eyes of the street' has dealt today's children a massive blow, because nowadays there are so few children on the street that any who are allowed outside are a good deal more vulnerable than they really should be. They have less of the natural protection offered by older children (who are generally to be found indoors on their screens, nurturing their diabetes, their heart problems and their obesity); what's more, because we live in a more selfish, individualistic society, friendly neighbours these days tend to look the other way if they see a child misbehaving or in need of help or guidance – everything is left up to the parents. Indeed, the child playing outside unsupervised today is more likely to be judged as neglected and uncared for than a child of educated, loving parents.

In our individualistic society we tend to look on adults who discipline our badly behaved children with suspicion or even outright hostility today; my friends would look askance at me if I reprimanded their children – this has become solely the parent's job and interference is not welcome. Previous generations had to get along with each other because we depended on each other more as a community, and so neighbours and family would freely discipline the children, but now each family strives to be a self-contained unit and we tend to be deeply uncomfortable if other adults comment on the difficult behaviour of our children. We don't ask for help or favours from our friends and neighbours unless we can pay them back very soon, and so in many ways we keep ourselves at a greater distance from others.

Lesson from the past No. 3: It takes a village to raise a child

Historically, children were considered to be entitled to societal goodwill as they were a community concern. These days, we parents are often left totally to our own devices, without a nanny, without a wet nurse, without fosterage and without an entire village feeling the duty of care towards their young. And so children are kept close by their parents' side, losing their freedom and fun in the process.

But perhaps the buck shouldn't entirely stop with the parents? Maybe our family, our society, our work culture, education and many other elements need to be brought back into the equation? And maybe it's time for parents to start pushing the duty of care out from the parents and begin sharing the burden among society in general – be it a kind neighbour, a relation, a childminder or whatever reduces the undiluted impact of parenting in isolation. Parents, in turn, could begin to look for opportunities for their families to contribute to the 'village', perhaps by dogsitting while your neighbour is on holiday, or sending your children in to run errands for an elderly neighbour.

COPING IN THE TWENTY-FIRST CENTURY

Alice is a highly successful corporate lawyer and Paul runs his own haulage company. Alice and Paul finally conceived Rory after many years of trying and they dote on him. Nonetheless, they are both finding the demands of parenting very difficult; Rory is often sick and this is when the demands tend to overwhelm the couple. Recently, the crèche called Alice to collect eight-month-old Rory as he was 'too sick for the crèche'. The timing couldn't have been worse, as Alice was in the middle of finalising a particular tricky situation at work. Alice simply *had* to appear at work the next day – if she didn't there was a risk the entire deal and a whole year's work could collapse. Paul also believed that he *had* to go to work the next day – there was a massive delivery to oversee and if things went wrong it would cost him dearly.

The next morning, Rory wasn't any better; he had a temperature and a hacking cough and Alice knew the crèche wouldn't take him in that state. Alice had been up all night with the baby and at 6.30 in the morning she made a decision. She put him in the car and took him to the local hospital and at the registration desk she told some lies. She explained how baby Rory was very sick and how she was a nervous new mother and how she would prefer if they admitted him in case he was seriously ill. The nurses were very nice and said that although it didn't appear as if there was anything seriously wrong with Rory, still they agreed that it was better to err on the safe side. Alice stayed with Rory (as she had planned) in the hospital for two hours until 8.30 a.m. and when she decided that Rory was well taken care of she slipped out of the hospital and drove into work as fast as she could. The feelings of guilt and anxiety over what a bad mother she was almost overwhelmed her.

The deal was sorted that day and that evening Alice took Rory home from hospital (to comments of disapproval from the nice nurses). Tada!

This may seem like a shocking story and yet, despite increased immunisations, *The British Medical Journal* in 2012 reported a 52 per cent increase in emergency admissions of babies (under twelve months) since 2003, and a persistent year-on-year increase in emergency admissions for children is apparent from 2003 onwards.[12] Of course, the explanations of such a marked increase are many and varied – not least that parents have lost their nerve and don't have the confidence in themselves to judge whether their baby is well or not, and yet this increase reflects a general trend to hand the responsibility of caring for our children over to the professionals, where the children get cool and clinical professional help.

In the past, Alice and Paul would have been more connected with the community and would have had a range of people on whom they could rely to deal with a crisis such as this – a neighbour living nearby, another mother who understood the situation, grandparents, extended family. Yet Alice and Paul felt they couldn't trust anyone sufficiently among their family and friends and so it was 'better to leave him to the professionals'. That this care would be colder and more clinical is waved away and yet few would argue that a mildly sick baby needs warmth, hugs and tenderness more than he needs professional help. It could even be argued that it is exactly these lifestyle choices that prefer clinical, professional help to the imperfect warmth of a neighbour which eventually gives rise to the feelings of alienation and depression that has become so common among teenagers.

It is perhaps all too easy for us to condemn Alice and Paul as bad parents; however, rather than condemning them, perhaps it would be more beneficial to reflect on a society that is creating a situation where episodes such as these can occur.

'A GEOGRAPHY OF CHILDREN'

In comparison to the hurried and stressful lives of children of today, childhood was very different in the 1970s, when British-born geography student Roger Hart settled for two years in a New England town to conduct a study on the activities of eighty-six children over the two years. Little did Hart know when he started his project that he was recording elements of the glory days of childhood, a lost moment in time, where children could roam free without constant harassment and interruption from their parents.[13] Hanna Rosin, in an article in *The Atlantic* magazine, describes in detail Hart's experiences, both in the 1970s and in 2004 when he returned.[14]

In the 1970s Hart was loaned a room in the local school, known as 'Roger's room', and his kindly and affable personality made it easy for the children to tell him about their secret places, their forts, dens and hideaways. Hart included actual maps showing where and how far the children roamed away from home, and he recorded the vast amounts of time children spent on their own creating imaginary landscapes. (Unlike today, their parents didn't praise and coo over their creative structures – more often than not, the parents never even saw them.)

Hart noted that when the children were about eight years old their 'radius of activity' – the distance they were allowed to roam without first asking permission from home – expanded significantly, because it was then that they tended to be allowed to ride bikes alone to their friends' houses or the local park. By the time they were ten years old, the children had gained a 'dramatic new freedom' and were able to go pretty much wherever they wanted (though girls were more restricted because they had to help with chores and babysit younger siblings). The children were proud of each little addition to their radius of activity – it was a sign that they were growing up.[15]

A BBC documentary based on Hart's research gives us glimpses of the lost days of a free childhood and the following excerpt by Hanna Rosin describes some of the scenes:

One long scene takes place across a river where the kids would go to build what they called 'river houses', structures made from branches and odds and ends they'd snuck out from home. In one scene, Joanne and her sister Sylvia show the filmmakers the 'house' they made, mostly from orange and brown sheets slung over branches. The furniture has been built with love and wit – the TV, for example, is a crate on a rock with a magazine glamour shot taped onto the front. The phone is a stone with a curled piece of wire coming out from under it.

The girls should be self-conscious because they are being filmed, but they are utterly at home, flipping their hair, sitting close to each other on crates, and drawing up plans for how to renovate. Nearby, their 4-year-old brother is cutting down a small tree with a hatchet for a new addition. The girls and their siblings have logged hundreds of hours here over the years; their mother has never been here, not once, they say, because she doesn't like to get her toes wet.

In another scene, Andrew and Jenny, a brother and sister who are 6 and 4, respectively, explore a patch of woods to find the best ferns to make a bed with. Jenny walks around in her knee-high white socks, her braids swinging, looking for the biggest fronds. Her big brother tries to arrange them just so. The sun is shining through the dense trees and the camera stays on the children for a long time. When they are satisfied with their bed, they lie down next to each other. 'Don't take any of my ferns,' Jenny scolds, and Andrew sticks his tongue out. At this point, I could hear in my head the parent intervening: 'Come on, kids, share. There's plenty to go around.' But no parents are there; the kids have been out of their sight for several hours now. I teared up while watching the film, and it was only a few days later that I understood why. In all my years as a parent, I have never come upon children who are so inwardly focused, so in tune with each other, so utterly absorbed by the world they've created, and I think that's because in all my years as a parent, I've mostly met children who take it for granted that they are always being watched.[16]

Hart returned in 2004 to do a follow-up study in the same town. He planned to reconnect with any of the kids he had written about who still lived in the general area. He wanted to see how they were raising their children, and he also aimed to track some local kids just as he had in the 1970s.

So, how do we think that went?

From the very first day he was there in 2004, Hart realised his task would be impossible. He began at the house of a boy he had interviewed in the 1970s who was now a father. Hart asked could he speak to his son outside and so they went to the backyard, but the mother followed them, always hovering nearby. Hart didn't believe the parents were suspicious of him, more that they had 'gotten used to the idea of always being close to their children, and didn't like them going off'.[17] Hart realised that in 2004 there would only be access to the children by going through the adults. The kids expected this; they were accustomed to having everything organised by their parents. This time round there was no 'Roger's room', because the new principal at the school said it wasn't directly related to the curriculum.

Hart went on to find some of the children he had tracked in the 1970s. Sylvia, one of the girls from the river house, was thrilled to speak to him. 'Roger Hart! Oh my God, my childhood existed,' she screamed.[18] Sylvia was now a suburban mum of two kids (aged five and four), and she lived nearby. She bought her house with a little wooded area at the back, with the express aim of giving her children similar childhood experiences to her own. But then Sylvia added, 'there's no way they'd be out in the woods … My hometown is now so diverse, with people coming in and out and lots of transients.' Later, Hart spoke to a law enforcement officer in the area, who pointed out that there weren't actually many transients in the area, and that over the years the crime rate has remained unchanged and steadily low. Hart remarked that among parents and children there was now a sense of fear: 'an exaggeration of the dangers, a loss of trust that isn't totally clearly explainable'.[19]

Hart reminded Sylvia of the hours she used to enjoy playing by the river. She recalled playing by the river with extreme pleasure but then added, 'There's no river here ... and I'm really glad about that.' Sylvia several times mentions the fence she plans to put around the yard 'so they'll be contained' and so she will always be able to see the kids from the kitchen window. During the interview, Sylvia's son makes a half-hearted attempt to cut the hedge with a pair of scissors, but it appears that he doesn't really know how to do it, so he stayed physically close to his father, afraid to venture forth and cut the hedge on his own.

Hart also showed the film to Jenny and Andrew, the four- and six-year-old siblings in the first film. They were both profoundly moved, because they'd hardly believed their memories of childhood – the memories had receded into a hazy, dreamlike reverie. Of all the people Hart interviewed the second time round, Jenny was one of the parents who seemed to have tried the hardest to recreate some of her childhood experiences for her own children. Jenny didn't let her children play with electronic devices too much, and encouraged them to play outside in the barn or the garden. She remarked that she wouldn't mind if they strayed into the woods, but that 'they don't want to go out of sight'. And in any case, she pointed out, they get their exercise from the sports they play. Jenny did initiate some activities with the boys, building a ski jump and making a fort, but she was the leader, as her boys didn't seem to know how to play like this on their own.

Hart is wary of nostalgia and he doesn't want to glorify childhood in the 1970s – for example, some things, according to Hart, have improved: in the 1970s, the power hierarchies that formed among children could be pretty harsh, with some children always remaining at the bottom or excluded completely. Also, fathers were, of course, largely absent, and children in general are much closer to their parents today (the laissez-faire style of parenting, along with the divorce boom of the 1970s in the USA perhaps left many children feeling neglected). And yet Hart nevertheless decries 'the erosion of child culture'.[20]

Hart's film shows how children used to grow up gradually; little by little they were allowed more freedom, more responsibility. They felt proud, competent and independent as they mastered activities they hadn't known how to do previously. But today, these milestones are skipped, the adults don't ask the children to run errands or take on much responsibility. And then suddenly their children are going to college and they have never had the opportunity to learn how to be independent and self-reliant.

Lesson from the past No. 4: Give your children a lifelong gift – teach them how to entertain themselves

Parents can lead by example by starting the conversation – should they make a picnic to take outside? Should they try and make a den? Or build a treehouse? But be very sure to allow the kids to finish the conversation – this is their concern, not yours. If they want a treehouse, puzzle with them about how to make it – no need for Daddy to be harassed into making a 'Grand Designs' structure in the back garden, complete with hi-tech wall insulation and vernacular windows; rather, encourage your children to make their own slightly lopsided, makeshift treehouse – much more satisfying for everyone concerned.

CHILDREN'S CHORES

Down through the ages, and even today, for most people the dominant consideration in life has been economic, and children until very recently have always been expected to contribute to the household; children as young as three years old were sent up chimneys, and children as young as six years old were sent to work in the mines. Indeed, nursery rhymes such as 'Little Boy Blue', 'See Saw Margery Daw' and 'Jack and Jill' show us the emphasis that was placed on child labour in years gone by.

But a study of articles, advice and letters published in more than 300 parenting magazines between 1920 and 2006 shows us how this has changed. Even a generation ago children had to do many more chores than they do today. Children these days are often asked to take on only trivial responsibilities such as feeding a pet, clearing the table after dinner or tidying up after themselves, but in previous generations they were given more meaningful opportunities to be responsible, such as planning menus, shopping and preparing family meals, decorating or even helping to maintain the family car.[21] 'Even very young children were assumed to be capable of contributing to necessary tasks,' said Markella Rutherford, author of the study. 'One mother's letter describes how she taught her four-year-old to lay kindling and strike a match to start a fire.'[22]

In contrast, children's primary concerns today are mainly about increasing their scores on their virtual games and making sure their mothers keep up with their homework and extra-curricular activities. Not only that, but children seem to be cleaning up in an entirely different way – children now expect to get paid for any significant chores they do carry out, and British children earn about £700m a year doing chores and errands for their parents these days.[23]

So can children really be helpful?

In 2004 Carolina Izquierdo, an anthropologist at the University of California, Los Angeles, spent several months with the Matsigenka, a tribe of about 12,000 people who live in the Peruvian Amazon. At one point, Izquierdo decided to accompany a local family on a leaf-gathering expedition down the Urubamba River. A member of another family, Yanira, asked if she could come along. Izquierdo and the others spent five days on the river. Although Yanira had no clear role in the group, she quickly found ways of making herself useful. Twice a day, she swept the sand off the sleeping mats, and she helped stack the kapashi leaves for transport back to the village. In the evening, she fished for crustaceans, which she cleaned, boiled and served to the others. Calm and self-possessed, Yanira 'asked for nothing', Izquierdo later recalled. The girl's behaviour made a strong impression on the anthropologist because at the time of the trip Yanira was just six years old.[24]

Lesson from the past No. 5:
Requiring children to contribute to the household is good for mankind in general

While I'm not anxious to shove the kiddies back up the chimneys, nevertheless the satisfaction of a job well done is hard to beat, so parents are doing their children a favour when they introduce them to the satisfaction of doing a job properly.

> *The following list caused heated debate on my Facebook page when I put it up – 'Allow children to handle knives, Stella? Are you all right in the head?' was one memorable response. But don't blame me! This is recommended by the last word in child development – Maria Montessori herself! We are just unused to expecting our children to be contributing members of the household; yet again, parents' shoulders are supposed to carry the entire weight of the burden.*

Age-appropriate housework for children[25]

Ages 2–3		
Clear toys away into toy box	Put rubbish into bin	Set the table
Stack books onto shelves	Carry turf or firewood	Fetch nappies and wipes
Put dirty clothes into laundry basket	Fold dishcloths	Dust skirting boards
Ages 4–5		
Feed pets	Tidy the bedroom	Use hand-held vacuum cleaner
Wipe up spills	Water the plants	Clear kitchen table
Put away toys	Sort cutlery drawer	Dry and put away dishes
Make bed	Prepare simple snacks	Disinfect doorknobs

Ages 6–7		
Gather rubbish	Empty dishwasher	Rake leaves
Fold towels	Match clean socks	Peel potatoes or carrots
Dust and mop floors	Weed garden	Prepare a salad
Replace toilet paper roll		

Ages 8–9		
Load dishwasher	Dust furniture	Hang and fold clean laundry
Change light bulbs	Clean patio	Bake simple dishes
Wash laundry	Put groceries away	Walk dogs
Make scrambled eggs	Sweep porch	Wipe table

Ages 10–11		
Clean bathrooms	Deep clean kitchen	Run simple errands
Vacuum clean rugs	Prepare simple meals	Sweep out garage
Clean countertops	Mow lawn	Do simple mending (hems, buttons etc.)

Ages 12 and up		
Mop floors	Paint walls	Do simple home repairs

Change overhead lights	Wash windows	Shop for groceries with list
Wash/vacuum car	Iron clothes	Cook complete dinner
Bake bread or cake	Trim hedges	Babysit younger siblings

FROM NOBLE PARENTING TO OVER-PARENTING

The culture of over-parenting began to gain momentum in the early 1980s as a rather obscure and neurotic style of parenting, but has now gained popularity and has become the norm of the Western World. Over-parenting can come in many guises – but the focus is usually on safety, risk and performance (the loud and clear message is that we can improve the safety and/or performance of our children if we buy more stuff, or use more media). While there are many different ways to be an over-involved parent, the initial motivation is always the same: parents are driven by the noble and natural desire to help their children flourish and to protect them, and yet, as a consequence of living in a society driven by the cynical pursuit of profit, the end result is often the same – the parents become paranoid and the children feel as though they're wrapped in cotton wool, frustrated and dependent as their independence is limited.

Lesson from the past No. 6:
Do what feels right for you, for your family and for your child

When we examine the history of child rearing we see so many

---

arguments and reversals that we can't really be too sure that modern-day practices are really so correct. We are now in a stage of history where parents are bearing almost the entire responsibility for their children on their shoulders. Academics continue to present new theories, experts continue to argue and parents continue to bite their lips and try to do what's right.

It wasn't that long ago, 1987 in fact, when the respected day care advocate Sandra Scarr told The New York Times *that, before the end of their first year, children's 'brains are Jell-O and their memories are akin to those of decorticate rodents'.*[26] *Of course, this has since been totally disproved, and these comments would be considered ridiculous today.*

Experts' advice changes radically from one decade to the next, and the advice in this era is causing both parents and children extreme distress. Within a couple of hundred years, parents have gone from being completely off the hook, free to treat their children as nuisance slaves, to blithely ignoring them, to them becoming of seminal importance, where one false step could ruin their children's lives.

While Supernanny and Co. are the dominant theorists of today, who knows what is to come in the future? After all, when we consider that blood-letting was the most common medical practice performed by doctors from antiquity until the late nineteenth century, we are reminded that public opinion isn't always right.

Might we simply be following a line of history, and might the pendulum one day swing in another direction? Can we perhaps let parents today off the horrific hook on which they are dangling?

Case Study

Pauline, a single parent, came to me for counselling in the hope that she could learn to control her fourteen-year-old child, Nadia. Nadia was refusing to go to school and Pauline was unable to force her. Nadia simply stayed in bed and screamed at her mother to go away every time Pauline tried to call her for school. Pauline was incredibly stressed by Nadia's behaviour. The school authorities had contacted Pauline and she regularly read accounts in the media of parents being punished for their child's school refusal. 'What will I do? I can't drag her in there!' she said.

Over a series of sessions, it emerged that Pauline had, if anything, killed with kindness the relationship with her only child. She had provided Nadia with total and absolute unconditional love when she was growing up, and when Nadia behaved badly Pauline would explain to her that this was 'not nice behaviour'. Pauline didn't believe in the 'naughty chair' or in sanctions; she believed that if you gave enough love to the child, this would be enough. And yet Nadia hadn't had enough love because of the profound experience of her father's abandonment of her – Pauline had, understandably, tried to compensate for this by loving her child too much.

Slowly but surely, the tyrant in the nursery had become the monster in the bedroom. Nadia had never learned the difference between right and wrong, and she believed herself to be far more important than anyone else. She had never learned to consider her mother's feelings on any level; instead, she had been taught by her mother to regard the latter's feelings as unimportant.

When Nadia initially refused to go to school, Pauline tried hesitantly to use some discipline on her, but unfortunately it was too late. Nadia towered aggressively over her mother and dismissed her objections. Nadia had a boyfriend and this was the most important thing to her. Nothing else mattered.

In counselling, Pauline is learning how to retrieve her relationship with her child. The first stage of recovery for Pauline was to learn to consider her own needs as being just as important as Nadia's. Pauline needed a lot of support within the counselling context initially to learn to cope with her daughter; however, she is learning to consider her own feelings in every situation and to quietly but firmly say 'no' and to stand her ground if a given situation calls for it.

Pauline is learning how to handle confrontation and is no longer devastated when Nadia loses her temper. Nowadays she gives her daughter sympathy for her problems but she doesn't tolerate the bad behaviour accompanying them; she simply leaves the room. Pauline is separating from her daughter and learning to appreciate that Nadia is a person in her own right. Consistency, firmness and understanding are the hallmarks of Pauline's new relationship with Nadia.

Nadia has found the change in Pauline difficult to take, but is slowly learning that she is not the boss of the household. From this, Pauline hopes to teach her daughter that she needs to learn to consider others in life. Counselling is ongoing and the road is long, but I hope, with enough time and effort, Pauline and Nadia's relationship could well recover.

THE LANGUAGE OF OVER-PARENTING

The language parents use with their children often suggests whether they are in danger of creating an oversized monster who never learns to live for him/herself. As a parent, do you use language that builds autonomy and independence? Or do you use words and phrases that teach your children dependence? This quiz will indicate whether you are performing tasks, rescuing and taking over to the degree that your child is deprived of learning experiences. To find out whether the way you communicate with your children should be addressed, tick the phrases that are a common part of your lexicon. A certain amount of imagination is required here as you must imagine these children in middle childhood, even if you are the parent of babies or older children:

1. *'Let me get that for you.'* ☐

2. *'I'll do it.'* ☐

3. *'Let me handle that.'* ☐

4. *'That's wrong, I'll finish it.'* ☐

5. *'I'll fix it for you.'* ☐

6. *'I'll send in a note and explain why you didn't do your homework.'* ☐

7. *'That's too difficult for you.'* ☐

8. *'It's late, so I'll cover for you this time.'* ☐

9. *'It was raining, so I put your bike in the garage.'* ☐

10. *'You're taking too long, let me do it.'* ☐

If you ticked five or more of these phrases, this suggests that you are regularly using the language associated with learned helplessness and you may be an over-functioning parent of a cotton wool kid. The following answers show where each statement is inadvertently creating a Frankenstein's monster.

1. *'Let me get that for you.'* Learn to have patience and allow children to get things for themselves, or else teach them to ask for help, otherwise they'll never learn.

2. *'I'll do it.'* If you do it for them, get ready to do it for them for the rest of your life, as you are creating dependence.

3. *'Let me handle that.'* Let children handle things; let them get things wrong – otherwise, how can they learn?

4. *'That's wrong, I'll finish it.'* So what if it's wrong? This might be a crucial 'teachable moment'.

5. *'I'll fix it for you.'* If we keep fixing things for youngsters, they will have no reason to learn to fix things for themselves.

6. *'I'll send in a note and explain why you didn't do your home-work.'* If you begin to make excuses about your child to their teacher, how will the teacher know what your child needs to learn? This is a classic rescue. Your children will learn a more valuable lesson if you allow them to experience consequences from another authority.

7. *'That's too difficult for you.'* Sometimes children need to fail at something to realise that they need to keep learning. Allow your child to conclude whether something is too difficult; it's not your decision.

8.   *'It's late, so I'll cover for you this time.'* Again, perhaps one of those golden 'teachable moments'. When will your child learn to live with the consequences of their actions if you keep bailing them out?

9.   *'It was raining, so I put your bike in the garage.'* If you do this once, okay. If you do it twice, you are setting up an expectation. If you do it three times, congratulations – you now have a new job.

10. *'You're taking too long, let me do it.'* Children often need to do things slowly as they are learning; they will speed up if given the opportunity to practise.

THE PSYCHOLOGY OF OVER-PARENTING

A profound fear of doing damage, and a misplaced sense of love and duty, convinces parents today that they must over-involve themselves in every aspect of their children's lives. In the early days of parenthood, parents can become over-involved in a bid to gain a sense of control over a life that appears to be spiralling out of control. Slowly, of course, they find their feet and begin to regain a sense of control in their new universe; then, propelled by commercial interests, the parents suddenly become aware of the thousands, nay millions, of potential hazards out there.

Then, having escaped the apparently dangerous jungle of babyhood, as the child grows up, well-meaning parents feel pressured into devoting all their free time to ensuring that their child is supervised, stimulated and developed. On an unconscious level, the parents are aware that their child is missing out on fun and freedom, and so they join the harried world of expensive extracurricular activities.

And so the madness begins ... urged on by society, by the media and by commercial interests, the parents feel compelled to constantly monitor their child's progress and its whereabouts. As a result, parents are encouraged into over-parenting, making them stressed, anxious and depressed. But what many parents don't realise is just how much of their behaviour has been shaped by big business.

PARENTAL CONTROL

In addition to media and commercial interests selling us the need for over-parenting, another element that drives parents' urge to over-involve themselves in their children's lives is the modern fixation on freedom and control. These days, most people are free to choose whatever career path they wish, can marry whomever they fall in love with and can travel the world over looking for a place to lay their hat. Adults in the West today have never been so free to be in control of their lives, and consequently adults in the twenty-first century often presume they should have a similar amount of control over their children. Ironically; children have never been so unfree.

Controlling parents do what it says on the tin. They are over-involved in every aspect of their children's lives and, depending on their priorities, these parents can be very strict about some things while being lax about others. Over-controlled children inevitably end up feeling frustrated, stifled and pressurised. They usually appear docile and obedient; however, there is often a simmering rage under the surface that emerges in later years, often in the form of bullying or passive aggression.

The following quiz will indicate where you appear on the scale of parental control. You may answer 'often', 'sometimes' or 'never'. Caveat to note: it is the rare individual who would have the honesty to assess themselves in this quiz and so it is recommended that your partner or someone who knows you well fills in this quiz on your behalf.

1. Do you give your child other options to the meal that you have prepared so you can be sure that the child eats something?

2. Do you violate your children's privacy? For example, do you read their texts, emails or private Facebook messages without their consent?

3. Do you find yourself making decisions on your children's behalf, even when you know it's inappropriate?

4. Do you intervene in your children's disputes with their friends?

5. Do you insist that your children always follow your instructions as you know what is best for them?

6. Do you feel you should have control over who your children should be friends with?

7. Do you have the last word on which activities or hobbies your children do?

8. Would you allow your child to wear something that you intensely dislike but your child likes?

9. Do you feel personally rejected by your children's growing sense of autonomy and independence?

10. Do you set perfectionist expectations or unattainable standards? (A clue here would be if your child has difficulty in achieving the goals set out for them.)

Give yourself three points if you answer 'always', two points if you answer 'often' and one point for 'sometimes'. If you have scored twelve or over it is likely that you have a tendency to over-parent.

THE MANY WAYS TO OVER-PARENT

Many people from older generations believe that parents today have it easier because nowadays Daddy is usually as involved as Mammy, but Judith Warner, in *Perfect Madness: Motherhood in the Age of Anxiety*, argues that the gains of feminism are no match for the frenzied perfectionism of contemporary parenting with 'pre-dawn violin and Ritalin on demand'.[27]

As a direct consequence of the intense effort parents put into raising their children, they now tend to expect and demand a lot more from themselves and their children, and so the emergence of ultra-parenting in our society has spawned the age of the toxic childhood. In previous generations there were always one or two super-nerds in each class (usually being hot-housed by an over-involved parent) but these days the super-nerd is commonplace. Five general styles of over-parenting have been identified and the following descriptions give a general idea of how each type behaves.

1. The Over-involved Parent

This parent finds it very difficult to leave his or her child alone. Constantly trailing after the child with small demands and requests is a feature of this type of parenting: 'Adam, blow your nose; Adam, stop running; Adam, slow down; Adam, share the toy with your brother; Adam, don't get annoyed now; Adam, I won't ask you again; blow your nose, Adam, blow your nose please.'

Oh God, it's all so joyless! It is exhausting to be an over-involved parent, and it is tiresome to be the child of an over-involved parent. These parents are driven by the feeling that if they aren't following the child and improving the child's world at any given moment then they are in some way failing in their duty. But the children of over-involved parents are being taught to be irresponsible and depend on Mum or Dad to do their thinking for them, so they lack the ability to assess risk or to think for themselves; other children may become needy and attention junkies.

2. The Over-protective Parent

The over-protective parent believes that the world is 'out to get them' and they also think the rest of the world is living in blissful ignorance. They are similar to 'helicopter parents' in that they constantly hover over their children, seeing hidden dangers everywhere. Over-protective parents send their children the message: 'It's a dangerous world out there, and you need me always to be there to protect you; you will be harmed if I'm not watching out for you.' They are determined to keep their children safe and attempt to have total control over their children's actions – even at a cost to the child's mental well-being. These parents are often stoical in the face of unhappiness. They usually believe this world is a vale of tears so they aren't as bothered by their children's unhappiness as other parents might be – their child's safety is far more important than his or her happiness. These parents show their love by keeping their children alive, safe and under constant supervision.

Over-protective parents are driven by fear and do their best to structure their child's time so that no moment is unsupervised. Long summer days playing with their friends are not an option for the children of these parents –

instead, the children are more likely to be fiends on the Xbox or Minecraft. These children are certainly physically safe in early and middle childhood; however, anxiety disorders or a pervasive unhappiness can overtake them as they become teenagers.

3. The Perfectionist Parent

As the author, Andrew Solomon, remarks in glorious understatement, 'Parenting is no sport for perfectionists.'[28] Perfectionist parents are paranoid about flaws, in themselves or in their children. These parents begin with the noble aim 'to be the best parent of the best child' but they soon tip into hyperparenting madness and can drive their children crazy with their desire to be the best and the brightest.

They may choose to fixate on order, sticking to a strict routine where tidiness and cleanliness are to the fore; or they can focus on status, whereby they ensure that their children's achievements give them a sense of superiority among their peers. Feelings of power are attractive to the perfectionist parent; as in the brightest child with the best parties, the best-dressed kid with the best toys and so on. Some perfectionist parents focus on perfect appearances or performances in order 'to be the best' while many others focus on the academic side of life.

Just like other over-involved parents, this parent is also motivated by fear; however, this parent's fear is generally based on an anxiety that they are inadequate as people and so they need a symbol of success to prove their worth. Children of perfectionist parents often grow up to be very self-critical, with little ability to find contentment, choosing instead to try to scale ever-increasing heights.

4. The Performance-based Parent

Performance-based parents are obsessed with their children's performances and abilities. These parents also begin with the understandable wish 'to be the best parent of the best child' but this soon gets lost as they become consumed by winning.

Winning is everything, but the problem is that the performance-based parent sends an ambivalent message to their child — on the one hand they are regularly heard saying 'It's the taking part that counts', and yet when the child doesn't win the constant post-mortems and the intense redoubling of efforts suggests that winning is, in truth, what it is all about.

Swimming, dancing, school tests or whatever; often it doesn't really matter what they are best at — archery, the cello or the violin — so long as they are the best. Some perfectionist parents devote their attention to one child, and the other children in the family can be neglected in the team effort to support the chosen child. The siblings often have conflicted feelings of intense resentment coupled with extreme relief that they aren't the family's chosen one.

This style of parenting can be very unsettling for the child, as he or she often begins to share the parents' ache to win, to achieve and to succeed in everything. The child becomes anxious and begins to confuse his or her identity and feelings of self-worth regarding their abilities and their successes. This can be the royal road to unhappiness as there is always,

always someone more talented coming down the tracks and consequently the child also begins to be driven by an intense fear of failure.

5. The Intensive Parent

Helicopter parents, hyper-parents, super-parents, ultra-parents, concerted cultivation; the list of different names for these parents is endless. However, these parents have one thing in common: over-scheduling and constant supervision. The parent is running on adrenaline and the children's over-scheduled lives often become harried and stressful as the parent is attempting to fit too many activities into the day. Every minute of the day is considered an opportunity, and is usually devoted to developing the child on some level.

'Helicopter parents' pay extremely close attention to their children's experiences and problems, and attempt to sweep all obstacles out of their paths, particularly at educational institutions. These parents will batter the school door down if they hear that little Cabáiste isn't getting an adequate amount of time or attention from the new teacher.

Every week the Sunday papers are filled with feature articles commenting on middle-class mums who are sending their children to extra-curricular classes and to tutors, hoping to 'give them the edge'. This parent is also driven by fear and anxiety, always needing their child to have a head start on others, with a rich and varied CV by the time they are twelve years old. The parents are always hovering, always focused on their child's improvement, and always intensely preoccupied with achievements.

> *Helicopter parents, or the even more aggressive 'black hawk' parents, have in recent years evolved into 'snow plough' parents, who determinedly clear a path for their bubble-wrapped kid and shove aside aggressively any potential obstacle that might get in their child's way.*
>
> *Ironically, all this effort can come to naught, as 'benign indifference' is often the hallmark of the children of these pushy parents. The children often become quite lazy as they are used to being pushed and propelled around the world; and they become totally out of touch with their feelings. Exhausted, these children often lack creativity and feel alienated by other people's passion. Feelings of joylessness may take over and the children frequently become whiny and eternally discontented.*

'WE'RE SWIMMING IN FEAR SOUP'

The reason that parents today feel the need to over-parent is that we are filled with fear and anxiety. Why can any twenty-first-century parent instantly reel off the names of children from around the world who suffered horrible fates? The mere names bring a shiver down parents' spines – JonBenet Ramsey, Madeleine McCann, Jamie Bulger … And yet, though the statistics concerning this subject were exactly the same way back when, *our* parents probably couldn't have reeled off the corresponding names from their generation! *Our* parents' brains weren't saturated with horrifying stories, with a peculiarly intense focus on gruesome stories about children. *Our* parents weren't swimming in fear soup, and so they had a much more pleasant time raising their children.

In the past, when our parents were trying to ascertain whether a certain event was likely to be safe, they could weigh up the situation calmly and rationally and make their decision accordingly.

However, when this generation of parents need to make a decision, their brain immediately flashes to the latest sensationally horrifying media story – our brains are made so that the most memorable story will come to mind first, and whatever comes to mind first we believe to be the most common – this is physiology, it's the way the brain works. And when you've even thought about the danger of child abduction in any given situation, well, that's it, game over. It's a very brave parent who will feel confident enough to defy the slightest, slightest chance of child abduction once it even enters our mind. And so the gates come down, the chains get locked, and the screens go on.

TOP TIP: Keep your distance from the ghouls!

Sensationalist stories infect your brain and impact your behaviour towards your children, which in turn has an impact on your children's lives. Until effective guidelines are in place ensuring responsible reporting, parents should be vigilant and wary when they find themselves reading sensationalist and sickening accounts of tragedies involving children, especially on social media: every couple of weeks or so I notice a different shared post on my Facebook page about a missing child. But when I do a search I find that the corresponding post that should be included – that the child was found safe and well – is almost never shared.

Keep a calm and cool eye on grisly and gruesome stories in the media and, as much as possible, simply stay away from them; they don't help you become a better parent – rather, they prey upon your innermost anxieties so as to hold your interest.

8

Your Child's Future – from Kiddies to Kidults?

There are only two lasting bequests we can hope to give our children. One of these is roots, the other, wings.

Johann Wolfgang von Goethe[1]

Not many parents set out to raise a thirty-year-old Xbox fiend living at home, sprawled on the couch all day, eating pizza and drinking beer, yet many parents are inadvertently doing just that by stifling their children's independence. Days of childhood innocence can end as early as eight years old these days, but some adolescents don't become adults until they're well into their thirties. And so, awful as it sounds, it seems that, in recent years, childhood has been shortened while adolescence has been lengthened.

In her critically acclaimed book, *Toxic Childhood: How the Modern World Is Damaging Our Children and What We Can Do About It*, Susan Palmer examines contemporary culture and its impact on contemporary children.[2] The fast-moving and fast-changing culture in which we are rearing our children is practically incomprehensible to grandparents, and there is much talk about 'digital natives' abounding today but, as Palmer points out, one only has to look at a ten-month-old baby trying to build a tower of blocks to realise that human development happens in 'slow time'– children need the same time and care that they have always had in order to develop into fully functioning adults.

Indeed, when a client of mine told her eight-year-old son, Darragh, that he had complete control over the events for the whole day, she was amazed by his low-tech choices. Darragh chose to go to the park with his mother, to play with his kite, then they went for an ice-cream, and after that they played in his tent in the garden. Finally, they went out for burgers and chips to finish off the day. 'It was very enjoyable, and really quite a cheap day out!' his mother enthused. 'And he acts as if it was the best day ever!'

Case Study

Kate is a lively and spirited teenager from Mayo who came to me for counselling when panic attacks started to control her life. It soon emerged that Kate was fixated on contact – she was a Facebook fiend, a manic texter and a rampant tweeter. She wouldn't let go of her phone during counselling sessions – even though it was turned off. She believed the phone calmed her down, but in many ways it was increasing her anxiety levels as she waited for responses to her relentless messages.

At nine years old, Kate was given her first mobile phone, to enable her parents to reach her when necessary. Now eighteen, Kate texts her mother as often as forty times a day. Whenever she is out with her friends and feels a moment of insecurity, she immediately texts either her mum or dad. Though Kate admits to texting her mum or dad simply for something to do when she is bored, she demands that they answer within five minutes 'so she doesn't look like Billy no-mates'.

When challenged that this constant texting wasn't helpful for Kate's autonomy, her mother, Joan, replied that she was happy with this arrangement, saying, 'At least I know where my daughter is and I know how she is feeling. And I can send her some love and support if she's feeling a bit insecure – it's so hard being a teenager these days!' Joan readily admits that she would have never given her own parents the same level of detail about her day, but she feels times have changed.

Both Kate and Joan believe that Kate is naturally indecisive, and Kate prefers her parents to make her decisions for her; often she texts in a jokey manner to ask what she should buy in the school canteen – 'tuna or ham?'. Joan laughs this off and says it's simply a bit of fun – even when I pointed out that experts believe that the struggle for this generation of children to learn to think independently will impact society for years to come.

As counselling progressed it became evident that it would be beneficial if Joan was invited into the process as she had such a high level of impact on Kate's behaviour. Joan was clearly an over-protective parent who worried about her children every minute of the day. These worries had influenced Kate's thinking, so she in turn believed that danger lurked in every corner. A culture of fear had grown up in the household, where unanswered texts signified horrific car crashes, and time spent alone was considered to be dangerous and was not encouraged.

Within a counselling context, Kate began to learn how to use a psychotherapeutic technique called self-monitoring, where she noted her responses to different situations, and later, still within the safe environment of the counselling session, she reflected on her behaviour and figured out whether it was healthy or dysfunctional. Kate became willing to try to wean herself off all forms of instant gratification by undergoing a slow process of change; she began to practise delayed gratification, making herself wait five minutes every time she felt the need to use her phone. Progress was slow, but the changes lasted.

> *Kate and I then worked together to reality-test her beliefs and she soon realised that she was prone to paranoia. She had lost the ability to be on her own with her own thoughts, and had almost lost her sense of self. After some months she began to calm down and relax the tight grip on her phone. She is now in the process of finding out who she is, what she likes and how she wants to live her life.*

The tethered generation

In recent years technology has brought us no less than mobile phones, text messaging, voicemail, laptops, email, blogging, the Internet, Google, YouTube, Facebook, Twitter, Instagram, satellite TV, digital TV, camcorders, computer games, Game Boys, Play-Stations, iPods, iPhones, iTunes, Skype, Swype … and whatever you're having yourself.

Many parents bite their lips about their children becoming more comfortable playing with Game Boys rather than actually playing games with their friends. However, others argue that these are adult moral panics about childhood based on nostalgia for mythical childhoods filled with sunny days and walks in the woods. Nevertheless, children today have access to technology from a very young age, and so parents have to contend with issues they never experienced in their own childhoods. The relationship between children, parents and IT is becoming ever more complex, with parents everywhere struggling to figure out what sorts of limits they should set for their children's access to technology, asking questions such as:

- At what age do we give our children a mobile phone?
- Is having a mobile phone safer or more dangerous?

- What do I do if my child is playing inappropriate video games at his friend's house?
- What age is it appropriate to allow my children to use social media?
- Should I have the password to my children's activities?
- Should I monitor their activities?
- Should I pry?
- Should I pry openly?
- What do I do when the children are more tech savvy than I am and so can easily bypass my attempts at control?
- What do I do when my children unfriend me on Facebook?
- What do I do when I am totally appalled by their computer games but they love them?
- What do I do if I am revolted by the violent porn on my teenager's computer history?

These digital natives are the first generation to use email and mobile phones since infancy, with the child's first mobile phone being a modern rite of passage. However, the insidious allure of the virtual world is causing some worrying developments among young people worldwide. The phenomenon of young people relying on technology to enable them to withdraw completely into their bedrooms is described by Alan R. Teo, from the Department of Psychiatry at the University of Michigan:

Masa [name changed], lives near Tokyo with his parents in a two-bedroom flat. The young man has barely set foot outside his room in the past two years, spending 23 hours a day in isolation. His mother leaves him meals on a tray put outside his door. He sleeps during the day, wakes up in the evening and spends all night browsing the net and chatting, and playing video games.[3]

'*Hikikomori*', the term used in Japan to describe the social with-drawal, mostly by young men, from real life into a virtual life, is a growing phenomenon, with an estimated 264,000 'core' *hiki-komori* cases, and with another 460,000 suspected cases out of a total Japanese population of 127 million. While Japan is the only country to have carried out extensive research on this topic, the epidemic is not only impacting the Japanese: there have been reports of cases in the USA, South Korea, Spain, France and Italy.

Another disturbing issue arising from developments in tech-nology is the way that parents can now hover over their children well into adulthood and many parents are present on university campuses today in a whole new way.

Stalker parents alert

In 2012 at the University of Cincinnati, Ohio, a twenty-one-year-old student, Aubrey Ireland, felt forced to take out a restraining order against her parents to put a stop to their helicopter parenting. Aubrey was an only child whose parents initially supported her and provided her with the best of everything. As Aubrey began to grow up and away from her parents, her overbearing guardians became more controlling and would often arrive unannounced at her university (a 600-mile journey) to check up on her.

The parents were reportedly worried that she was too busy taking drugs or sleeping around to focus on her studies and they withdrew their financial support in an attempt to retain a hold on their daughter. The university then stepped in and offered Aubrey funding to complete her studies and so the parents upped the ante and demanded back the $66,000 they had already spent on her education.

(How nice!)

After it transpired they had installed spyware software on her mobile phone and computer, the court eventually ordered that parents David and Julie Ireland must stay at least 500 feet away from their daughter for at least a year.[4]

CHILDREN AT UNIVERSITY

As society is pressurising parents to over-parent, consequently more and more great big babies are arriving at university without a clue as to how to take responsibility for themselves. In a brave new world where more parents than children called a Leaving Cert helpline (1,393 calls from parents versus 535 from students), and colleges report that the majority of the calls they receive before term begins come from 'emotional' parents, third-level institutions are struggling to figure out to whom they should respond – the parent or the student.[5]

Frank Costello, head of admissions at Dublin Institute of Technology, agrees that helicopter parents can be overly involved in their children's third-level education: 'If the children are calling, it's often because the parents are having the child make the phone calls,' he said. 'Parents ask questions such as, "Why didn't my son get an offer?" and "What can you do?" Parents who call are concerned, crying, angry – we get the gamut of emotions.'[6] Richard Murphy, school liaison officer at Griffith College in Dublin, said '99.9 per cent' of the calls he receives when the Leaving Cert results come out are from parents: 'They can be quite emotional, so you need to be a sort of care worker in this role. I've had parents crying on the phone because they are just so anxious. It's surprising that parents take on such a role, because their children are now adults.'[7]

Many college authorities today are now wondering whether third-level students are adults who can be considered responsible for their own actions, or children who need the support of their parents and the institution? In truth, today's parents are very clear that their children who attend third-level institutions (with an average age of 18–22) are children and not young adults. Of course, these parents are unwittingly making their children hopelessly dependent, and their children know no better so they complacently agree – they're happy to have a perpetual connection to their parents. Mothers regularly clean their children's apartments they pay for their children's essays to be written by graduates; they collude in lies of a death in the family to get an extension – no jump is too high if it gets their children over the line.

Mum always knows best!

Seán is a nineteen-year-old business student who missed his exams because he slept in. When the college administrators said that this was an inadequate excuse, Seán's mother became involved and sent copious numbers of emails to the class tutor, the head of the department and every other influential person on campus. Eventually, the college relented and allowed Seán to resit his exams.

Seán didn't turn up for the exam resit. The mother phoned to apologise.

Often the kids haven't grown up enough to know what they're missing out on. Indeed, many of these 'kidolescents' have never had a taste of independence and so have no concept of the proud feelings associated with the competency and mastery that independence can provide.

The current expensive and competitive third-level system in Ireland now looks set to become entrenched even further in our society. Parents these days regularly attend open days at third-level institutions and even graduate career fairs. Gerry

Flynn, president of the Institute of Guidance Counsellors, said a 'significant number of parents' go along to college open days – indeed, many third-level colleges have now begun to cater for this by having a 'parents' section' on the open day.[8] The cost of third-level education has soared, with registration fees for college increasing tenfold since the end of the 1990s, and a survey by the Irish League of Credit Unions in August 2013 showed that 43 per cent of parents have saved for at least a decade to fund student living costs.[9] And so it is little wonder that parents seek a worthy return on their heavy investment. But where do we draw the line? If the parents have invested untold effort and money into their child's future, when can they back off and allow their child to fail or succeed? After third-level? After the kidult's first job? After the kidult buys his or her first house? Has his/her first child?

The following excerpt from *The Guardian* illustrates just how long the umbilical cord is stretching these days:

Donna Miller, European HR director for Enterprise Rent-A-Car, did a double-take when she started noticing parents at careers fairs two years ago. 'They come right up to us and say, "What would my son be doing if he worked for you?" while the son is standing right there. It's like they're asking about a nursery place,' she says.

The next thing she knew, parents were turning up at their off-spring's job interviews. 'Again, we were amazed, although we try to be polite and say, "Gosh, it's lovely you're here, but can you wait in reception?" Most recently, we've seen parents responding to the job offer, asking, "What will they be doing? Can you explain the benefits? My son doesn't understand what a stakeholder is." We've even had parents turning up for the induction and they've been really surprised when we've said they can't spend the first week of their child's job with them. But this isn't a first day at school.'

Miller, who works both in the United States and UK, believes that

what sociologists have called the 'infantilisation' of society is more prev-
alent over here. 'It has become so common that we've taken the attitude,
"If you can't beat 'em, join 'em." It's the way it is for this generation so if
you can't include their parents, you risk missing out on talent.'[10]

LEARNED HELPLESSNESS

Learned helplessness is a theory first conceptualised by the psychologist, Martin Seligman, at the University of Pennsylvania in 1967 to describe the condition of a human or animal that has learned to behave helplessly.[11] In a behavioural experiment, Seligman accidentally discovered that if an animal is repeatedly hurt by a stimulus beyond his control, the animal will eventually stop trying to avoid the pain and begin to behave in a helpless manner, as if he is powerless to change the situation. Tragically, even when the environment is changed and opportunities to escape are presented, this 'learned helplessness' has taught the animal to do nothing. The only coping mechanism the animal uses is to be stoical and endure the pain, thereby not expending energy getting worked up about difficult conditions.

Seligman expanded this theory of learned helplessness and applied it to aspects of human development; for example, if children perceive an absence of control over a given situation, they soon believe at a very early age that they are ineffective, with no option but to accept the rules and learn to 'shut up and put up'.

The story of two-year-old Evan neatly encapsulates how quickly a baby can learn a sense of helplessness against stronger forces. Baby Evan was diagnosed with diabetes and had to undergo a series of injections to help control his blood sugar levels. On the first day, Evan roared and cried when the nurse administered the injection. The second day, Evan put up a strong resistance, kicking and screaming when he saw the nurse and the needle, but he was held down and in the needle went. On the third day, Evan started to cry the moment he saw the nurse, but it was relatively easier to inject him. The fourth day, he whimpered and turned towards his mother's breast, and winced as the needle went into his skin. On the fifth day, the nurse arrived with the needle and two-year-old Evan sadly proffered his little arm with no resistance; he knew that resistance was futile – he had learned helplessness. And this is exactly how over-parented children go from feeling ineffective to actually living ineffectively.

Seligman linked his theories on learned helplessness to the onset of depression in humans, as it has been shown that feeling ineffective in your life is associated with depression. It is well-documented that if a parent over-controls the child's life, overriding the child's wishes and needs, children with certain dispositions surrender all control to the parent and learn to live with whatever the parent plans for them.

ADULT CHILDREN OF OVER-INVOLVED PARENTS

So what is the future for this generation of over-controlled and excessively pressurised children? Will there be magnificent leaps in science and creativity as a result of all this concerted cultivation? And will the children of the future lead the way into a brave new world? Or will these children boomerang back home to Mammy with an armful of impressive qualifications and plump for the superficially easy life?

The answer, of course, is that pampered, over-educated millennials would much rather feel safe and a failure at home than face the many challenges of adulthood. The combination of the forces of the global recession and a millennial trend of over-parenting have combined to send millions of young men and women (nicknamed 'boomerang children') back home to Mammy and Daddy. This is the first generation that doesn't believe it is at all likely that they will attain a better standard of living than their parents, and tragically, boomerang children often feel intimidated or belittled by their parents' success.[12] Sometimes called 'the L'Oréal generation' ('because we're worth it'), they have been taught to believe that the world revolves around them, but they have never been given the brain space to find out who they are, and so they feel hemmed in, disaffected, entitled and yet without choices.

'DEM OUT DERE'

Even though research shows that this generation of children is more confident, assertive and entitled than previous generations, they are also more miserable, anxious and depressed. They prefer to remain in old, dysfunctional relationships than to begin new friendships, they are cynical and suspicious of other people's motives and have an attitude of 'dem out dere' towards outsiders.

Therapists agree that it is relatively easy to spot the child who has been affected by hyper-parenting. When these adult-children come for therapy they are indecisive and easily persuaded because they haven't learned to think for themselves. They are always asking the therapist for his or her opinion, and they will usually have one or two mentors (often their parents) who they view as having much better judgement than they do.

Some adult children worry more about pleasing their parents and others than pleasing themselves, as they have been taught that pleasing their parents is the most important thing. And yet these adult-children habitually wish to reduce contact with a parent – though they rarely carry this out in any meaningful way. They find it hard to separate emotionally from their parents and have an overweening sense of duty and obligation towards their parents. Alternatively, some over-parented adult children are completely self-absorbed and will trample over other people's lives as and when they wish, because they have been taught to believe that the world revolves around them.

So how do we move from cotton wool kids to free-range kids?

The role of the parents is not to raise a child but to raise an adult – the child is the raw material and the adult is the finished product. It is only right that parents move from being doting parents to our babies to being adult mentors to our adult children; indeed the Irish author Dr Harry Barry has stated that most of the problems for our young people occur between the ages of eighteen to twenty-five; according to Dr Barry 'that's when the carnage will occur', and so it is our job to ensure our children are ready for the storms and stresses of early adulthood by the time they are eighteen.[13] As we know, raising children isn't a one-size-fits-all scenario; instead each child has individual challenges and for you to ascertain what sort of parent you want to be you may need to write out the challenges you would wish for each of your children to overcome. The big advantage to doing this now is that from reading this book you are now well-informed about childhood and parenting in the twenty-first century, and so you can calmly, and with consideration, assess the situation. From taking some time to write your own thoughts about each situation, you can establish what you and your family need and how you should behave.

The most important questions many parents wish to answer are: How do we raise safe and happy children? And can we create a safe and happy lifestyle for every member of the family? To discern how we might create this lifestyle we could try to answer this question first: *How can you help your children to contribute to the happiness of the family?* You don't need to write a thesis for this exercise; it's more a back-of-an-envelope job that needn't take more than ten minutes. Each child is different, so you may wish to write a different plan for each child. Divide your wishes into age-appropriate and child-appropriate categories, and you should include whatever is important for your family – cleanliness, academia, independence, friendship, kindness and so on. Some examples are included below, *not as recommendations*, but rather to jog your inspiration.

How can you help your children contribute to the happiness of the family?

By the age of six:
- ✓ I would like my children to be able to enjoy themselves without always needing other people or technology.
- ✓ I would like them to do a couple of jobs around the house.
- ✓ I would like them to be able to dress themselves, unprompted.
- ✓ I would (dearly) like them to keep their rooms tidy!
- ✓ _____
- ✓ _____
- ✓ _____

By the age of eight:
- ✓ I would like my children to be walking to school on their own.
- ✓ I would like them to be able to do simple errands, such as going to the shop to buy milk.
- ✓ I would like them to be able to keep their own rooms tidy and regularly help with some basic chores around the house such as filling/emptying the dishwasher, caring for pets and tidying the sitting room.
- ✓ I would like them to have become aware of the great solace to be found in nature.
- ✓ _____
- ✓ _____
- ✓ _____

By the age of ten:
- ✓ I would like them to have found some hobbies that give them great joy and allow them to escape from any stressors in their lives.
- ✓ I would like them to have found some good friends.
- ✓ I would like them to appreciate music and books.
- ✓ I would like them to be a general help around the house.
- ✓ _____
- ✓ _____
- ✓ _____

By the age of twelve:
- ✓ I would like them to be able to use their pocket money in their own way, without needing my input.
- ✓ I would like them to be able to cook a meal for the family.
- ✓ I would like them to appreciate our culture.
- ✓ I would like them to be interested in being educated.
- ✓ _____
- ✓ _____
- ✓ _____

By the age of fourteen:
- ✓ I would like them to have some good friends.
- ✓ I would like them to contribute meaningfully to the family – through cooking, cleaning and so on.
- ✓ I would like them to have found a passion.
- ✓ _____
- ✓ _____
- ✓ _____

By the age of sixteen:

✓ I would like them to have an interest in the world.

✓ I would like them to be able to see ways in which they could contribute to the world.

✓ I would like them to have learned to withstand peer pressure on some level.

✓ _____

✓ _____

✓ _____

WHAT IS YOUR ATTITUDE TO YOUR CHILDREN'S EDUCATION?

Many experts believe that homework is of questionable value, and yet most parents continue mindlessly following the rules laid down by the teacher.[14] If children are doing excessive homework and then having to go to endless after-school activities they are thereby missing out on other activities, such as looking for snails in the garden, building a hut in the garden and pretending to be a superhero, because they are bent over their books. Indeed, the whole concept of homework is anathema to some people who believe home life should be about leisure time and not bringing work home. Even teachers frequently disagree with the excessive homework given out in today's schools, but as our culture is caught up with performance and results, teachers are often too fearful not to give plenty of work to do at home. The debatable success of cramming schools and private tutors have encouraged many parents to seek help to push children into achieving higher academic results. And yet, in the countries with the most successful education systems the children start school when they are older and spend fewer hours on the school premises![15] Despite this, cramming schools and tutors have never been busier in Ireland, with Kumon expanding its franchise operation all over the country. These extra-curricular classes can exhaust children and often require them to exclude other, more enjoyable, activities. The price is high, and though the exam results might be impressive, we all know that there is more to success than exam results.

The following questions will help you understand your own attitudes to education and provide a useful guide for you with your own children:

Is there such a thing as too much education, and if so, how much education is too much?

_____
_____
_____

How little is too little?

_____
_____
_____

How do you know if your child has too much homework?

_____
_____
_____

Should you have a say in how much homework your child does?

_____
_____
_____

After thirty minutes of their seven-year-old doing homework, is it fair and reasonable for parents to say 'that's enough' and close the books, even if the child hasn't concentrated for more than ten seconds at a time during the thirty minutes? _____

_____
_____

How much of your own time and energy should you devote to your child's education? _____

_____

_____

_____

How much time and energy should you devote to extra-curricular education? _____

_____

_____

_____

Should a rule of thumb be adhered to – for example, when the pain outweighs the pleasure (for either parent or child) is it time to stop for the evening? Or stop ten minutes past that pain barrier? Or should a more specific rule be introduced such as ten minutes for five-year-olds, twenty minutes for six-year-olds, thirty minutes for seven-year-olds, etc.? _____

_____

_____

_____

_____

Should tutors be brought into the equation if the child's teacher is lazy and ineffective? _____

_____

_____

_____

Should the child seek to achieve certain goals in education so as to keep up with his/her peers? _____

_____

_____

_____

How much of your money should go towards education in the long run?

_____

_____

_____

*Is education more important than holidays?*_____

_____

_____

_____

General thoughts on education: _____

_____

_____

_____

WHAT IS YOUR ATTITUDE TO RISK?

For a whole raft of reasons, we live in a risk-averse society, increasingly unable to even contemplate risk in any given situation. This has led to parents preventing children from facing any kind of risk, and while this attitude is culturally approved, it stunts children's development. As already discussed, life itself is risky and children will never learn how to deal with risk unless they are allowed to experience it: as a simple example, without risk how will children learn to swim or to ride a bike?

Ellen Sandseter, mentioned in Chapter 3, has noted that parents' fear of children being harmed in very minor ways will probably result in more long-term problems such as fearful children and increased levels of psychopathology.[16] When a third of children have never climbed a tree, one in ten can't ride a bike and a quarter of children have never experienced the unique thrill of rolling down a hill, the fear is that contemporary children will grow up to be stunted adults who cannot handle risk or responsibility in their own lives.[17] As Sir Digby Jones puts it:

Overprotecting our children – swaddling them in cotton wool – is bad for society, the economy and young people's preparation for adulthood in a world full of uncertainties. Of course we want our children to be safe, but risk taking is inherently in their nature and unless we give them controlled opportunities to experience it, judge it and manage it we will inhibit their development and capacity for innovation. At worst, we will be unwittingly complicit in channelling their natural thirst for adventure in completely the wrong direction.[18]

If you outline in a few words what your attitude to risk is, it will help you as you go forward in the world of parenting. It is important to assess risk when you're feeling calm – and not after a grisly episode of *CSI* or *Law & Order Special Victims Unit*! This should be a comfort to you in the future because, if you have already thought out and decided on your version of healthy and unhealthy risk you will ensure that your children don't grow up to be dependent and overly fearful automatons who have never learned to think for themselves. Again, proposals are listed here, *not as recommendations*, but to help inspire ideas:

My children need to learn risk so that:

- They can develop properly.
- They can have a happy childhood.
- They can learn to assess risk properly.
- _____
- _____
- _____

In what ways can I expose my children to appropriate risk?

- I could leave them in a local play area for half an hour.
- I could send them on an errand to the local shop.

- They could walk to school alone.
- _____
- _____
- _____

I can expose my children to risk when:

- They can find their way back to me if they need to.
- They are very comfortable in the surroundings.
- They know what to do if they feel threatened.
- _____
- _____
- _____

The most important factor when assessing risk is:

- Figuring out if it is really risky or if it is fabricated.
- What could go wrong.
- That the children know how to respond correctly if things don't go to plan.
- _____
- _____
- _____

WHAT IS YOUR ATTITUDE TO CHILDCARE?

This is a highly contentious issue, with friends and family afraid to even bring up the subject of childcare while all the time silently condemning their peers' high or low usage of professional childcare. The problem with this is that parents often spend so much time silently defending their lifestyle to the rest of the world that they don't have a chance to pause for thought.

In their responses below, parents can outline their private feelings about childcare and possibly admit to themselves if they aren't parenting in a manner that corresponds with these ideals.

Self-awareness around this subject will probably make parents less sensitive and defensive, and more inclined to live and let live.

Perhaps you would like more help to raise your children but are too ashamed (and/or too poor) to obtain it? Or perhaps you wish you could have more time with your children but can't face the drop in income? It really doesn't matter what the conflict is – you will benefit by giving the discord some airtime and this in turn will encourage you to take the first steps that will lead to a life that is more in keeping with your values.

Childcare should be used when:

- The parents are at work.
- The parents need a break.
- _____
- _____
- _____

I require the following from childcare:

- A warm and friendly atmosphere.
- No TV.
- Healthy food.
- Children encouraged to play outside.
- _____
- _____
- _____

I'll know if childcare is suiting my child or the family because:

- I'll feel it in the atmosphere when I go there.

- My children will tell me.
- It relieves stress and hassle in our lives.
- _____
- _____
- _____

Too much childcare:

- Is bad for everyone.
- Is sometimes necessary if there is no other support.
- Is a warning sign that family life is falling out of balance.
- _____
- _____
- _____

TOP TIP: Free play is more effective than structured play

Many parents think that exercise is more effective within a structured environment such as a football club. However, it has been documented that free, unstructured play in the fresh air expends significantly more energy than supervised and structured activities. If you cast your mind back to when you were a child, a lot of time in structured sports is spent waiting around in a line, waiting for your turn, waiting while the supervisors organise things, and so on. Ensuring your child gets adequate exercise is actually fairly easy – you just put them out to play and you let them walk to school. That'll be enough for them.

For younger children, create safe areas, and for older

> *children teach them how to handle any potential dangers.*
> *Road safety is imperative. The children will need firm rules*
> *initially (for example, 'You can't come back in till I call*
> *you'), as they might not be used to playing outside alone and*
> *it will take time before they realise the fun that can be had*
> *out there. But if the children get used to playing outside they*
> *will naturally expend energy and exercise without needing*
> *to be driven to their latest activity.*

EXTRA-CURRICULAR ACTIVITIES

Again, in this hyper-culture we must ask: How much activity is too much? For some people a rule of thumb about extra-curricular activities is that if the journey to the activity causes stress, it will possibly cause the family as much pain as it will give the child in question pleasure. The entire family's needs must be assessed as to whether it suits them for the child (and often all the other siblings) to be ferried in a car on a Monday evening to karate at 6 p.m., when the child could instead walk to a different (though less attractive) activity at another time. On the other hand, if the child can source a lift to and from the venue, then perhaps his or her resourcefulness should be rewarded with permission to attend.

Extra-curricular activities:

- Should be chosen by the parents while keeping the children's wishes in mind.

- Shouldn't be further than 20 minutes' drive away from home.

- Shouldn't be taken up and dropped willy nilly.

- _____

- _____

- _____

If extra-curricular activities are costly:

- They should be strictly rationed.
- They should only be allowed if the child is willing to forgo another activity.
- _____
- _____
- _____

If your child wants to give up an activity:

- He or she should be ignored for a time, while you consider whether it is beneficial to keep the activity up or drop it.
- The parents should help the children to enjoy it more, or else let them drop it.
- _____
- _____
- _____

And now for some quick-fire questions; fingers on the buzzers please!

Should you still go to extra-curricular activities if the kids are tired?

_____
_____
_____

Should it be your job to make them practise for their extra-curricular activities?

_____
_____
_____

Should they attend all the classes because you have paid for them?

_____

_____

_____

What should you do if your life is frazzled as a consequence of keeping to the extra-curricular timetable, but your children are thriving?

_____

_____

_____

Is your children's pleasure more important than your happiness? (Keeping in mind that children are often only as happy as their parents.)

_____

_____

_____

_____

_____

_____

YOUR FAMILY'S LIFESTYLE

There are many, many different lifestyles, with most parents preferring to muddle through, making it up as they go along. The issue with this is that our present cultural obsession with gruesome crime, combined with commercial interests whose primary motive is to scare parents into buying stuff, has created a culture of stressed parents and frustrated children. This toxic culture is the reason why parents today need to be more vigilant to ensure that their family isn't being affected adversely by fabricated fears.

Today, by far the most likely issue to have an impact on your children's health is mental health problems: your child is statistically much more likely to experience emotional distress, such as stress, anxiety, depression, addiction and a risk of suicide, than be hurt in a road traffic accident, be abducted by a predator or experience sexual abuse. And so parents need to be more sensitive and responsive to emotional upset than to any other safety concern.

This doesn't mean that parents need to roll over and give their children whatever they want; rather, it suggests that parents need, first and foremost, to think about what it would take to create a happy family environment. When considering this question, it might be beneficial to be reminded that one of the best ways you can raise a happy child is to lead an authentic, fulfilling and happy life yourself surrounded by a culture that is largely happy and fulfilled.

There is space below for you, the parent, to create your family's individual manifesto. So get your pen and write out your individual family's guide to living. (If you run out of ideas, you might be inspired by the Parenting Manifesto in the next chapter.)

My family's guide to a happier lifestyle:

9

Is Féidir Linn –
But It Takes a Village!

I don't think one parent can raise a child. I don't think two
parents can raise a child. You really need the whole village.

Toni Morrison[1]

Now that we are up to date with the common issues impacting
our children's lives today, readers may be wondering how we can
raise happy and healthy children despite the rampant paranoia
and toxic culture. We now know that while the baby books are
informative, we can't trust them fully; ditto the baby experts. In
truth, all we can rely on is our own faltering and unsteady views,
and our brains are malleable, biddable organs that are being
shaped and swayed continuously by the crazy stuff on the TV,
on social media, in the news and in the shops. And so all we can
do is to keep ourselves informed and keep in touch with our own
instincts as flawed-but-good-enough parents.

PARENTS NEED TO FIGHT BACK
As Philip Larkin's poem, 'This Be the Verse' goes, *'They f**k you up,
your mum and dad / They may not mean to, but they do'*.[2]

Wait! Hold on now, let's back up there a little bit. *'They f**k
you up, your mum and dad'*? And what about society? And what
about your friends? And your lovers? And your career? And
this crazy world in general? Surely it is life itself that breaks our
hearts? Living in this complicated and complex world requires

boundless courage, stoic endurance, worldly wisdom, a sense of humour, forbearance, resilience and much, much more. Can we really justify pinning all our problems on our parents? What about everyone else? Let's get the extended family, the community, the town planners, the education system and wretched consumerism into the firing line too!

DOES IT OR DOES IT NOT TAKE A VILLAGE TO RAISE A CHILD?

So what should parents expect from their community? It might be helpful if you take some time to study your environment and consider how you could lighten your load by bringing the 'village' into your family's life. You may need to grit your teeth and summon up your courage for some of these initiatives and, initially, these ideas may take up even more of your time, but inevitably, as our children learn to have a sense of ownership over their own time, the burden on parents will be lightened considerably.

Again, the following ideas are merely suggestions; it's up to parents to modify, amend and dump as necessary:

- Parents could begin to look upon their extended family and friends as a natural part of the network of people who have an input in their children's lives. And by extension, return this favour and look upon other children and elders as your responsibility too. Children could perhaps offer to do some odd jobs for neighbours, to help create a sense of neighbourliness.

- A children's tidy-roads contest in your town, where children are responsible for the upkeep of their individual road would cultivate a sense of responsibility, confidence, maturity and pride in their homeplace. (You might obtain sponsorship for prizes from local businesses, and you will certainly get support from the Tidy Towns committee.)

- Hold a garage sale with your children. Encourage them to tap into the spirit of enterprise: clear out all their unused toys, declutter the house and tell the kids to run the stall themselves. (Let them keep all the money they make so that they have an interest in the whole thing.)

- Could a babysitting ticketing system run in your community? This would entail swapping tickets with other like-minded parents and would foster a sense of community and a sense that 'we are all in it together'. Some communities have guidelines for such a strategy, while others prefer to use old-fashioned common sense.

- The next time you stand bored, cold and resentful at the playground or on the sideline of your child's football training session, with an excessive number of adults standing gormlessly and restlessly nearby, strike up a conversation and offer to watch their kids for a while; if they refuse, ask them nicely if they could watch your children. Then go and have a latté – and congratulate yourself on your courage. (This requires a certain chutzpah that not everyone feels up to.) Better still, tell your children beforehand that you need a break, drop them off and leave them to it.

- Throw an old-fashioned street party! Each household provides some food or drink and you haul tables out onto the street, throw in a bit of music, close the street to traffic and let the conversation flow. When everyone is relaxed and chatting happily, at the risk of being sneaky, that's when to nab them – this is a good time to suggest some more adventurous initiatives.

- Perhaps you could organise one day a week when parents take it in turns to keep an eye on the children as they play in the local park? This could be done by you initially, then over time it's hoped that one or two other parents could offer their services too.

TOP TIP: Small and local initiatives

Parents and adults can begin some small-scale local initiatives that would help take the pressure off parents, build a shared sense of community and at the same time enrich their children's lives, for example 'Walk on Wednesdays', 'Car-free Sundays' or 'Odd-jobs Day', which some communities adopt to enhance a community spirit and foster independence among children.

WHAT IS NEEDED FROM OUR SOCIETY?

First and foremost, the impact of the car on our children's freedom has to be addressed urgently. This is the single most relevant reason for parents refusing to allow their children outside to play. There are interesting innovations in Germany and Sweden giving emphasis to children's play space over car usage.[3] Ireland's eco-village in Cloughjordan, Co. Tipperary, is also structured to put less emphasis on the convenience of the car and give more importance to children's play areas.[4]

Parents need to put pressure on society to further improve road safety and create safe spaces in which children can play. Politicians, town planners and councillors all need to be made aware of the lack of child-friendly resources in your locality. And this is not just confined to playgrounds and youth clubs. Cycle lanes, safe routes to schools and amenities, adequate zebra crossings, places in nature for children to play; these are not idealised castles in the air, they are accepted necessities for our children to live happy, healthy lives.

TOP TIP: Teach your children good road safety!

To raise safe kids, children must learn at an early age how to keep themselves safe. Ask your children to be the 'Captain' when crossing the road. Discuss road safety with them, pointing out dangerous drivers, dangerous pedestrians, cycle lanes, lack of cycle lanes, blind spots, safe spots and so on. Make sure your children take pride in their extraordinary expertise in road safety.

IMPROVING ROAD SAFETY

Teaching your children road safety is one of the most important lessons you can teach them; do it yesterday! When you feel confident that your children know how to behave in traffic it clears the situation for you to spot any vague, media-fabricated fear that is influencing your thought processes.

A 2010 survey by 'Cycling England' criticised overprotective parents for stifling the chances of children cycling to school, and the poll of more than 1,000 parents found that 80 per cent of children were banned from doing so.[5] (A shockingly small number (1 per cent) of children cycle to school in Ireland, so in this country we're probably even worse than in England.)[6] According to the same report, our pervasive sense of anxiety and fear is creating 'cul-de-sac kids' who are limited to cycling only outside their own house and in their own road. Few parents can argue that cycling to school is not feasible – it is only infeasible because society hasn't been minded to create safe paths for children on which to walk, cycle or play. A safe route for children to travel to schools should be a given in every town.

The majority of car accidents happen less than five miles from home and, considering that the average gas-guzzling, environmentally ruinous journey to primary schools is less than two miles and to the majority of secondary schools less than three miles, children are often much safer walking or cycling to school than being stuck in the metal box.

As we have seen, even though traffic accidents cause significantly fewer deaths today than in previous years, nevertheless, after mental health issues, they are easily the greatest threat to our children's safety (see Figure 9.1). Strategies are now needed to build the children's licence to be independently active – for example, safe routes to parks, safe routes to schools and safe routes to play areas in every town should be *part* of the planning – what use is a fabulous park nearby if the children can only go there with their parents? There are a multitude of traffic-calming measures that could be increased to encourage safe, independent physical activity in estates.

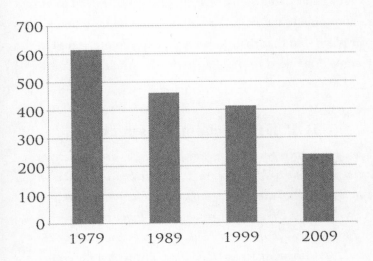

Figure 9.1: Number of road deaths in Ireland.
Source: National Roads Authority, table 2.[7]

Play equipment is not the sole method to encourage free play – landscaping, planting and community art installations offer as much play value as does apparatus. As Play England's *Charter for Children's Play* states:

> *Children should be able to play freely in their local areas. Children have the same right to use and enjoy public space as others. Local streets, estates, green spaces, parks and town centres should be accessible for children and young people to move around in safety and offer places where they can play freely, experience nature, explore their environment and be with their friends.*[8]

Charles Montgomery's book *Happy City* suggests ways to retrofit our cities to create happy environments, and urban designers are now considering how the actual design of towns can induce happiness.[9] When asked to define 'play', children have frequently described it as 'what children and young people do when not being told what to do by adults'.[10] Consequently, parents need to look at their environment and consider how it could be modified to be a happier place – so that their kids are free to explore and play, and the parents don't need to trail haplessly after their every move.

TOP TIP: Reclaim the streets!

Some progressive parents have organised a 'reclaim the streets' attitude for our children, focusing on their housing estates on Sundays with an aim of allowing their children to roam free every Sunday. Drivers are requested to limit their driving in the area and to drive particularly slowly, overcoming the social traps, discussed earlier, that often exist in housing estates today – children don't play outside because it is perceived to be dangerous, and so fewer kids play outside, and so the cars drive faster, making it even more dangerous for children to play outside.

If Sunday is declared the day for children to be encouraged to play outside, then there are more 'eyes on the street' and suddenly playing outside will be safer. This can be set up very simply by taking leaflets around the housing estate, and placing some very large and imposing signs at strategic spots along the estate roads.

But the big, green, dead spaces in the middle of new housing estates all over Ireland are also a sort of social trap, as the children are given the message that that is the best that can be offered for playing outside – and so they feel uninspired and retreat back home to their screens. Children, and adults, need more than a wide expanse of green to inspire their imaginations. We need interesting layouts such as a maze or woods and hills; we also need permission to engage with the environment – the children need to be allowed to climb trees, build dens and roll down the hills.

RESTRAINT IN THE MEDIA

There are other forces in contemporary culture that need to be addressed – primary among these being the fear-mongering that is rampant in the media. As we now know, the reason why the media focuses on child horror stories is that they guarantee sales – everyone buys, everyone tunes in. However, with a little effort, the media could be restrained when reporting sensationalist horror stories. It has been acknowledged that a suicide in the community will often spark copycat events and so the media has learned restraint in this area, and these days it reports suicide in a responsible, sensitive and mature manner.

Equally, there should be similar campaigns to ensure that any horror stories involving children are reported in a serious, newsworthy manner, with restraint, sensitivity and a strict adherence to specific guidelines. The primary reason for this is that parents and children aren't left cowering behind the couch during the best years of their lives. Secondly, we don't yet know how much impact sensationalist stories about abduction and sex slaves have on already troubled minds, but it certainly normalises abnormal behaviour and we need to keep an eye on how hysterical messages from society might impact an already disturbed mind.

WHEN YOU GO TO THE SHOPS, BRING YOUR WHIP ALONG!

To misquote Nietzsche, we need to be properly armed and vigilant when we shop. The shops sell us so-called educational toys, encouraging parents to think their children will benefit from having these. They sell us safety gadgets, encouraging parents to fear that something disastrous will happen if they don't buy them. They sell us junk food, leading our children into obesity and beyond, and inciting them to harass us in the pester power war. They sell us days out in theme parks, raising our children's expectations that fun is to be provided by the adults. They also sell us (and I'm a tad embarrassed about a conflict of issues here, but it has to be said) literature that we simply *must* read, about the latest parenting fads, again preying on our worries so we will buy more, more and more.

Societal pressure needs to be placed on the canny marketers who are enticing our children towards consumerism. This is another long war to be fought; however, certain guidelines may one day be introduced whereby advertising can only be directed at those aged over eighteen; no more appealing to the five-year-olds and pitting them against their so-called 'boring' parents. This is literally taking candy from babies, who, in their innocence, ally themselves with the global, child-labour, profit-at-all-costs-even-if-it-nurtures-child-obesity enterprises. Rather, we must keep the real enemy in our line of fire – not the pestering child, not the so-called boring parent, but the cynical marketing managers in their shiny offices.

TOP TIP: Teach your children how advertising and marketing works!

Parents need to teach their children about the mad, bad world of advertising. Show them the tricks advertisers use to try to get their money. Make it a game, so that children can feel proud of themselves when they aren't conned into spending increasing amounts. Parents can also show their children how it is that some carefully chosen products can bring us great happiness, but others will disappoint. Children need to learn vigilance in shops so that they aren't conned.

LEARN TO HANDLE THE SCAREMONGERS

Some people will always be more fearful than others, but that doesn't mean that your children's freedom and fun should be ruined because of misinformed hysteria. Sometimes parents fall in with the over-parenting system as they don't want to appear neglectful, but as can be seen in this book, pampering children is, in a curious way, also neglectful. The worst-case-scenario group-think that prevails these days has been shown to be damaging for both children and parents; the adults need to fight back so this fear-mongering, alarmist culture doesn't ruin everyone's lives. Learning to face down feverish, doom-laden, over-the-top responses to your more easy-going parenting style might be the biggest challenge for you, but it may also be the most rewarding.

When the scaremongers attack, challenge them right back

(you will need certain facts in your head to be ready for them). Put all your ducks in a row: the danger of mental ill-health, the rise in obesity, the issue of teen suicide, the joylessness of restrictive and formalised games, and argue your point – list the advantages of teaching your children resourcefulness, independence, resilience and responsibility. If you feel uneasy about doing it for yourself, then do it for your kids!

RESIST OVER-PARENTING FOR SHOW

Time and again clients in my office regale me with stories about how they felt they had to over-parent their children, just for the sake of appearances. This particular emperor is wearing no clothes. We don't have to pretend to over-parent just to show we love our kids. As Daisy Waugh points out in *I Don't Know Why She Bothers*, we all love our kids; it was ever thus: 'Mother love is ferocious, intense, fathomless, unconditional, absolute. It is no myth. We know this! But the pastel-shaded, guilt-driven, bake-your-own, bend-over-and-take-it-up-the-tailpipe saintliness that we have allowed to grow up around it is sheer humbug.'[11]

SPEAK OUT AGAINST CRUELTY TO PARENTS!

My six-year-old child has been dressing herself every day since she was three years old. At the moment she has swimming lessons during school and a parent or guardian has to be available every Friday morning at 12 noon to undress her for swimming and then again at 1 p.m. to dress her again – the rule is, no adult present, no swim. This is, of course, causing great stress to the family as we both work and my little boy has to be picked up from his playschool at noon – so it's all slightly impossible every single Friday. Every week approximately thirty adults are gathered outside the swimming pool, with around twenty of them muttering furiously about the pointlessness of it all (and maybe ten eager beavers, delighted to be on hand to dress their six-year-olds) but there is little interest in revolution – people believe that if you complain too furiously it looks as though you're selfish. But we're not selfish and we should complain – it's a stupid system! Let the kids who need a hand have a hand and leave the rest to their own devices!

Learn from the dads

Many people argue that it is the supremacy of feminism that accounts for the growth in fearful and anxious children – previous to this generation, fathers over-ruled mothers' more extreme protectiveness and allowed their children to roam free and to make their own mistakes. However, these days, with mothers earning as much as fathers, Father doesn't reign supreme any more and mothers have won the battle over how to raise the children – and so children are suffering from more feminised, neurotic parenting that is all too often driven by fear and guilt.

Helpful strategies for the community

- Parenting experts could come to your community hall to discuss such issues as excessive homework, our competitive culture, and the benefits of free play for children. The fun of belonging to organisations such as the local Scouts or Girl Guides can be spoiled by too many petty regulations and the continual need to convince fear-consumed parents that it is sometimes appropriate to loosen the reins on their children. And yet your local Scout and Girl Guide Leaders will undoubtedly remember the glorious, golden days of their own childhoods – that's probably why they became leaders. If you can organise an expert to give a talk to parents about the benefits of risk and adventure in your child's life, you could be making the Scout Leader's day.

- The 'Walking Bus' is perhaps the best-known and easiest innovation that readers can establish immediately in their own community. This is a simple strategy whereby children meet at a designated 'bus stop' and they walk to school two-by-two in the form of a walking bus, supervised by a couple of parents or other volunteers. It should be an all-weather initiative as otherwise it will probably fall apart at the slightest sign of rain. And yet many freestyle parents are critical of the walking-bus idea as they point out (understandably) it does not encourage independence, it is strictly supervised and it is probably quite boring for the kids. Personally I couldn't agree more with the nay-sayers, and yet surely it's better than being chauffeur-driven to school? And it is a challenge to car culture, which is always good in my view. As with all matters to do with parenting, parents need to assess the issue and make up their own minds.

- There are other initiatives that promote walking to school such as 'WOW – Walk on Wednesdays'. Wow is right, as presumably the children who walk on Wednesdays could also walk on Mondays, Tuesdays, Thursdays and Fridays as well. Still Rome wasn't built in a day and all that …

- An after-school activities group could be established in communities that have little emphasis on homework and a heavy emphasis on fun and a culture of togetherness in the community. This could entail thirty minutes each day devoted to homework (that is, get it out of the way) and then after that, free play, old-school games and being around nature. It would need to be done with volunteer parents working on a rota system to keep the cost down.

- Free Play Initiatives, where you and anyone sympathetic

to your cause (ideally, three or four adults) volunteer to be available from 2–4 p.m. every Saturday in the woods. Caveat to remember: don't describe yourself as a 'supervisor' as this is a free play initiative and nervous parents will interrogate 'supervisors' about their health and safety qualifications and their skills among children. Instead, encourage parents to come along and bring their children, then the message of the benefits of free play can slowly but surely be learned. Back yourself up with the relevant leaflets highlighting these issues that can be handed out assiduously (yes, difficult, but oh so necessary!) at appropriate opportunities.

- Locally based organisations – parent–toddler groups, local health centres, etc. – could cultivate a culture of social supports for parents. The entire concept of the parent–toddler groups could be extended into the wild and to groups for older children; and so 'Free Play Projects' could be established on a voluntary basis around the country. Modelled on the parent–toddler system, parents could meet at the local forest, or failing that, the local park or the local beach, with the primary objective of their children playing outside together. This would need to be an all-weather initiative and the organiser would need to be prepared to lead with enthusiasm initially. Free Range Kids in Dublin operate an initiative such as this (see them on Facebook) with the apparent emphasis on spending time among nature and not spending money.

Pioneering projects already in existence
Outdoor crèches

As the saying goes, there is no such thing as bad weather, only bad clothes. Ireland's first outdoor crèche opened in Donegal in 2009.[12] Glen Outdoor School for Early Learning is run by

Donegal teacher Sally O'Donnell, and caters for children up to twelve years of age. The entire focus is on the great outdoors and the children play and learn outside for around 90 per cent of the day. Sally, a mother of five, visited several similar crèches across Europe, including one in Scotland, and noted that, as long as the children wear appropriate clothing, they are not affected by adverse weather conditions.

The mission statement is a quote by Margaret McMillan, a health and education reformer, in 1925: 'The best kept classroom and the richest cupboard are roofed only by the sky'. The children learn to play safely and make the most of the environment around them. They use pebbles for tasks like sorting and classifying, bug catchers and a microscope for looking at the bugs, and they also use chalk and blackboards, paints and easels. Children have access to small huts and are given the opportunity to create their own games and gather round campfires – glorious!

FOREST SCHOOLS

Forest schools have been defined as 'an inspirational process that offers children, young people and adults regular opportunities to achieve and develop confidence through hands-on learning in a woodland environment'.[13] This outdoorsy approach to education and play encourages children to become comfortable among wild nature. Some parents suggest that Forest Schools and other similar projects combat the issues of the 'indoors kid', while others argue that less political involvement with schools and authorities would be more effective, as too many child-based activities have already been over-regulated. Hmmm, can we agree with both sides of this argument?

The Forest School Leaders use the woods and forests as a means of building independence and self-esteem in children. The emphasis is on the natural environment, but personal skills such as teamwork and problem solving are also prized, and the woodland environment is habitually used to learn about more abstract concepts such as maths and communication. Forest schools have been found to help children who need more attention or support, such as children with ADHD or autism.[14]

NATURE CAMPS

Though in many ways camps of all types are to be regarded with suspicion as they are expensive, nonetheless many of us work and many kids need to go to camps if they are to meet their friends at all during the summer holidays. Nature camps will at least keep the children outside and give them an appreciation of nature.

TOP TIP: Create your own children's play areas in the wild

Luckily there still remain many areas given over to green-ery and to the wild in Ireland. The tragedy is that these areas aren't being used, nor have they been designated for children's play. Urban design could be further examined to encourage children to play outside; and rural design could begin to address the lack of play areas for children. In this way, in the future, play areas in the wild could be flagged as being somewhere that parents could be encouraged to leave their children to play unsupervised.

GIVE YOUR CHILD A CARD EXPLAINING YOUR ETHOS (ANNOYING BUT NECESSARY)

Lenore Skenazy, in her book *Free-Range Kids: How to Raise Safe, Self-Reliant Children* (*Without Going Nuts with Worry*) has a very helpful membership card that is available for parents to cut out and give to their children, and to use themselves.[15] We have since adapted this and my husband has found it very useful when he is out with the kids in the big, bad jungle that is rural Ireland. He reports that adults in general take these laminated cards with good grace. For a moment or two they begin to argue but then when they are requested nicely to read the entire card they do so and they begin to unwind and interesting conversations often unfold as adults start to recall their own childhoods and agree that perhaps the world isn't really filled with crazed cross-eyed axemen lurking around every corner …

Defending our children's right to have fun

MEMBERSHIP CARDS
Clip 'n Save!

I'm not lost and I'm not neglected but neither am I a Cotton Wool Kid.

I am well-loved and cared for and the adults in my life prefer to allow me the opportunity to go outside and explore the world; as they did when they were children.

I have been taught how to cross the street safely. I can speak with strangers but I know never to GO OFF with strangers. I like having fun outside and the adults in my life prefer me to have fun outside rather than sitting inside playing on screens.

The adults in my life know where I am, but if you want to talk to them, please feel free to give them a call.

The number is: _____

Signed: _____

Parenting manifesto

1.   *Teach your children appropriate safety measures.*
Essential. Teach your children how to cross the road, how to spot a
nice lady and ask for help if needed, and how to act responsibly. You
will also need to discuss with them the different and complicated
ways that bad people will use to try to lure children away. Again,
as with the roads, help your children to become experts in these
situations. Just like many aspects of safety, these are complicated
messages that need to be taught in baby steps and slowly, over
time.

2.   *Teach your children to talk to strangers!*
Ernie Allen, head of the US National Center for Missing &
Exploited Children, agrees that 'stranger danger' is overblown:
'We have been trying to debunk the myth of "stranger danger".'[16]
Instead, Allen believes parents would be better off teaching their
children to talk to strangers. This will teach children how to
discern the difference between trustworthy and untrustworthy
strangers. Considering that Allen's Center instituted the infamous
kids' pictures on milk cartons all over the USA, this shows us how
badly stranger danger has been misconstrued. (The tragedy of the
milk carton campaign was that they forgot to mention that the
vast majority of the children on the milk cartons were runaways
or children taken by non-custodial parents in divorce cases.)

3.   *Teach your children not to GO OFF with strangers.*
This may involve conversations you are reluctant to have; however,
it is worth it if you teach your children to understand the difference
between dangerous behaviour and adventurous behaviour. And,
because they have already learned to speak with confidence to
strangers, they can appeal to passing strangers if they feel they

need help. Children who feel competent and confident in the world are safer than those who have never learned how to assess risk or danger. When Ernie Allen interviewed children who had escaped potential abductions, they all had one thing in common: they resisted and they stood up for themselves. They shouted, kicked, punched, bit and ran away. The number of children who are abducted simply because they follow the adult obediently is scary.

Teach your children that most adults don't ask children for help and they should be wary of any who does, and that bad people may use tricks such as sweets, puppies or another child to lure them, but that they're simply not allowed to go off with any strangers that you haven't pre-approved beforehand. That way your children should be quite clear about everything.

4. *Teach your children how to rebuff unwanted attention from adults.*
This can be rehearsed at home so that it is fun and instils confidence. The child's most important weapon is their voice; teach your children how to say clearly and loudly, 'No. My mammy wouldn't let me.' Predators interviewed in jail were asked what made them choose one child over another. Almost all of them agreed that they go for the docile children, the obedient, the naïve, the less confident and the quiet children – basically, the ones they believe would do as they're told and wouldn't tell on them.

5. *Create safe areas for your children to play in.*
This will give your child the confidence necessary to enjoy the world; it will also normalise playing outside as they grow up, instead of teaching them the natural reaction to boredom is to look for their electronic toys.

6   *Provide breakfast, dinner and tea for your children. No choices and no snacks.*
This should be cheaper, reduce the pressure on you and help your children's eating habits. Also, snacking is bad for your teeth.

7.   *When your children ask 'What are we doing today?', don't rise to it.*
You are not their summer camp leader; nor are you a children's entertainer. It is not your role to provide fun; and if you provide it you are neglecting to teach your children the lifelong gift of self-sufficiency. It is noticeable that there has been a complete reversal in that some parents today seek approval from their children instead of vice-versa; consider disappointing your children in the short-term for a more long-term gain.

8.   *Figure out who should do which chores and keep to it.*
Again, this is good for everyone in the household. While paying your children for doing chores is probably not helpful in the long term, chores can be linked to pocket money – no chores; no pocket money.

9.   *Send your children outside and tell them you will call them in at dinner time. They are only allowed in the house for toilet breaks (you have to be cruel to be kind!).*
At first your children will be whiny and furious at being thrown out, but keep the faith and don't let 'em back in; it took my children some time before they began to enjoy being outside on their own, but they can't get enough of it now. There is a wonderful world out there that your children possibly haven't even noticed yet. Encourage your children to make a fort or build a treehouse. If that doesn't work, tell them that they have to invent a game and you will join in the game if it's any good. (Join in anyway, these kids probably need a bit of support to help them hear the call of the wild!)

10. *De-schedule your child's life.*

Perhaps begin with a baby step: look at your child's schedule. Is there anything that you can dump just for this week? Following on from this, is there anything you can dump for the long term? Can you push your child into the great outdoors during the de-scheduled time?

11. *Bring nature back into your family's life.*

Nature deficit disorder is alive and kicking among urban children (see Chapter 5). Give your child the soul nourishment that only nature can give. You can begin by taking your children to the nearest park and asking them to find ten different leaves (if they are young), or perhaps see who can climb the highest tree – including Mammy (Mammy needs to leave her dignity aside in the spirit of it all). This is giving your children a gift they can access for free for the rest of their lives.

12. *Allow your kids to get bored.*

Twenty-first-century children have learned that, when they get bored, the screens go on. But boredom can lead to true creativity. Remember when your own mother used to say 'Boredom isn't in my vocabulary'? Bring that phrase back! We actually need more boredom in this hurried world – we all seem to be terrified of boredom, and yet it gives you the mental brain space to work out who you are and what you like. Apparently, Albert Einstein spent hours staring into space at his office at Princeton. (Wow! That's mad – I, too, spend hours staring into space ...)

13. *Spread the word and create a community.*

Of course, every movement has adamant unbelievers – just leave them be. Instead, like a sniper, notice the more positive or ambivalent parents and pick them out one by one. Begin parenting discussions with them. Many parents are outwardly parenting according to the values they perceive are acceptable to society, but secretly flouting many of society's rules. A thoughtful discussion about media myths and scaremongering stories can begin to free parents to openly raise their children in the way they wish. This will also give you back-up when you try to begin initiatives in your area.

14. *Stand up to hysteria.*

The next time you find yourself behaving as you think a 'good parent' should, stop, straighten your shoulders and consider what is driving your behaviour. Are you parenting from guilt? From fear of disapproval? Are you thinking, 'I couldn't live with myself if ...' or are you thinking about your children's welfare? You will need to have certain facts at your disposal as you may need to stand up to the nearest fearful and paranoid parent who is urging you to hover over little Johnny on the swings; remember, little Johnny is perfectly capable of running to you if he needs you.

15. *Stay away from the likes of CSI and 24-hour news ... turn off the TV once in a while and stay away from gory stories involving children as much as possible.*

The TV and the Internet are filled with horrific stories about sex crimes and violent assault, which directly affect our brains. And our brains are simply too malleable to be able to withstand these stories without becoming paranoid and nervous, leading us to believe that there are psychotic serial killers the length and breadth of the country.

Switch off these stories. As I've said before, they are very rare, but because vast amounts of filthy lucre is made from sicko stories, every last drop of horror will be squeezed out of them (to you and your children's detriment). Or at the very least, only read well-informed and thoughtful articles about such events.

16. *Have some fun.*

Pause for a moment and write down the five things that make you happiest. This list may surprise you, so don't shirk! Now make sure you do one of these things today, and tomorrow, and so on. Begin to live your life for pleasure, not pain.

1. _____

2. _____

3. _____

4. _____

5. _____

17. *Show your children that you can handle failure.*

If we look to the wild, we will see how a lioness only 'succeeds' in finding food in, at best, one in eight attempts at hunting. The cub goes with the lioness and thereby learns that success doesn't come instantly – sustained effort and determination is also required. Rather than immediately questioning your children about their day at school, instead, make like a lioness and begin to share with your children about your day; tell them about your little successes and failures (without falling into heavy, adult conversation), and then your children will feel more able to share their own successes and failures with you.

18. *Show your children how to fail better.*

Thomas Edison was once allegedly asked by a slightly snarky reporter, 'How does it feel to fail 2,000 times at inventing the light bulb?' And Edison famously replied 'Mommy! It's not fair, I can't do it!' … Er, no, that's not right, wrong file … actually the words he used were: 'I have not failed. I've just found 2,000 ways that won't work.'

The only way your children will learn how to ride a bike is by you letting go of the handlebars. Your children will fall. Your children will cry. Your children will learn to dust themselves off and start all over again, and again, and again. Then they will learn. It is your role, as the concerned parent, to back off, and bestow upon your children the gift of confidence and trust that they can do it for themselves. Yes they can! (If you let them, that is).

19. *Take what you like, leave the rest.*
This manifesto is not foolproof and it is not for everyone – as with everything in life, you should take what you like and leave the rest.

20. *Is féidir linn!*
Despite the media and co. trying valiantly to start a civil war between parents, we parents have largely nobly resisted. Likewise, the path you are following might annoy many misinformed parents and so you may find yourself increasingly embattled and needing the courage of a lion to parent according to your own beliefs. Keep the faith and keep smiling – one hopes that, as the backlash to our hysterical culture grows, the truth will eventually win out and we will all be able to kick back and enjoy parenting together.

As the much misinterpreted violin master Dr Suzuki (What is it with these Suzuki classes?! They are nothing like how Dr Suzuki envisaged them!) said, 'Children learn to smile from their parents', and so it follows that the easiest way for you to teach your children to live a happy and healthy life is to be happy and healthy yourself.

Suggested Reading

Certain movements have emerged all over the world and there is now a considerable backlash fighting against the syndrome of over-parenting. And while this book seeks to let parents encourage individuality so that they will have the brain-space and confidence to create their own unique family, nevertheless some readers may find the following texts interesting.

- Tom Hodgkinson, *The Idle Parent: Why Less Means More When Raising Kids* (Penguin, London, 2010).

  In 2009 the writer (and father) Tom Hodgkinson released *The Idle Parent* as an entertaining alternative to over-parenting. Hodgkinson argues that most of the time children can take care of themselves, and that the entire family would be happier if parents spent more time doing the same. The idler's ideal scenario is to be near his children, though not too near, and Hodgkinson says he is happiest when he sees his children playing happily 'in the distance'.

- Carl Honoré, *Under Pressure: Rescuing Our Children from the Culture of Hyper-Parenting* (Orion, London, 2008).

  Carl Honoré was inspired to establish the Slow Parenting Movement (a by-product of the burgeoning Slow Movement) as a backlash against parents over-managing and over-scheduling kids' lives with excessive extra-curricular activity and organised play dates. This style of parenting instead encourages parents to do less for their children; plan less and organise less, advising them to let their children explore the world at their own pace.

Honoré proposes that slow parenting will give children the gift of ample time for free play and relaxed family bonding. His book advises a measured and caring way of stepping back and allowing children to mature as naturally as possible.

- Lenore Skenazy, *Free-Range Kids: How to Raise Safe, Self-Reliant Children (Without Going Nuts with Worry)* (Jossey-Bass, San Francisco, 2009).

Lenore Skenazy wrote her hilarious book as a consequence of the hysterical reaction in the media when she wrote about letting her nine-year-old son ride the subway alone. While establishment America asked 'Is this the worst parent ever?', Skenazy, on the other hand, felt so empowered by other parents contacting her to cheer her on that she developed her own 'Free-Range Kids' parenting style. As Skenazy points out:

A Free-Range Kid is a kid who gets treated as a smart, young, capable individual, not an invalid who needs constant attention and help. For instance, in the suburbs, many school PTAs have figured out a new way to raise money (God bless 'em): They auction off the prime drop-off spot right in front of the school – the shortest distance between car and door.

But at the mall, or movie theater or dentist's office, that would be considered the handicapped parking spot – the one you need if you are really disabled. So somehow, in our understandable desire to do the very best for our kids, we have started treating them as if they're handicapped! As if they couldn't possibly walk a couple of blocks, or make their own lunch or climb a tree without hurting themselves, or struggling too much.[1]

Excerpts from 'The Overprotected Kid'

by Hanna Rosin

A trio of boys tramps along the length of a wooden fence, back and forth, shouting like carnival barkers. 'The Land! It opens in half an hour.' Down a path and across a grassy square, 5-year-old Dylan can hear them through the window of his nana's front room. He tries to figure out what half an hour is and whether he can wait that long. When the heavy gate finally swings open, Dylan, the boys, and about a dozen other children race directly to their favorite spots, although it's hard to see how they navigate so expertly amid the chaos.

'Is this a junkyard?' asks my 5-year-old son, Gideon, who has come with me to visit. 'Not exactly,' I tell him, although it's inspired by one. The Land is a playground that takes up nearly an acre at the far end of a quiet housing development in North Wales. It's only two years old but has no marks of newness and could just as well have been here for decades. The ground is muddy in spots and, at one end, slopes down steeply to a creek where a big, faded plastic boat that most people would have thrown away is wedged into the bank. The center of the playground is dominated by a high pile of tires that is growing ever smaller as a redheaded girl and her friend roll them down the hill and into the creek. 'Why are you rolling tires into the water?' my son asks. 'Because we are,' the girl replies.

It's still morning, but someone has already started a fire in the tin drum in the corner, perhaps because it's late fall and wet-cold, or more likely because the kids here love to start fires. Three boys lounge in the only unbroken chairs around it; they are the oldest ones here, so no one complains. One of them turns on the radio – Shaggy is playing (Honey came in and she caught me red-handed, creeping with the girl next door) – as the others feel in their pockets to make sure the candy bars and soda cans are still there. Nearby, a couple of boys are doing mad flips on a stack of filthy mattresses, which makes a fine trampoline. At the other end of the playground, a dozen or so of the younger kids dart in and out of large structures made up of wooden pallets stacked on top of one another. Occasionally a group knocks down a few pallets – just for the fun of it, or to build some new kind of slide or fort or unnamed structure. Come tomorrow and the Land might have a whole new topography.

Other than some walls lit up with graffiti, there are no bright colors, or anything else that belongs to the usual playground landscape: no shiny metal slide topped by a red steering wheel or a tic-tac-toe board; no yellow seesaw with a central ballast to make sure no one falls off; no rubber bucket swing for babies. There is, however, a frayed rope swing that carries you over the creek and deposits you on the other side, if you can make it that far (otherwise it deposits you in the creek). The actual children's toys (a tiny stuffed elephant, a soiled Winnie the Pooh) are ignored, one facedown in the mud, the other sitting behind a green plastic chair. On this day, the kids seem excited by a walker that was donated by one of the elderly neighbors and is repurposed, at different moments, as a scooter, a jail cell, and a gymnastics bar.

The Land is an 'adventure playground', although that term is maybe a little too reminiscent of theme parks to capture the vibe. In the U.K., such playgrounds arose and became popular in the 1940s, as a result of the efforts of Lady Marjory Allen of Hurtwood, a landscape architect and children's advocate. Allen was disappointed by what she described in a documentary as 'asphalt square' playgrounds with 'a few pieces of mechanical equipment'. She wanted to design playgrounds with loose parts that kids could move around and manipulate, to create their own makeshift structures. But more important, she wanted to encourage a 'free and permissive atmosphere' with as little adult supervision as possible. The idea was that kids should face what to them seem like 'really dangerous risks' and then conquer them alone. That, she said, is what builds self-confidence and courage.

... Today, these playgrounds are so out of sync with affluent and middle-class parenting norms that when I showed fellow parents back home [in the USA] a video of kids crouched in the dark lighting fires, the most common sentence I heard from them was 'This is insane.' (Working-class parents hold at least some of the same ideals, but are generally less controlling – out of necessity, and maybe greater respect for toughness.) That might explain why there are so few adventure playgrounds left around the world, and why a newly established one, such as the Land, feels like an act of defiance.

If a 10-year-old lit a fire at an American playground, someone would call the police and the kid would be taken for counseling. At the Land, spontaneous fires are a frequent occurrence. The park is staffed by professionally trained 'playworkers', who keep a close eye on the kids but don't intervene all that much. Claire Griffiths, the manager of the Land, describes her job as 'loitering with intent'. Although the playworkers almost never stop the kids from what they're doing, before the playground had even opened they'd filled binders with 'risk benefits assessments' for nearly every activity. (In the two years since it opened, no one has been injured outside of the occasional scraped knee.) Here's the list of benefits for fire: 'It can be a social experience to sit around with friends, make friends, to sing songs to dance around, to stare at, it can be a co-operative experience where everyone has jobs.

It can be something to experiment with, to take risks, to test its properties, its heat, its power, to re-live our evolutionary past.' The risks? 'Burns from fire or fire pit' and 'children accidentally burning each other with flaming cardboard or wood'. In this case, the benefits win, because a playworker is always nearby, watching for impending accidents but otherwise letting the children figure out lessons about fire on their own.

'I'm gonna put this cardboard box in the fire,' one of the boys says.

'You know that will make a lot of smoke,' says Griffiths.

'Where there's smoke, there's fire,' he answers, and in goes the box. Smoke instantly fills the air and burns our eyes. The other boys sitting around the fire cough, duck their heads, and curse him out. In my playground set, we would call this 'natural consequences', although we rarely have the nerve to let even much tamer scenarios than this one play out. By contrast, the custom at the Land is for parents not to intervene. In fact, it's for parents not to come at all. The dozens of kids who passed through the playground on the day I visited came and went on their own. In seven hours, aside from Griffiths and the other playworkers, I saw only two adults: Dylan's nana, who walked him over because he's only 5, and Steve Hughes, who runs a local fishing-tackle shop and came by to lend some tools.

Griffiths started selling local families on the proposed playground in 2006. She talked about the health and developmental benefits of freer outdoor play, and explained that the playground would look messy but be fenced in. But mostly she made an appeal rooted in nostalgia. She explained some of the things kids might be able to do and then asked the parents to remember their own childhoods. 'Ahh, did you never used to do that?' she would ask. This is how she would win them over ...

... I used to puzzle over a particular statistic that routinely comes up in articles about time use: even though women work vastly more hours now than they did in the 1970s, mothers – and fathers – of all income levels spend much more time with their children than they used to. This seemed impossible to me until recently, when I began to think about my own life. My mother didn't work all that much when I was younger, but she didn't spend vast amounts of time with me, either. She didn't arrange my playdates or drive me to swimming lessons or introduce me to cool music she liked. On weekdays after school she just expected me to show up for dinner; on weekends I barely saw her at all. I, on the other hand, might easily spend every waking Saturday hour with one if not all three of my children, taking one to a soccer game, the second to a theater program, the third to a friend's house, or just hanging out with them at home. When my daughter was about 10, my husband suddenly realized that in her whole life, she had probably not spent more than 10 minutes unsupervised by an adult. Not 10 minutes in 10 years.

… What's lost amid all this protection? … By engaging in risky play, children are effectively subjecting themselves to a form of exposure therapy, in which they force themselves to do the thing they're afraid of in order to overcome their fear. But if they never go through that process, the fear can turn into a phobia. Paradoxically, Sandseter [Professor of early-childhood education in Trondheim, Norway] writes, 'our fear of children being harmed,' mostly in minor ways, 'may result in more fearful children and increased levels of psychopathology.' She cites a study showing that children who injured themselves falling from heights when they were between 5 and 9 years old are less likely to be afraid of heights at age 18. 'Risky play with great heights will provide a desensitizing or habituating experience,' she writes.

We might accept a few more phobias in our children in exchange for fewer injuries. But the final irony is that our close attention to safety has not in fact made a tremendous difference in the number of accidents children have. According to the National Electronic Injury Surveillance System, which monitors hospital visits, the frequency of emergency-room visits related to playground equipment, including home equipment, in 1980 was 156,000, or one visit per 1,452 Americans. In 2012, it was 271,475, or one per 1,156 Americans. The number of deaths hasn't changed much either. From 2001 through 2008, the Consumer Product Safety Commission reported 100 deaths associated with playground equipment – an average of 13 a year, or 10 fewer than were reported in 1980. Head injuries, runaway motorcycles, a fatal fall onto a rock … turn out to be freakishly rare, unexpected tragedies that no amount of safety-proofing can prevent …

[What] makes this current generation of parents most nervous is … children getting lost, or straying from adult supervision. 'Children love to walk off alone and go exploring away from the eyes of adults,' [Sandseter] writes. They 'experience a feeling of risk and danger of getting lost' when 'given the opportunity to "cruise" on their own exploring unknown areas; still, they have an urge to do it.' Here again Sandseter cites evidence showing that the number of separation experiences before age 9 correlates negatively with separation-anxiety symptoms at age 18, 'suggesting an "inoculation" effect' …

As the sun set over the Land, I noticed out of the corner of my eye a gray bin, like the kind you'd keep your recycling in, about to be pushed down the slope that led to the creek. A kid's head poked out of the top, and I realized it was my son's. Even by my relatively laissez-faire parenting standards, the situation seemed dicey. The light was fading, the slope was very steep, and Christian, the kid who was doing the pushing, was only 7. Also, the creek was frigid, and I had no change of clothes for Gideon.

I hadn't seen much of my son that day. Kids, unparented, take on pack habits, so as the youngest and newest player, he'd been taken care of by the veterans of the Land. I inched close enough to hear the exchange.

'You might fall in the creek,' said Christian.

'I know,' said Gideon.

Christian had already taught Gideon how to climb up to the highest slide and manage the rope swing. At this point, he'd earned some trust. 'I'll push you gently, okay?' 'Ready, steady, go!,' Gideon said in response. Down he went, and landed in the creek. In my experience, Gideon is very finicky about water. He hates to have even a drop land on his sleeve while he's brushing his teeth. I hadn't rented a car on this trip, and the woman who'd been driving us around had left for a while. I started scheming how to get him new clothes. Could I knock on one of the neighbors' doors? Ask Christian to get his father? Or, failing that, persuade Gideon to sit a while with the big boys by the fire?

'I'm wet,' Gideon said to Christian, and then they raced over to claim some hammers to build a new fort.

Endnotes

Introduction

1   Finkelhor, David, Jones, Lisa, Shattuck, Anne and Saito, Key, 'Updated Trends in Child Maltreatment, 2012' (Crimes Against Children Research Center, Durham, NH, January 2013).

2   Twenge, Jean M. and Campbell, W. Keith, *The Narcissism Epidemic: Living in the Age of Entitlement* (Atria Books, 2010).

3   Simon, Robin W., 'The Joys of Parenthood, Reconsidered', *Contexts* (American Sociological Association), Vol. 7, No. 2, 2008, p. 41.

4   Tom Hodgkinson, *The Idle Parent: Why Less Means More When Raising Kids* (Penguin, London, 2009), p. ix.

5   Novotney, Amy, 'The Price of Affluence', *Monitor*, Vol. 40, No. 1, 2009.

6   UNICEF, *Children's Well-being in UK, Sweden and Spain: The Role of Inequality and Materialism*, Ipsos MORI Child Well-being Report, June 2011; Bingham, John, 'Cycle of "Compulsive Consumerism" Leaves British Family Life in Crisis, UNICEF Study Finds', *The Daily Telegraph*, 14 September 2011.

Chapter 1: The Culture of Fear

1   Martin, George R. R., *Game of Thrones: Book One of A Song of Ice and Fire* (Harper Voyager, London, 2011).

2   Killingsworth, Matthew A. and Gilbert, Daniel T., 'A Wandering Mind is an Unhappy Mind', *Science*, Vol. 330, No. 6006, November 2010, p. 932.

3   Cited in Senior, Jennifer, *All Joy and No Fun: The Paradox of Modern Parenthood* (Harper Collins, New York, 2014), pp. 5–6.

4   'Louis C.K. on Father's Day'. Available at: http://www.youtube.com/watch?v=KJI8wLao1yY (accessed November 2014).

5   Kahneman, Daniel, Krueger, Alan B., Schkade, David, Schwarz, Norbert and Stone, Arthur, 'Toward National Well-Being Accounts', *American Economic Review*, Vol. 94, No. 2, 2004, p. 432.

6   Zelizer, Viviana A., *Pricing the Priceless Child: The Changing Social Value of Children* (Basic Books, New York, 1985), p. 14.

7   Senior, *All Joy and No Fun*, p. 8.

8   Kettering, Charles F., 'Keep the Consumer Dissatisfied', *Nation's Business*, Vol. 17, No. 1, January 1929, pp. 30–1, 79.

9 Young, Toby, 'Why Our Children Will Never Have a Summer Like '76', *Daily Mail*, 21 July 2013.

10 Heffernan, Virginia, 'Sweeping the Clouds Away: Not the Same Street', *The New York Times*, 18 November 2007.

11 Available at: www.thudguard.com.

12 Aviva One Poll Research, 'UK: First-time Parents Spend £492 million Preparing for Baby', 22 April 2014.

13 Morrongiello, Barbara A., Walpole, B. and Lasenby, J., 'Understanding Children's Injury-risk Behavior: Wearing Safety Gear Can Lead to Increased Risk Taking', *Accident Analysis & Prevention*, Vol. 39, No. 3, 2007, pp. 618–23.

14 Cited in Rosin, Hanna, 'The Overprotected Kid', *The Atlantic*, 19 March 2014. Available at: http://www.theatlantic.com/features/archive/2014/03/hey-parents-leave-those-kids-alone/358631/.

15 Fairbairn, Jordan and Dawson, Myrna, 'Canadian News Coverage of Intimate Partner Homicide: Analysing Changes Over Time', *Feminist Criminology*, Vol. 8, No. 3, 2013, pp. 147–76.

16 Elliott, Michele, *501 Ways to Be a Good Parent: From the Frantic Fours to the Terrible Twelves* (Trafalgar Square Publishing, London, 1996), p. 42.

17 Healy, Jonathan, *Newstalk Lunchtime*, Newstalk FM, 24 October 2013.

18 Road Safety Authority (RSA), *Deaths and Injuries on Irish Roads*, 2012.

19 *Ibid.*

20 Niles, Chris, 'Report Reveals Kenya Child Sex Industry of "Horrific" Magnitude', 19 December 2006. Available at: http://www.unicef.org/infobycountry/kenya_37817.html (accessed September 2014).

21 Eirienne, Arielle K., 'Child Sex Tourism: "Us" and "Them" in a Globalized World', *Student Pulse*, Vol. 1, No. 11, 2009. Available at: http://www.studentpulse.com/articles/34/child-sex-tourism-us-and-them-in-a-globalized-world (accessed September 2014).

22 *Ibid.*

23 Lucey, Jim, 'Do Our Young People Really Have Mental Health Problems?', St Patrick's Mental Health Services. Available at: http://www.stpatricks.ie/blog/do-our-young-people-really-have-mental-health-problems (accessed September 2014).

24 Smyth, Noel, *Today with Seán O'Rourke*, RTÉ Radio 1, 20 May 2014.

25 National Office for Suicide Prevention (NOSP), Annual Report 2012, *Reaching Out to Communities to Build Resilience and Reduce*

Suicide in Ireland, September 2013; Lucey, Jim, 'Do Our Young People Really Have Mental Health Problems?'.

26   MacKay M. and Vincenten J., *National Action to Address Child Intentional Injury – 2014: Europe Summary*, Birmingham: European Child Safety Alliance, 2014, p. 12. Available at: http://www.childsafetyeurope.org/archives/news/2014/info/ciir-report.pdf (accessed September 2014).

27   NOSP (2013); RSA, *Deaths and Injuries on Irish Roads*.

28   Ó Caollaí, Éanna, 'Ireland Has "Exceptionally High Rates" of Suicide', *The Irish Times*, 21 March 2014.

29   Condon, Deborah, 'Depression Main Cause of Illness in Teens', IrishHealth.com, 14 May 2014. Available at: www.irishhealth.com/article.html?id=23619 (accessed September 2014).

30   McSharry, John, 'Stranger Danger: How Can I Teach Safety Without Scaring My Child?', *The Irish Times*, 26 June 2012.

31   McCann, Kate, *Madeleine* (Transworld Publishers, London, 2012).

32   Greenslade, Roy, 'Express and Star Apologies to McCanns Bring All Journalism Into Disrepute', *The Guardian*, 19 March 2008.

33   UK Parliament, House of Commons Culture, Media and Sport Committee, *Press Standards, Privacy and Libel: Second Report of Session 2009–10*, Vol. 2, 2010, p. 161.

34   *Ibid.*, p. 160.

35   *Ibid.*

36   *Ibid.*, p. 68.

37   Gibson, Owen, 'Newspapers Apologise to McCanns', *The Guardian*, 20 March 2008.

38   Halm, Laura, 'Mom Speaks Out About Neglect Charges', WCYB.com, 8 June 2012. Available at: http://www.wcyb.com/Mom-Speaks-Out-About-Neglect-Charges/15240294 (accessed September 2014).

39   Skenazy, Lenore, 'This Is Not a Crime', Free-Range Kids.com, 11 April 2012. Available at: http://www.freerangekids.com/this-is-not-a-crime-cops-charge-dad-who-let-kids-play-alone-in-park-for-2-hours/ (accessed September 2014).

40   Celizic, Mike, 'Mom Lets 9-year-old Take Subway Home Alone', *Today News*, 3 April 2008.

41   Skenazy, Lenore, *Free-Range Kids – How to Raise Safe, Self-Reliant Children (Without Going Nuts with Worry)* (Jossey-Bass, San Francisco, 2010).

42   Celizic, 'Mom Lets 9-year-old Take Subway Home Alone'.

43   Skenazy, Lenore, 'Why I Let My 9-year-old Ride the Subway Alone', *New York Sun*, 1 April 2008.

Chapter 2: Life is a Risky Business

1   Shedd, John A., *Salt from My Attic* (Mosher Press, Portland, ME, 1928), cited in Fred R. Shapiro (ed.), *The Yale Book of Quotations* (Yale University Press, New Haven, CT, 2006), p. 705.

2   Didion, Joan, *Blue Nights* (Fourth Estate, London, 2011).

3   Szalavitz, Maya, '10 Ways We Get the Odds Wrong', *Psychology Today*, January 2008.

4   *Ibid.*

5   Gallagher, Bernard, 'Fear of the Unknown', *Safer Communities*, Vol. 7, No. 3, 2008, pp. 22–5; Noll, Jennie G., Shenk, Chad E., Barnes, Jaclyn E. and Putnam, Frank W., 'Childhood Abuse, Avatar Choices, and Other Risk Factors Associated with Internet-Initiated Victimization of Adolescent Girls', *Pediatrics*, Vol. 123, No. 6, 2009, pp. e1078–83; Pain, Rachel, 'Paranoid Parenting? Rematerializing Risk and Fear for Children', *Social & Cultural Geography*, Vol. 7, No. 2, 2006, pp. 221–43.

6   Palmer, Sue, *Toxic Childhood: How The Modern World Is Damaging Our Children and What We Can Do About It* (Orion, London, 2006).

7   Louv, Richard, *Last Child in the Woods: Saving Our Children from Nature-Deficit Disorder* (Algonquin Books, New York, 2005).

8   Wardle, Claire, 'Monsters and Angels, Visual Press Coverage of Child Murders in the USA and UK, 1930–2000', *Journalism* 8(3), 2007 (Sage Publications, London, 2007), pp. 263–84.

9   Szalavitz, '10 Ways We Get the Odds Wrong'.

10   *Ibid.*

11   Department of Justice and Equality, 'Minister Shatter Releases Figures on Applications Dealt with by the Central Authority for International Child Abduction in 2012', Press Release, 11 March 2013.

12   NOSP (2013); RSA, *Deaths and Injuries on Irish Roads*; Department of Justice and Equality, 'Minister Shatter Releases Figures on Applications Dealt with by the Central Authority for International Child Abduction in 2012'.

13   McSharry, 'Stranger Danger'.

14   Dublin Rape Crisis Centre, Annual Report 2011.

15   Sedlak, Andrea J., Finkelhor, David, Hammer, Heather and Schultz, Dana J., *National Estimates of Missing Children: An Overview*, Office of Juvenile Justice and Delinquency Prevention, NISMART: National Incidence Studies of Missing, Abducted, Runaway and Thrownaway Children, US Dept of Justice, 2002. Available at: https://www.ncjrs.gov/pdffiles1/ojjdp/196465.pdf (accessed September 2014).

16   *Ibid.*
17   *Ibid.*, Table 3: Reasons Children Became Missing: Reported Missing Children, p. 6.
18   Gregoire, Christine O., Attorney General of Washington and US Dept of Justice, 'Case Management for Missing Children Homicide Investigation', May 1997. Available at: http://www.pollyklaas.org/media/pdf/Abduction-Homicide-Study.pdf (accessed September 2014).
19   US Dept of Transportation, National Highway Traffic Safety Administration, 'Traffic Safety Facts, Research Note', December 2012. Available at: http://www-nrd.nhtsa.dot.gov/Pubs/811701.pdf (accessed September 2014).
20   Weather Safety: Lightning, 'Lightning Safety for You and Your Family', US Department of Commerce, NOAA (National Oceanic and Atmospheric Administration) http://www.nws.noaa.gov/os/lightning/resources/lightning-safety.pdf (accessed September 2014).
21   Centers for Disease Control and Prevention (CDC), 'Violence Prevention, Suicide Data Sheet', 2012.
22   Parker-Pope, Tara, 'Suicide Rate Rises Sharply in US', *The New York Times*, 2 May 2013.
23   Tavernise, Sabrina, 'To Lower Suicide Rates, New Focus Turns to Guns', *The New York Times*, 13 February 2013.
24   Furedi, Frank, 'Paranoid Parenting – Making Sense of Parental Paranoia', *The Guardian*, 25 April 2001.
25   US Dept of Justice, Federal Bureau of Investigation (FBI), 2010, 'Crime in the United States', table 1.
26   Keohane, Joe, 'The Crime-Wave in Our Heads', *Dallas News*, 26 March 2011; Oke, Femi, 'What 99.5% of People in America Will Never Experience, Despite the Hype', Upworthy.com. Available at: http://www.upworthy.com/what-99-5-of-people-in-america-will-never-experience-despite-the-hype (accessed September 2014).
27   National Highway Traffic Safety Administration, *Fatality Analysis Reporting System (FARS) Encyclopedia*; Skenazy, Lenore, 'Crime Statistics', Free-range Kids.com. Available at: www.freerangekids.com/crime-statistics/ (accessed September 2014). Sedlak *et al.*, *National Estimates of Missing Children*; CDC, 'Violence Prevention, Suicide Data Sheet'; US National Weather Service Lightning Safety: 'How Dangerous Is Lightning?'; Copeland, Larry, 'In a Sharp Trend Reversal, Highway Fatalities Rise', *USA Today*, 3 May 2013; Merritt, Nancy, *Teen and Young Adult Suicide: Light and Shadows* (Do It Now Foundation, 2002); Furedi, Frank, *Paranoid*

Parenting: Why Ignoring the Experts May Be Best for Your Child (Continuum Publishing, London, 2008)

28   Finkelhor *et al.*, 'Updated Trends in Child Maltreatment, 2012'.

29   *Ibid.*

30   *Ibid.*

31   Solomon, Andrew, *Far from the Tree: A Dozen Kinds of Love* (Chatto & Windus, London, 2013).

32   Finkelhor, David, *Childhood Victimization: Violence, Crime and Abuse in the Lives of Young People* (Oxford University Press, Oxford, 2008).

33   Dublin Rape Crisis Centre Annual Report 2012, 'Relationship between the Victim and the Offender (Where Known)'. Available at: http://www.drcc.ie/media1/publications/ (accessed September 2014).

34   The Rape Crisis Network of Ireland, 'Hearing Child Survivors of Sexual Violence: Towards a National Response', 2013, p. 33. Available at: http://www.rcni.ie/wp-content/uploads/Hearing-Child-Survivors-of-Sexual-Violence-2013.pdf (accessed September 2014).

35   Sullivan, Bob, 'What You Don't Know Can Hurt Your Child', *NBC News*, 2013.

36   Bartlett, Jamie, 'The Tap, Tap, Tap of Child Abuse', *The Sunday Times*, 20 July 2014.

37   Reilly, Capps, '"Pick-Up" Insanity at an Ordinary Suburban School', Free-Range Kids.com, 2 October 2013. Available at: www.freerangekids.com.

38   Furedi, *Paranoid Parenting*, p. 119.

Chapter 3: Childhood in Captivity

1   Eisenhower, Dwight D., quotation. Available at http://thinkexist.com/quotation/if_you_want_total_security-go_to_prison-there_you/202895.html.

2   Fanning, Martha, 'Wild Child Poll, Quantitative Survey, Behaviour & Attitudes', Heritage Council of Ireland, 2010.

3   Heritage Council Press Release, 'Supervision is a Key Issue in Children Playing Outdoors', 22 February 2011.

4   Fanning, 'Wild Child Poll, Quantitative Survey, Behaviour & Attitudes'.

5   Louv, Richard, 'A Timely Truth', *National Trust Magazine*, 2010, p. 27.

6   Cited in Louv, *Last Child in the Woods*, p. 116.

7   *Ibid.*, p. 27.

8   Moss, Stephen, 'Natural Childhood', National Trust (document -1355766991839/), 2012; Heritage Council Press Release, 2011.

9   Griffiths, Jay, 'Wild Child', *Psychologies*, September 2013.

10   Cited in Rosin, 'The Overprotected Kid'.

11   TVNZ One News Report, 'School Ditches Rules and Loses Bullies', *National News*, New Zealand, 26 January 2014.

12   Carver, Alison, Timperio, Anna and Crawford, David, 'Playing It Safe: The Influence of Neighbourhood Safety on Children's Physical Activity – A Review', *Health & Place*, Vol. 14, No. 2, 2008, pp. 217–27.

13   Moss, 'Natural Childhood'.

14   Based on Mullan, Elaine and Lodge, Jean, 'Active Transport to School: Ideals and Realities' in Connor, Seán (ed.), *The Sporting, Leisure and Lifestyle Patterns of Irish Adolescents: The Impact of the Celtic Tiger Years* (The Liffey Press, Dublin, 2012), pp. 85–106.

15   Dowling, Kevin, 'Row Over Child's Right to Roam', *The Sunday Times*, 4 July 2010.

16   Road Safety Authority, '89% Reduction in Children Killed on Our Roads between 1997 and 2012', 2 September 2013. Available at: http://www.rsa.ie/ga-IE/Utility/Nuacht/2013/89-Reduction-in-Children-Killed-on-Our-Roads-Between-1997-and-20121/ (accessed September 2014).

17   Jones, Sir Digby, 'Releasing the Potential for Children to Take Risks and Innovate', *Cotton Wool Kids*, Issues Paper 7, 2007, p. 13.

18   Shaw, Ben, Watson, Ben, Frauendienst, Bjorn, Redecker, Andreas and Jones, Tim with Hillman, Mayer, *Children's Independent Mobility: A Comparative Study in England and Germany* (1971–2010) (Policy Studies Institute, London, 2013), fig. 108, p. 165.

19   Williams, James, Greene, Sheila, Doyle, Erika, Harris, Elaine, Layte, Richard, McCoy, Selina, McCrory, Cathal, Murray, Aisling, Nixon, Elizabeth, O'Dowd, Tom, O'Moore, Mona, Quail, Amanda, Smyth, Emer, Swords, Lorraine and Thornton, Maeve, *Growing Up in Ireland, National Longitudinal Study of Children 'The Lives of 9-year-olds'* (Minister for Health and Children, 2009).

20   *Ibid.*

21   Moss, 'Natural Childhood'.

22   Sheehan, Aideen, 'Irish Children Get D Minus for Physical Activity in Global Test', *Irish Independent*, 21 May 2014; Williams *et al.*, *Growing Up in Ireland*; Moss, 'Natural Childhood'; Butterly, Amelia, 'Online Porn Seen by One-quarter by Age 12, Survey Says', *BBC News*, 10 April 2014.

23   Cited in Louv, 'A Timely Truth', p. 168.

24   *Ibid.*, p. 169.
25   Richardson, Hannah, 'Children Should Be Allowed to Get Bored, Expert Says', BBC Report, 23 March 2013. Available at: http://www.bbc.com/news/education-21895704 (accessed September 2014).
26   *Ibid.*
27   Rosin, 'The Overprotected Kid'.
28   Sandseter, Ellen and Kennair, Leif, 'Children's Risky Play from an Evolutionary Perspective: The Anti-Phobic Effects of Thrilling Experiences', *Evolutionary Psychology*, Vol. 9, No. 2, 2011, pp. 257–84. Available at: www.epjournal.net/wp-content/uploads/EP0 92572842.pdf (accessed September 2014).
29   Sandseter quoted in Rosin, 'The Overprotected Kid'.
30   Tuckman, Bruce and Monetti, David, *Educational Psychology* (Cengage Learning, Boston, MA, 2010), p. 560.
31   Frank, Anne, *Diary of a Young Girl*, diary entry for 23 February 1944 (reprint edn, Bantam, New York, 1993).
32   Driscoll, Margaret, 'If Your Child Says They Feel Low and Need a Hug, Don't Dismiss It', *The Sunday Times*, 8 June 2014.
33   Palmer, *Toxic Childhood*.
34   'Modern Life Leads to More Depression Among Children', *Daily Telegraph*, 12 September 2006.
35   Palmer, *Toxic Childhood*.
36   Ginsburg, Kenneth R. and the Committee on Communications and the Committee on Psychosocial Aspects of Child and Family Health, 'The Importance of Play in Promoting Healthy Child Development and Maintaining Strong Parent–Child Bonds', *Pediatrics*, Vol. 119, No. 1, 2007, pp. 182–91; Guldberg, Helene, *Reclaiming Childhood: Freedom and Play in an Age of Fear* (Taylor & Francis, London, 2009); Louv, *Last Child in the Woods*; Medina, John, *Brain Rules: 12 Principles for Surviving and Thriving at Work, Home and School* (Pear Press, Seattle, 2009).
37   Cooper, Rafi, 'How Safe Are Our Children?', Press Release, The Children's Society, April 2010.
38   *Ibid.*
39   Prigg, Mark, 'Children Play With Touchscreens More Than Traditional Toys, Researchers Find', *Daily Mail*, 21 February 2014.
40   Bielenberg, Kim, 'Why more "Helicopter Parents" hover in their children's college lives', *Irish Independent*, 20 November 2013; Howard, Philip, 'Why safe kids are becoming fat kids', *The Wall Street Journal*, 13 August 2008; Mills, Eleanor, 'Slave mothers wield a love that smothers', *The Sunday Times*, 20 April 2014.

41 Cited in Tyler, Katherine, 'The Tethered Generation', *HR Magazine*, Vol. 52, No. 5, May 2007.

42 Gill, Tim, *No Fear: Growing Up in a Risk-Averse Society* (Calouste Gulbenkian Foundation, 2007).

43 Jones, 'Releasing the Potential for Children to Take Risks and Innovate', p. 6.

Chapter 4: Education and Performance Anxiety

1 LaChapelle, Dolores, *D.H. Lawrence: Future Primitive* (University of North Texas Press, Denton, TX) p. 95.

2 Robinson, Ken, 'How Schools Kill Creativity', Ted.com, February 2006. Available at: http://www.ted.com/talks/ken_robinson_says_schools_kill_creativity (accessed September 2014).

3 Hurst, Greg, 'Pupils Being Damaged by Endless Tests Set by Gove', *The Times*, 1 October 2013.

4 O'Regan, Michael, 'Child not read to at Bedtime is "Abused", says Quinn', *The Irish Times*, 25 March 2011.

5 Honoré, Carl, *Under Pressure: Rescuing Our Children from the Culture of Hyper-Parenting* (Orion, London, 2008).

6 *Ibid.*

7 Waugh, Daisy, *I Don't Know Why She Bothers: Guilt-free Motherhood for Thoroughly Modern Women* (Orion, London, 2013).

8 Bruer, John, *The Myth of the First Three Years: A New Understanding of Early Brain Development and Lifelong Learning* (Free Press, New York, 1999).

9 Carey, Tanith, 'Can You Teach a Baby to Read? It's the Latest Obsession for Pushy Parents', *Daily Mail*, 12 December 2012.

10 Graimes, Nicola, *Brain Foods for Kids: Over 100 Recipes to Boost Your Child's Intelligence* (Delta Publishing, Peaslake, Surrey, 2005).

11 Borrill, Rachel, 'A World of a Difference', *The Irish Examiner*, 15 April 2011.

12 Shpancer, Noam, 'The Myth of Infant Determinism: Early Childhood Experiences Do Not Determine Adult Outcomes', *Psychology Today*, 26 September 2010.

13 Furedi, *Paranoid Parenting*, p. 65.

14 Solomon, *Far from the Tree*.

15 Lewin, Tamar, 'No Einstein in Your Crib? Get a Refund', *The New York Times*, 27 October 2009.

16 Carey, 'Can You Teach a Baby to Read?'.

17 Gopnik, Alison M., Meltzoff, Andrew M. and Kuhl, Patricia K., *The Scientist in the Crib: What Early Learning Tells Us About The Mind* (revd edn, Harper Perennial, New York, 2011).

18 O'Connor, Brendan, 'As I watch my eldest dancing, I realise I'm already losing her to One Direction and The Wanted and the whole awful world ... and one day she'll forsake me for some hairy goon', *Sunday Independent*, 23 December 2012.

19 Interview with Seán O'Connor on *The Marian Finucane Show*, RTÉ Radio 1, 31 August 2013.

20 Kyung, Hee Kim, 'The Creativity Crisis: The Decrease in Creative Thinking Scores on the Torrance Tests of Creative Thinking', *Creativity Research Journal*, Vol. 23, No. 4, 2011, pp. 285–95.

21 Carey, 'Can You Teach a Baby to Read?'.

22 Elkind, David, *The Hurried Child: Growing Up Too Fast Too Soon* (25th anniversary edn, Perseus Publishing, New York, 2006); Elkind, David, *The Power of Play: Learning What Comes Naturally* (reprint edn, Da Capo Press, Boston, MA, 2007); Elkind, David, *Miseducation: Preschoolers at Risk* (Knopf, New York, 1987).

23 Chua, Amy, *Battle Hymn of the Tiger Mother* (revd edn, Bloomsbury, New York, 2012).

24 *Ibid.*

25 Khan, Noorain, 'Tiger Mom Amy Chua Has Feelings Too', 24 January 2011. Available at: http://jezebel.com/5741872/tiger-mom-amy-chua-has-feelings-too (accessed September 2014).

26 Chua, *Battle Hymn of the Tiger Mother*.

27 Chua-Rubenfeld, Sophia, 'Why I Love My Strict Chinese Mom', *New York Post*, 18 January 2011. Available at: http://nypost.com/2011/01/18/why-i-love-my-strict-chinese-mom/ (accessed September 2014).

28 Chua, Amy and Rubenfeld, Jed, *The Triple Package: How Three Unlikely Traits Explain the Rise and Fall of Cultural Groups in America* (Penguin, New York, 2014).

29 Dutton, Kevin, *The Wisdom of Psychopaths: What Saints, Spies and Serial Killers Can Teach Us About Success* (New York Scientific American, London, 2012).

30 Bernstein, Gaia and Triger, Zvi, 'Over-Parenting', UC Davis Law Review, Seton Hall Public Law Research Paper No. 1588246, 2010.

31 Cited in Bruer, *The Myth of the First Three Years*.

Chapter 5: The Impact of the Age of Anxiety

1 Bell, Iris, *Chew on Things: Workbook for Fellow Worriers* (Creative Bookworm Press, Tucson, AZ, 2007), p. 164.

2 Sheehan, Aideen, 'Children Do Best When Parents "Are Firm But Kind"', *Irish Independent*, 1 December 2012.

3 Palmer, *Toxic Childhood*, p. 2.

4   World Health Organization, *Projections of Mortality and Global Burden of Disease 2004–2030* (WHO, Geneva, 2004).

5   'One Million Commit Suicide Each Year', *Medical News Today*, 10 September 2011.

6   NOSP (2013).

7   Williams *et al.*, *Growing Up in Ireland*; Moss, 'Natural Childhood'; Palmer, *Toxic Childhood*; Louv, *Last Child in the Woods*; Smith, Rebecca, 'Thousands of Children on Antidepressants', *The Daily Telegraph*, 30 October 2009.

8   'Fitzgerald Welcomes New Statistics on Children in Ireland', Merrion Street Irish Government News Service; National Office for Suicide Prevention (NOSP), *Research Evaluation of the Suicide Crisis Assessment Nurse (SCAN) Service, November 2012*, 7 March 2013; Williams *et al.*, *Growing Up in Ireland*; Central Statistics Office (CSO), Press Release, *Vital Statistics Fourth Quarter and Yearly Summary 2012*, 31 May 2013; Sullivan, C., Arensman, E., Keeley, H. S., Corcoran, P. and Perry, I. J., *Young People's Mental Health: A Report of the Results from the Lifestyle and Coping Survey*, National Suicide Research Foundation, 2004; Dooley, Barbara and Fitzgerald, Amanda, *My World Survey: National Study of Youth Mental Health in Ireland*, Headstrong and UCD School of Psychology, May 2012; Coughlan, Helen, *Youth Mental Health: Making the Vision a Reality in Ireland*, Irish College of Psychiatry, January 2013.

9   James, Oliver, *Affluenza* (Vermilion, London, 2007).

10   Centers for Disease Control and Prevention (CDC), *Twenty Leading Causes of Death Among Persons Ages 10 Years and Older, United States*, 2009.

11   *Ibid.*; NOSP (2013); WHO cited in *Medical News Today* (2011). Available at http://www.medicalnewstoday.com/articles/234219.php (accessed September 2014).

12   Boseley, Sarah, 'Study Finds Children Less Fit With Lack of Exercise', *The Guardian*, 22 December 2009; Campbell, Denis, 'Children Growing Weaker As Computers Replace Outdoor Activity', *The Observer*, 21 May 2011.

13   Horan, Niamh, 'Irish Will Be Fattest Europeans by 2030, Claim Researchers', *Sunday Independent*, 11 May 2014.

14   Williams *et al.*, *Growing Up in Ireland*.

15   Sheehan, 'Irish Children Get D Minus for Physical Activity in Global Test'.

16   Hayes, Katherine, 'Teen Girls Risk Hearts Sitting for 20 Hours a Day', *Irish Independent*, 15 May 2014.

17   Layte, Richard and McCrory, Cathal, *Growing Up in Ireland: National Longitudinal Study of Ireland, Physical Activity and Obesity Among 13-year-olds; Overweight and Obesity Among 9-year-olds – Report 2; Development from Birth to Three Years*, September 2013.

18   Cited in Palmer, *Toxic Childhood*, p. 22.

19   *Ibid.*, p. 23.

20   Chandon, Pierre and Wansink, Brian, 'Is Food Marketing Making Us Fat? A Multi-Disciplinary Review', *Foundations and Trends in Marketing*, Vol. 5, No. 3, 2011, pp. 113–96.

21   Palmer, *Toxic Childhood*, p. 29.

22   Harding, Karen L., Judah, Richard D. and Gant, Charles E., 'Outcome-Based Comparison of Ritalin® versus Food-Supplement Treated Children with AD/HD', *Alternative Medicine Review*, Vol. 8, No. 3, 2003, pp. 319–30.

23   Palmer, *Toxic Childhood*.

24   Pell, Sheila, 'Family Dinner Minus Family', *Washington Post*, 11 January 2005.

25   Orbach, Susie, *Fat Is a Feminist Issue* (new edn, Arrow, London, 2006).

26   'Rise in Bowel Diseases in Young People', *Morning Ireland*, RTÉ Radio 1, 20 June 2014.

27   Palmer, *Toxic Childhood*, p. 4.

28   Saul, Richard, *ADHD Does Not Exist: The Truth About Attention Deficit and Hyperactivity Disorder* (HarperWave, New York, 2014); Davie, James, *Cracked: Why Psychiatry Is Doing More Harm Than Good* (Icon Books, London, 2014).

29   Cited in 'What's Looks Got to Do With It?', *The Sunday Times, Style* magazine, 20 April 2014.

30   Associated Press, 'News Release', *Journal of the American Academy of Child and Adolescent Psychiatry*, 22 November 2013.

31   Farrelly, C. K., 'New Study Shows Parent Power May Be Best For Kids with ADHD Symptoms', *NUI Maynooth Foundation*, 27 November 2013.

32   McKee, Selina, 'UK ADHD Drug Use Rockets 50% in Just Six Years', *World News, Pharma Times*, 14 August 2014.

33   Dommett, Ellie, 'The Young Mind – The Effects of Proscribed and Prescribed Drugs on Learning and Memory', Research Report, Institute for the Future of the Mind, Oxford. Available at: http://www.futuremind.ox.ac.uk/research/drugs-on-learning-and-memory.html (accessed 9 November 2013).

34   Sahakian, Barbara, 'The Impact of Neuroscience on Society: The Neuroethics of "Smart Drugs"', Cambridge University, 27–29 September 2013.

35   'Child Antidepressant Use "Rising"', *BBC News*, 18 November 2004.

36   'Number of Children with Autism Soars by More Than 50 per cent in Five Years', *The Daily Telegraph*, 22 March 2012.

37   Cone, Marla, 'Autism increase not caused only by shifts in diagnoses; environmental factors likely, new California study says', *Environmental Health News*, 9 January 2009.

38   Baron-Cohen, S., Scott, F. J., Allison, C., Williams, J., Bolton, P., Matthews, F. E. and Brayne, C., 'Prevalence of Autism-Spectrum Conditions: UK School-Based Population Study,' *British Journal of Psychiatry*, Vol. 195, No. 2, August 2000, p. 182; 'Autism in Schools: Crisis or Challenge?', The National Autistic Society.

39   Blumberg, Stephen J., Bramlett, Matthew D., National Center for Health Statistics; Kogan, Michael D., Maternal and Child Health Bureau; Schieve, Laura A., National Center on Birth Defects and Developmental Disabilities; Jones, Jessica R. and Lu, Michael C., Maternal and Child Health Bureau, 'Changes in Prevalence of Parent-reported Autism Spectrum Disorder in School-aged U.S. Children: 2007 to 2011–2012', *National Health Statistics Report*, no. 65, 20 March 2013. Available at: http://www.cdc.gov/nchs/data/nhsr/nhsr065.pdf (accessed September 2014).

40   Irish Autism Action, Autism Advice and Support leaflet, 'Don't wait and see: early intervention works'. Available at: http://www.autismireland.ie/assets/files/IAA%20Advice%20&%20Support%20Brochure.pdf (accessed September 2014). Shaw, W., 'Evidence that Increased Acetaminophen use in Genetically Vulnerable Children Appears to be a Major Cause of the Epidemics of Autism, Attention Deficit with Hyperactivity, and Asthma', *Journal of Restorative Medicine* 2, 2013, pp. 14–29; Autism Speaks, 'New Study Reveals Autism Prevalence in South Korea Estimated to be 2.6% or 1 in 38 Children', 9 May 2011. Available at: http://www.autismspeaks.org/about-us/press-releases/new-study-reveals-autism-prevalence-south-korea-estimated-be-26-or-1-38-chil (accessed September 2014). Blumberg *et al.*, 2013.

41   Theroux, Louis, *America's Medicated Kids*, BBC TV programme, 18 April 2010.

42   Boyle, C. A., Boulet, S., Schieve, L., Cohen, R. A., Blumberg, S. J., Yeargin-Allsopp, M., Visser, S. and Kogan, M. D., 'Trends in the Prevalence of Developmental Disabilities in US Children, 1997–2008', *Pediatrics*, Vol. 127, No. 6, 2011, pp. 1034–42.

43   Galloway, Sinéad, Ní Mháille, Gráinne, Leckey, Yvonne, Kelly, Paul and Bracken, Mairéad, 'Proving the Power of Positive Engagement', NUI Maynooth, November 2013.

44 Saul, *ADHD Does Not Exist*.

45 Louv, 'A Timely Truth', p. 36.

46 National Trust, *Wildlife Alien to a Generation of Indoor Children* (2008).

47 Cross, Charles R., *Heavier Than Heaven: The Biography of Kurt Cobain* (Hyperion, New York, 2001), p. 20.

Chapter 6: Bring on the Professionals

1 Goodall, Jane, *In the Shadow of Man* (Collins, London, 1971).

2 DeMause, Lloyd, *The Emotional Life of Nations* (Other Press, New York, 2002), p. 362.

3 *Ibid.*

4 Freud, Sigmund, *On Sexuality: Three Essays on the Theory of Sexuality and Other Works* (Penguin, Harmondsworth, 1991).

5 Robertson, James, *A Two-Year-Old Goes to Hospital: A Scientific Film*, 1952.

6 Bowlby, Dr John, *Maternal Care and Mental Health* (WHO, Geneva, 1952).

7 Bowlby, Dr John, *A Secure Base* (Routledge, London, 2005).

8 Watson, John B., *Psychological Care of Infant and Child* (New York: W. W. Norton & Co., 1928), pp. 81–2.

9 Spock, Dr Benjamin, *The Common Sense Book of Baby and Child Care* (2nd edn, W. H. Allen Co. Ltd., London, 1946), p. 1.

10 *Ibid.*

11 Spock, Dr Benjamin, *The Common Sense Book of Baby and Child Care*, 1946, with revisions up to ninth edn (W. H. Allen Co. Ltd, London, 2012); 1957 (2nd edn); Bodley Head, London, 1968 (3rd edn); Pocket Books, New York, 1976 (4th edn); Dutton, New York, 1992 (6th edn); with Steven, Parker, Pocket Books, New York, 1998 (7th edn); with Robert Needlman, Pocket Books, New York, 2004 (8th edn); with Robert Needlman, Gallery Books, New York, 2012.

12 Gilbert, Ruth, Salanti, Georgia, Harden, Melissa and See, Sarah, 'Infant Sleeping Position and the Sudden Infant Death Syndrome: Systematic Review of Observational Studies and Historical Review of Recommendations from 1940 to 2002', *International Journal of Epidemiology*, April 2005.

13 *Ibid.*

14 Spock and Parker, *The Common Sense Book of Baby and Child Care* (7th ed).

15 *Ibid.*

16 Winnicott, D. W., 'Transitional Objects and Transitional Phenomena', *International Journal of Psycho-Analysis*, Vol. XXXIV, 1953.

17   Winnicott, D. W., *The Child, the Family, and the Outside World* (Penguin Psychology, Harmondsworth, 1973), p. 138.

18   Liedloff, Jean, *The Continuum Concept: In Search of Happiness Lost* (Da Capo Press, Boston, 1986).

19   Sears, William and Sears, Martha, *The Baby Book: Everything You Need to Know About Your Baby from Birth to Age Two* (Little, Brown, London, 1992).

20   Leach, Penelope, *Your Baby and Child: From Birth to Age Five* (Dorling Kindersley, New York, 2010), p. 12.

21   *Ibid.*, p. 146.

22   Ford, Gina, *The New Contented Little Baby Book: The Secret to Calm and Confident Parenting* (new edn, Vermilion, London, 2006).

23   James, Oliver, 'I Would Love Someone to Look After Me', *The Guardian*, 29 January 2003.

24   Ferber, Richard, *Solve Your Child's Sleep Problems* (Fireside Publishing, Whitby, ON, Canada, 1986).

25   Cited in James, 'I Would Love Someone to Look After Me'.

26   Himmelstrand, Jonas, 'Universal Daycare Leaves Sweden's Children Less Educated', *National Post*, 26 April 2011.

27   Perez-Rivas, Manuel, 'Autistic Girl Unsafe at Home, Judge Says', *The Washington Post*, 27 April 2001.

Chapter 7: From Under–Parenting to Over–Parenting

1   Evans, Sarah, 'Feckless or Pushy, Parents Just Can't Win', *Birmingham Post*, 14 December 2012.

2   Randall, Kay, 'Mom Needs an "A": Hovering, Over-involved Parents the Topic of Landmark Study', 2 April 2007. Available at http://www.utexas.edu/features/2007/helicopter/ (accessed September 2014).

3   Cited in Anderssen, Erin, 'Why the 1970s Were the Best Time to Be a Mom', *The Globe and Mail*, 5 May 2011.

4   *Ibid.*

5   *Ibid.*

6   Pickert, Kate, 'Are You Mom Enough?', *TIME*, 21 May 2012.

7   Young, Toby, *The Sound of No Hands Clapping* (Abacus, London, 2006), p. 166.

8   DeMause, *The Emotional Life of Nations*, p. 382.

9   Bianchi, Suzanne, Robinson, John and Sayer, Lionel, 'Are Parents Investing Less in Children? Trends in Mothers' and Fathers' Time with Children', *American Journal of Sociology*, Vol. 110, No. 1, July 2004, pp. 1–43; Ramey, Garey and Ramey, Valerie, *The Rug Rat Race*, National Bureau of Economic Research (NBER), San Diego

April 2010.

10   Hodgkinson, Tom, *The Idle Parent: Why Less Means More When Raising Kids* (Hamish Hamilton, London, 2009), pp. 28–9.

11   Power, Brenda, 'Turning a Blind Eye is a Crime', *The Sunday Times*, 4 May 2014.

12   Gill, Peter J., Goldacre, Michael J., Mant, David, Heneghan, Carl, Thomson, Anne, Seagroatt, Valerie and Hamden, Anthony, 'Increase in Emergency Admissions to Hospital for Children Aged Under 15 in England, 1999–2010: National Database Analysis', *The British Medical Journal*, 4 December 2012.

13   Chamberlin, Jamie, 'Childhood Revisited,' *Monitor*, Vol. 37, No. 3, March 2006.

14   Rosin, 'The Overprotected Kid'.

15   *Ibid.*

16   *Ibid.*

17   *Ibid.*

18   *Ibid.*

19   *Ibid.*

20   *Ibid.*

21   Hill, Amelia, 'Lack of Household Chores Making Children Less Responsible, Claims Survey', *The Observer*, 15 November 2009.

22   Rutherford, Markella, 'Children's Autonomy and Responsibility: An Analysis of Child Rearing Advice', *Qualitative Sociology*, 18 November 2009.

23   Hill, 'Lack of Household Chores Making Children Less Responsible, Claims Survey'.

24   Cited in Kolbert, Elizabeth, 'Why Are American Kids So Spoiled?', *The New Yorker*, 2 July 2012.

25   This is based on the Age Appropriate Chores for Children chart, accessible at http://www.flandersfamily.info/web/wp-content/uploads/2013/11/Age-Appropriate-Chore-Chart-for-Children.pdf.

26   Karen, Robert, *Becoming Attached: First Relationships and How They Shape Our Capacity to Love* (Oxford University Press, New York, 1998), p. 325.

27   Warner, Judith, *Perfect Madness: Motherhood in the Age of Anxiety*, reprint edn (Riverhead Trade, New York, 2005).

28   Solomon, 'Far from the Tree'.

Chapter 8: Your Child's Future

1   von Goethe, Johann Wolfgang, BrainyQuote.com, Xplore Inc, 2014. Available at: http://www.brainyquote.com/quotes/quotes/j/johannwolf137527.html.

2   Palmer, *Toxic Childhood*.
3   Gozlan, Marc, 'The Growing Band of Young People Living a Re-clusive Life', *The Guardian*, 17 July 2012.
4   Kuruvilla, Carol, '21-year-old Ohio Honor Student Wins Stalking Order Against Helicopter Parents', *The New York Daily News*, 27 December 2012.
5   National Parents Council Post Primary (NPCpp), *Newsletter 1*, December 2012.
6   Quoted in Monaghan, Gabrielle, '"Helicopter" Parents Swamp Helpline', *The Sunday Times*, 18 August 2013.
7   *Ibid.*
8   *Ibid.*
9   *Ibid.*
10   Hilpern, Kate, 'Umbilical Cords Just Got Longer', *The Guardian*, 10 September 2008.
11   Seligman, Martin, *Helplessness: On Depression, Development, and Death* (W.H. Freeman, San Francisco, 1975).
12   Boffey, Daniel, 'Middle-class Young Will Fare Worse Than Their Parents', *The Observer*, 12 October 2013.
13   Interview with Dr Harry Barry, *Today with Seán O'Rourke*, RTÉ Radio 1, Friday 25 September.
14   Goodman, Vera, Chapman, Rod and Collins Oman, Elizabeth, *Simply Too Much Homework! What Can We Do?* (Reading Wings, Calgary, Canada, 2007).
15   Hancock, LynNell, 'Why Are Finland's Schools Successful?', *Smithsonian Magazine*, September 2011.
16   Sandseter and Kennair, 'Children's Risky Play From an Evolution-ary Perspective'.
17   Spencer, Charlotte and Bicknell, Alexis, 'New Research: Outdoor Play in Danger of Disappearing', *Play England*, 8 July 2011.
18   Jones, 'Releasing the Potential for Children to Take Risks and In-novate', p. 4.

Chapter 9: Is Féidir Linn

1   Morrison, Toni, *Conversations with Toni Morrison* (University Press of Mississippi, Jackson, MS, 1994), p. 131.
2   Larkin, Philip, *High Windows* (Faber & Faber, London, 2012).
3   Gillies, Andrew, 'Is the Road There to Share? Shared Space in an Australian Context', Thesis, University of New South Wales, Octo-ber 2009.
4   Walsh, Ciaran, 'On the Edge of Utopia in Rural Ireland', *Irish Independent*, 3 February 2014.

5   McVeigh, Tracy, 'Cycling to School: Is It Really Such a Terrible Risk?', *The Guardian*, 11 July 2010.

6   Williams *et al.*, *Growing Up in Ireland*.

7   National Roads Authority, 'Road Deaths in Ireland 1959–2009', table 2. Available at www.rsa.ie (accessed September 2014).

8   Play England, *Charter for Children's Play*. Available at: http://www.playengland.org.uk/media/71062/charter-for-childrens-play.pdf (accessed September 2014). Shackell, Aileen, Butler, Nicola, Doyle, Phil and Ball, David, *Design for Play: A Guide to Creating Successful Play Spaces* (FreePlay Network, June 2008). Available at: http://www.playengland.org.uk/media/141887/design-for-play-introduction.pdf (accessed September 2014).

9   Montgomery, Charles, *Happy City: Transforming Our Lives through Urban Design* (Allen Lane/Penguin, London, 2013).

10   Play England, *Charter for Children's Play*.

11   Waugh, *I Don't Know Why She Bothers*, p. 18.

12   Wayman, Sheila, 'It is what is on the outside that counts', *The Irish Times*, 27 November 2012.

13   O'Brien, Liz and Murray, Richard, 'Forest School Research Summary', *Forest Research*, 2008.

14   Forestry Commission Scotland, *Woods for Learning Education Strategy*, 2005.

15   Skenazy, *Free-Range Kids*.

16   Skenazy, Lenore, interview with Ernie Allen, Head of the National Center for Missing & Exploited Children, Free-range Kids.com. Available at: http://www.freerangekids.com/faq/ (accessed September 2014).

Suggested Reading

1   Skenazy, Lenore. Available at: http://www.freerangekids.com/faq/ (accessed September 2014).

Acknowledgements

I've always wondered why people who write books tend to include such over-the-top effusive thanks to everybody around them – well, me oh my, now I know why! Simply put, by the time I'm getting to write these acknowledgements I'm mortified by how much time and energy I have spent in the writing of this book and I really need to extravagantly thank everyone who knows me for being so patient with me!

My writing of 'the book' has gone on and on and on and I would like to take this opportunity to thank all my friends and family who have had to put up with me ranting, raving and foaming at the mouth about modern-day parenting practices, about cotton wool kids, about abduction statistics, about mental health issues, covers, titles and about the book in general – far more often than anyone could have found even remotely interesting. I know that I have become the most peculiar, long-winded bore in the Western World – so thanks all for putting up with me – Ali, Antoinette, Rosie and everyone else who I've bored senseless!

Of course there are many people who totally disagree with the message in this book – the 'non-believers' think that I am totally wrong and that, in fact, we need to keep our children by our side more than ever. I'm very thankful that my nice and generous friends didn't let the fact that they thought I was completely round the bend get in the way of showing me love and support.

I will be forever grateful to my pals Fiona and Pauline for unlocking the door and leading me to realise that ordinary people like ourselves could write books.

I couldn't have done without the professional guidance and support that I was lucky enough to receive and I am particularly grateful to Sarah Liddy for her almost instinctive understanding of where I was coming from, to Emma Walsh for enthusiastically helping me to structure a book out of my impassioned ramblings, and also to Wendy Logue for her patience and tolerance when I was a bit all over the place.

I wouldn't be here without my lovely mother, so a special thank you to Mam for not making a cotton wool kid out of me; I was one of those kids who really needed freedom and independence.

A special thanks to Ciara Crowe Leahy for reading the book, very, very quickly, when I suddenly and desperately needed feedback – your insightful, thoughtful and honest response was like gold dust. I was inspired by how quickly you incorporated a freestyle approach to parenting as a consequence of reading the book and I was delighted to hear how much happier your family was as a consequence. I will never forget the day you texted me saying that you were having a lovely day out with the family and had it not been for reading this book, you would have been running all over Tayto Park shrieking at the kids to get down, to slow down, to calm down and to stay by your side. Nice one, Ciara, your texts gave me the nerve to continue whenever I lost the faith!

Hugs, kisses and thanks to my darling kids, Róisín and Muiris; had you not been such great kids who had such funny wild streaks and who enjoyed independence and freedom so much, I would never have had the courage to write this book. Thanks kiddos!

Far and away, most of all I would like to thank my lovely husband for putting up with me, for giving me time alone when I needed it, for giving me lots of wise advice and practical help, but especially for giving me the courage to try to be a loving but easy-going parent. The freedom and forbearance that I asked from you was way above and beyond the call of duty, so thanks Henry for that – I owe you so much that I don't even know how to begin, so all I can do is dedicate this book to you.